# International News Coverage and the Korean Conflict

"As a long-term international news focus, the Korean conflict provides a lens into journalistic perspective. Using the Hierarchy of Influences model, Miri Moon sorts out the rich array of content and interview data to reveal the factors underlying news frames."

—Stephen D. Reese, *Jesse H. Jones Professor,*
*University of Texas at Austin, USA*

Miri Moon

# International News Coverage and the Korean Conflict

## The Challenges of Reporting Practices

palgrave
macmillan

Miri Moon
Sookmyung Women's University
Seoul, Soul-t'ukpyolsi
Korea (Republic of)

ISBN 978-981-13-6290-3      ISBN 978-981-13-6291-0   (eBook)
https://doi.org/10.1007/978-981-13-6291-0

Library of Congress Control Number: 2019930287

Cover design by Tom Howey

This Palgrave Macmillan imprint is published by the registered company Springer Nature Singapore Pte Ltd.
The registered company address is: 152 Beach Road, #21-01/04 Gateway East, Singapore 189721, Singapore

# PREFACE

A conflict can be a reflection of social, political, economic, and cultural issues facing society. The way the public, we, comprehend and perceive the conflict, however, is through the media. Thus, news through the media is our important source of making sense of a conflict or an issue in our everyday life. As is emphasized in media and communication theories, the news is a social construction of reality, a conflict within news producers' particular framework. As Hall Critcher, Jefferson, Clarke, and Roberts (1978) assert, the process of the construction of a news story is significant due to its involvement in the presentation of the article disseminated to the assumed audience, which means that the news story is encoded within a context of social and cultural frames to make the message understood by the audience. This book not only examines the prevailing media's mapping that is news framing, which is the ways in which the media defines and interprets an event in journalism studies but also exploring the "field" (Bourdieu, 2005) that affects the news frames that influence the public's perceptions.

The Korean Peninsula is "technically" at war because the Korean War was concluded not by a peace treaty but by an armistice. The clashes between the two Koreas have generated tensions and conflicts and have also become a global threat because the United States has its military stationed in South Korea to ensure security in the region. It means that journalists are at war on the frontline. Even if the global audiences watched the U.S. President Donald Trump and North Korean leader, Kim Jung Un at the historic Singapore Summit, following the historic meeting that a North Korean leader crossed the 38th line and shook hands with the South Korean President Moon Jae-In in 2018, North Korea is still one of the world's most secretive societies. Under these circumstances, how does the news media report conflicts? Are there any differences in news production on the conflicts between the two Koreas, compared with other international conflicts? North Korea is a severely closed state with limited accessibility. What about the use of news sources by international journalists and Korean journalists in the new media era? Bourdieu (2005) explains the notion of a field—a sphere of actions and reactions executed by social agents and how they react to relations of the pressures from economic and cultural forces by constructing, perceiving, forming, and representing those relations. Thus, this book investigates the news production and its process, especially news about war conflicts and how it operates.

This book focuses on the nature of news production mainly by international journalists, particularly, the ways in which they cover new stories about the Korean conflict. There is a good body of work on studying reporting of war and international conflicts. However, exploring international correspondents' journalistic practices in covering North Korea is scarce. North Korea's nuclearization is involved in the two superpowers, the United States and China and their foreign policies. The issue is a global threat, so we share it real time as the world is linked to each other as a "global village" (McLuhan, 1964). Hence, it is imperative to examine the ways in which international news reports the North Korean issues. Moreover, the news media shape our mind and perceptions and affect foreign policies. Despite its impact on a global society, there is relatively little research on this area of journalism studies. Hence, this book would allow students and researchers to broaden their understanding of the role of journalism by critically analyzing by looking at why media coverage of North Korea was reported in this way and what factors affected the news frames.

This book draws upon a comparative analysis of major news coverage pertaining to the Korean conflict with a sample of US/UK and South Korean media (*AP, CNN, The New York Times, BBC, The Guardian, Yonhap, The Hankyoreh Shinmun, The DongA Ilbo*). On the one hand, the study of news narratives leads to a deeper understanding of journalism and its practices. On the other hand, a study of content alone is not sufficient to understand either the force that produced that content or the nature or extent of its effects. Interviews are a way of gaining views, opinions, and perceptions of interviewees through their confessional responses or biographic narratives. In particular, the interviews focus on investigating what influences their practices and how they collect information because a comparative news analysis alone could not offer detailed background information about the processes and nature of news production. Thus, 18 semi-structured interviews with foreign correspondents (*AP, AFP, Reuters, The New York Times, The Financial Times, BBC, CNN, Le Figaro, The Washington Times, The Voice of America, The Mainichi Shimbun, The Wall Street Journal, Christian Science Monitor*) and Korean journalists (*KBS, Yonhap, The DongA Ilbo, The Hankyoreh newspaper*), were conducted to explore news gathering practices concerning the Korean conflict and to investigate factors that influence journalists' news production. I have hope that this book opens a little sphere where readers can prognosticate and mold the core necessity in reporting a conflict in the process of news construction for future journalism.

Seoul, Korea (Republic of)                                        Miri Moon

# Acknowledgements

I am truly thankful for all the support from those who have shared intellectual and academic experience, which made completing this research possible. I would like to give my sincere thanks and respect to Peter Lunt, Lesley Henderson, Clive Seale and Chris Rojek in the UK whom I met at Brunel University London, UK for the first time.

Peter Lunt taught me critical ways of reasoning and constructing a logical structure in literature reviews. Lesley Henderson gave me constructive comments and her feedback has enabled me to gain academic strengths and pursue new avenues in academic research. I would also like to give my heartfelt thanks to Clive Seale for all his penetrating questions and thoughtful notes. I was inspired by his scholarly mind and I have learned profoundly about researching culture, society, and social science methodologies from him. I remember he gave me feedback on my writings even around a Christmas season. Chris Rojek is a renowned scholar for the emerging popular academic study area, Celebrity. He was the one who told me to conduct in-depth interviews with journalists, which I had never thought about. I thank him for enlightening me and respect him for his challenges to explore social theories limitlessly.

I would also like to show my gratitude toward Julian Petley and Daya Thussu. They did not only enlighten me and lead me to broaden my scholarship in journalism and global media studies with detailed comments, but also appreciated my research and added value to it. I would never have even imagined publishing a book if Daya had not said that there is a book in here, putting his hand on my thesis in my viva voce. Whenever I questioned publishing my own book, his comments led me to concentrate on writing.

Looking back, I owe great thanks to Christine Geraghty for her unconditional academic support since I was a student at Goldsmiths College. I have learned both what true learning and teaching is from the ways she helped students. I would also like to send many thanks to Colin Sparks. His good advice always helped me to come up with a good decision in studies and in life.

While researching my Ph.D. thesis, I completed all the required taught Ph.D. course Department of Journalism & Communications at Korea University. While studying there, I have met excellent scholars. My special thanks go to Professor Jae Chul Shim for his immeasurable support. His advice and encouragement truly helped me to work through my struggles in studying. I also would like to thank Professor Jaeyung Park for his consistent help and guidance as my supervisor. His remarkable mentoring and advice influenced every step of my studies as well as my teaching at Korea University. I am also truly grateful to Professor Dong Hoon Ma. Without his commitment to being my local supervisor, I would not have been able to continue my Ph.D. studies in the UK. I would also like to thank Professor Young Min for her amazing lectures and academic inspiration. Thanks to her reading lists, I believe I have extended my knowledge in political communication and was given a rationale to be equipped with statistical analysis.

Thankfully, I have met a new advisor as well as a colleague, Professor Byung Jong Lee, former Seoul Bureau Chief of Newsweek at Sookmyung Women's University where I just started my work as Adjunct Professor. It is such a pleasure for me to work with him and other colleagues here. I would like to thank him for all his advice and help in lecturing as well as settling down in this beautiful campus with dazzling students in the department of International Service. Classes with mixed students in diverse cultural backgrounds from all over the world stimulate me to explore global society furthermore.

I would like to send my warm thanks to Sophie Basilevitch, a dear friend of mine at Oxford, who is always happy to read my writing and share the details of our everyday life since our start at Goldsmiths College. Thank you, Sophie for standing by me as always.

I would like to sincerely thank all the journalists who generously took time out of their busy schedule to take part in interviews. I felt that I was so blessed. They were genuinely willing to help my studies by talking frankly with me and engaging with my research. Above all, I truly thank them for sharing their own journalistic experience and opinions with me through emails, telephone calls, and interviews. Without them, the strengths of my book would not have been achievable.

During my further studies, I realized how much support my family continues to give me. They were there always next to me and stood by me. I would like to express my warmest thanks and love to my family for their support and patience. Especially, I would like to express my wholehearted gratitude to my parents for their never-ending support and unconditional love through my life. With their consistent love and care, I was able to arrive here where I am now in my precious life. I also would like to send my love to Jin and Albert who came along to my life as very special gifts and blessings.

Last but certainly not least, I thank God for giving me wisdom and for establishing my steps faithfully. Thank you. I trust you.

# CONTENTS

# LIST OF TABLES

# JOURNALISTIC FIELD BETWEEN NEW MEDIA AND RAW CULTURE

International conflicts reflect the most complex state of an international community involved in unresolved problems and issues interwoven with the international relations and foreign policies as the crises such as the divided Germany 1948–1989, the Vietnam war 1954–1975 and the Soviet's invasion of Afghanistan in 1979 illustrate the nature of the Cold War. Reflecting on international conflicts is part of striving after truth (Cottrell, 2003). Hence, through reflection, we can acknowledge what really lies beneath that we might have lost in the normal decoding process of international conflicts in modern times. People make sense of international conflicts primarily through the news that is encoded and mediated. Hence, it is imperative to examine the ways in which news is constructed and encoded by news producers, journalists and investigate what challenges international journalists face in covering North Korea, where accessibilities and gathering information and data are severely limited. In addition, this book intends to explore the factors that influence journalists' news frames. To conduct the analysis, first, this study examines the narratives of international news coverage and conducts in-depth interviews with international journalists and Korean journalists. The principal case this study focuses on is the major skirmishes that occurred around the disputed Western sea border, the Northern Limit Line (NLL) where South Korea and North Korea agreed to establish a peace and cooperation zone in 2018 (Yonhap, April 27, 2018).

This book discusses the reasons why the conflict has brought us even more confusion and complexity, followed by the Yeonpyeong artillery bombing and the raised tensions in March 2013 in the Korea Peninsula, bringing more than 40 journalists flocking to South Korea from all over the world to cover what might happen, which is a war.

Like the Financial Times, Seoul correspondent Simon Mundy said, "the global media embarrassed it up during the time on North Korea because a lot of international TV and the media and network made clear that they didn't understand the dynamics here. They didn't understand when North Korea says there is going to be a war tomorrow that's not actually what it means." Thus, this study intends to reflect critically on the dynamics and challenges of international news coverage of the Korean conflict, mainly the sinking of the Cheonan warship as a case study that happened in March 2010 in the Yellow Sea, killing 40 sailors with 6 sailors missing, in a geographical, political, social and economic context, focusing on the current international relations, political powers and the foreign policies in the Korean Peninsula with the United States, China, to explore what the conflict connotes and implies in Journalism Literature in the post-Cold War era.

The Republic of Korea (ROK) naval 1200-ton vessel, Cheonan sank about 2 km below Baekryong Island, a South Korean island in the Yellow Sea at around 9.30 pm local time on March 26, 2010, killing 46 sailors. The patrolling corvette was ripped in half. Following the sinking, the South Korean government established the international Joint Military–Civilian Investigation Group (JIG), including the US, the UK, Australia, Canada, and Sweden, to investigate the cause of the sinking. Finally, 55 days after the sinking, the investigation team completed its report and the South Korean government announced firmly on March 20, 2010, "The evidence points overwhelmingly to the conclusion that the torpedo was fired by a North Korean submarine. There is no other plausible explanation." According to the investigation result by the Ministry of National Defense, Republic of Korea on the sinking of ROKS "Cheonan," the JIG concluded that the South Korean navy ship, Cheonan was sunken by a "shockwave and bubble effect" from an explosion set off by a North Korean torpedo, which caused "significant upward bending" of the center keel. As further clear evidence shown to the public, components of a torpedo matched that of a diagram that the South Korean military had, the North Korean CHT-02D torpedo. In addition, inside the rear section of the propulsion systems were the Korean letters "1 Buhn," meaning number 1 in blue ink, which is similar to the marking of a North Korean test torpedo obtained in 2003.

Although both Korean governments officially announced the result, based on the conclusion reported by the international Civilian–Military Joint Investigation Group, a torrent of suspicion and questions has come out. For example, two South Korean-born US physicists, Yang who is a laboratory manager in mass spectrometry at the University of Manitoba in Canada, and Lee who works at the University of Virginia in the US updated reports on the Cheonan, claiming some problems about the South Korean investigation. They also had a press conference in Tokyo, on July 9, raising some issues about the JIG investigation and maintaining that "a piece of torpedo propeller with a handwritten mark in blue ink reading "Number 1" in Korean, the smoking gun, is suspicious." Katsumi Sawada, Bureau Chief in Seoul for the Mainichi Shimbun in Japan who first covered Kim Jong-Il's third son, Kim Jung Un going to a school in Switzerland, said that he and his boss attended the conference and did not understand why South Korea questioned the government's official announcement on the attack.

Amid the continuing debates on what caused the tragic incident and the public's distrust toward the government, why North Korea did it and why there were not still uncovered. The important thing to note is to think about the reason why the Cheonan incident has these endless debates and questions going on, unlike the Yeonpyeong artillery bombing that occurred about seven months after the Cheonan sinking. I do not think that it is an issue of whether the scenes of the artillery bomb shelling are available or not. It is of significance to reconsider the implication of the incident and revisit the ways in which North Korean issues have influenced Korean society, policies and international relations. To discuss the implication, I categorized three major dimensions to focus on.

First, I discuss the geopolitical dynamics in the Korean Peninsula. Second, domestic political issues with regard to North Korea will be explored. Third, I examine the ways in which the news media reports the Korean conflict. Perhaps, it could be argued that as Choe Sang Hun at the New York Times said, due to the turbulent military governments that South Korea had historically, the public does not trust the government in general. Hence, the Korean conflict is related to one's belief or trust toward the South Korean government. On the other hand, as Sawada at the Mainichi Shimbun said, the reported conclusion is not seen as a result of an investigation team's probe about the incident but seen as a political issue in South Korea, which shows its failing social integration. The Cheonan incident has tested China's foreign policy and relations in the region and it can be explained by continuing concerns about North Korea's instability, especially with regard to leadership succession (Thompson, 2010; Snyder & Byun, 2011).

However, few previous studies approached the conflict from the media and journalistic perspectives. The unprecedented and the most tragic incident after the Korean War was one of the media agendas at that time but the deaths of 46 young sailors who were doing their compulsory military service were not justified because no one was willing to take part in resolving the festering conflicts. Doubtlessly, it might also be of significance equally to define whether the Cheonan was an attack by North Korea because so many questions and conspiracies are still in the media discourse, even after the South Korean government and the international joint investigation team concluded on May 20, 2010 that the North torpedoed the South Korean naval ship. Hence, this book approaches the international conflict as a global event in an international communication and geopolitical context. Second, from the domestic perspective, I would like to examine the ways in which the South Korean government dealt with the incident and what the Cheonan incident reflects in Korean society. Third, because the public understands the reality of the outside world through the media, it would be important to examine the ways in which the news was constructed about North Korea. Starting from Water Lippmann with "pictures in our heads" to the agenda-setting theory of McCombs and Shaw and media framing, a great body of studies has researched the power of the mediated politics that shapes public understandings of the world (Williams & Delli Carpini, 2011). Thus, this exciting book analyses the ways in which international journalists report the Korean conflicts and its process of news production. Prior to reviewing approaches to this study, it would be essential to look at the historical and political upheavals in the Korean Peninsula, in particular, explicating before and after the Korean War.

## REFERENCES

Bourdieu, P. (2005). The Political Field, the Social Science Field, and the Journalistic Field. In R. Benson, & E. Neveu (Eds.), *Bourdieu and the Journalistic Field* (pp. 29–47). Cambridge: Polity Press.

Cottrell, S. (2003). *Skills for Success*. Basingstoke: Palgrave Macmillan.

Hall, S., Critcher, C., Jefferson, T., Clarke, J., & Roberts, B. (1978). *Policing the Crisis: Mugging, the State and Law and Order*. London: Macmillan.

Lippmann, W. (1922). *Public Opinion*. New York: The Free Press.

McLuhan, M. (1964). *Understanding Media: The Extensions of Man*. New York: Signet Book.

Snyder, S., & Byun, S.-W. (2011). Cheonan and Yeonpyeong: The Northeast Asian Response to North Korea's Provocations. *The RUSI Journal, 156*(2), 74–81.

Thompson, D. (2010, August 13). *China's Perspective of Post-Cheonan Regional Security*. presented at the Asan Institute for Policy Studies Symposium, Seoul, Korea.

Williams, A. B., & Delli Carpini, X. M. (2011). *After Broadcast News: Media Regimes, Democracy, and the New Information Environment*. New York, NY: Cambridge University Press.

# CHAPTER 1

# The Historical Context of the Korean Conflict

## THE KOREAN WAR BETWEEN GREAT POWERS

Korea, located between China to the west and north and neighboring Japan to the east, has historically been the subject of intervention by greater powers for centuries. The geographical situation of the Korean peninsula has made Korea vulnerable to invasion by great powers. Korea has been a subject of various Chinese empires since the Chinese Han dynasty invaded the peninsula in 109 B.C. China often demanded contributions and took members of the royal family from Korea as hostages. Moreover, Japan invaded Korea, which was ruled by the Chosun Dynasty at that time, in 1592, and the resulting war lasted for seven years, ending with the Chosun Dynasty's victory. Even before a complete recovery from Japanese rule, the Chinese Later Jin attacked Chosun in 1627. Incessant foreign invasions led Korea to insist on a closed-door policy during the rule of the prince regent, or "Taewon gun," 1863–1873. However, Japan assassinated Queen Min in 1895, leading Korea to open its doors to western countries (Jung, Kim, Shin, Shin, & Cho, 2011; Sheen, 2009).

Japan's fear of a rival power, Russia, and its desire to prevent Russia's military conquest led it to war with Russia in 1904–1905; in the wake of the war with Russia, Japan annexed Korea in 1910, and its colonization of the Korean peninsula lasted until the end of the Second World War (Williams, 2004). During the period of Japanese colonization, hundreds of thousands of Koreans were sent to Japan, and a continuing debate on Korean sex slaves, also known as "comfort women" for Japanese soldiers,

© The Author(s) 2019
M. Moon, *International News Coverage and the Korean Conflict*,
https://doi.org/10.1007/978-981-13-6291-0_1

remains unresolved because Japan denies the existence of the comfort women system and consequently refuses to offer an official apology.[1] This issue, as well as the Dokdo Island dispute with Japan, has caused great resentment among Koreans. Korea became independent from Japan on August 15, 1945, when Japan declared its unconditional surrender, and the Second World War ended. Earlier that year, at the Yalta Conference on February 11, 1945, Stalin had promised to fight against Japan, and in return, the United States, the United Kingdom and the Soviet Union would regain the authority and rights that they had possessed before the Russo-Japanese War. On August 9, 1945, the Soviets began to attack Manchuria and the Korean peninsula, and on the following day, Japan accepted the UN suggestion for an unconditional surrender. At that time, the United States divided Korea along the 38th parallel of latitude. Therefore, Japan's surrender and disarmament were managed by the Soviets in North Korea and the United States in South Korea.[2] Even at the end of the Pacific War, it appeared that the fate of the two Koreas remained undecided.

By July 1945, the U.S. concern about the spread of Soviet influence in the Far East was growing, and on August 10, 1945, two American army colonels were ordered to draw a line across Korea that followed the 38th parallel, the demarcation line of the demilitarized zone on the Korean peninsula (Lee, 2001). Lowe (1997) explains that in the aftermath of the sudden death of President Franklin Roosevelt on April 12, 1945, Vice President Harry S. Truman, who had little foreign affairs experience, assumed the presidency (Truman was President from April 1945 to January 1953). One argument holds that Truman's trenchant dislike for communism and hostility toward Russia led him to deploy the atomic bomb against Japan partly to persuade the Soviet Union to pursue a less abrasive policy in Eastern Europe (Cumings, 1983: 67–91). However, according to Lowe (1997), the colonel who believed that the 38th parallel was the most satisfactory line of division, the goal of the United States was to prevent the Russians from occupying all of Korea and to restrict the Soviet Union from expanding its occupation to the entire peninsula. It seems that containment existed between the Soviet Union and the United States, but the two powers agreed that the north and south zones divided by the 38th parallel would be controlled by the Soviets and Americans, respectively; consequently, neither the Soviet Union nor the United States wanted to expand the war without achieving a clear-cut victory. Halberstam (2007) calls this situation a failure by

Secretary of State Dean Acheson to include noncommunist South Korea in America's Asian "defense perimeter." To summarize the lengthy historical background, it is worthwhile to concentrate on the role of China in the Korean War and briefly on its role in the region. Many revisionists and scholars have studied the Korean War. I will not examine the debate in detail; rather, I seek to describe general facts about the Korean War to prevent my studies from becoming a topic of further debate. As shown above, throughout centuries of history, Korea has been a victim of power politics in the region. It seems as if this situation has never ended.

In South Korea, the Korean War is better known as the "6.25 war." It began at dawn on 25 June when armed North Korean infantry units attacked the Republic of Korea, and within three days, Seoul, the capital of South Korea, was occupied by the North. Kim Il Sung, the grandfather of Kim Jong Un, the current supreme leader of North Korea, had sought authorization from Stalin in 1949 to launch the invasion of South Korea, and Stalin had consented. With air support from the Soviet Union, North Korea launched a surprise attack on June 25, 1950.[3] In defense, President Truman sent American troops from Japan, and the attack was so effective that it has been said that the first nuclear crisis may have been the use of nuclear weapons against North Korea by U.S. forces. British Prime Minister Atlee made an emergency trip to the United States and argued against the use of nuclear weapons (Perry, 2006). Truman agreed and instead built up a massive quantity of conventional arms. In addition, General Douglas MacArthur, who was the supreme commander of the UN forces, made a successful landing at Inchon, forcing the North Koreans to retreat to the north. UN military forces, with soldiers from 21 countries, joined the war. They were from Australia, Belgium, Luxembourg, Canada, Colombia, Denmark, Ethiopia, France, Greece, India, Italy, the Netherlands, New Zealand, Norway, the Philippines, South Africa, Sweden, Thailand, Turkey, Great Britain, and the United States. As Leckie (1962) notes, the number of "dead" and "wounded and missing" for the communist forces is not known; 900,000 and 520,000 are the total numbers for those on the side of the South, respectively. The Korean casualties alone were approximately 8 times greater than the casualties in the Iraq War, during which there was a suicide bombing almost every day. Additionally, the fact that the Korean War lasted less than 3 years, compared to nearly nine years in Iraq, provides a sense of the scale of the Korean War.

East Asia was secondary to Europe in the U.S. struggle with the Soviet Union (Stueck, 2002). Cumings (2010) and Halberstam (2007) note that America intervened in this war without a plan, and MacArthur, as commander, did not even consider that China would dare present a challenge. What was China's interest in the war? There are lengthy discussions about whether China knew of the North Korean invasion, which means questioning whether Stalin informed Mao Tse-tung of the forthcoming attack. Whiting (1960) notes that the transfer of troops from China to Korea certainly shows that Beijing knew of North Korea's attack on the South well in advance. In addition, the hasty redeployment of Lin Piao's crack Fourth Field Army from southeastern to northeastern China during May and June 1950 indicates that China anticipated direct involvement in the war (1960: 45). In terms of Sino-Soviet and Sino-American relations, these facts are significant because victory in the war would serve China's interests. North Korea launched a surprise attack on June 25, 1950. However, the Korean War, refers not only to North Korea's invasion of South Korea but also to a brutal war game between the great powers during the Cold War era. Leckie says, "So the decision to invade was made probably by Premier Stalin, whose retouched photograph graced the wall behind Premier Kim's massive mahogany desk in Pyongyang" (1962: 38). As Johnson writes, "It is also worth remembering that what we call the Korean War ended as a war between the United States and China fought on Korean soil" (2000: 140).

When Eisenhower was elected President, he promised to bring the war to an end, but he found it difficult to end the conflict (Perry, 2006). In 1953, North Korea and China agreed to an armistice. This means that the South and the North are still at war because the two sides merely called a truce to cease the bloodshed. As framed by the documentary "Battle for Korea," produced by the American public broadcaster PBS and Malin Film and Television Ltd., the Korean War was a battle of the Western powers after the Second World War and showed international power relations in the context of the Cold War (Choi, 2009).

The Korean War of 1950–1953 reflects China's foreign policies during the Cold War era. Victory in the war by China would mean an expansion of communism. Moreover, the conflict could place Communist China in a position that would bring the Soviet Union, owing to the communist connection, closer as an ally; at the same time, China could act as a ruling group in relation to the West, mainly the

United States. Therefore, Communist China's voluntary entry into the war represented another rising ruling power group in Asia. As intended, the consequences of the Korean War for China show that even in the present day, China plays an important military and political role in the international community in both the East and the West. In the aftermath of the fall of the Soviet Union and the reunification of Germany, we perceive the world to be in a post-Cold War era. However, the rise of China, as many economists anticipated, and the new capitalist order have brought about a new Cold War. The rising superpower's highly calculated strategies have been concretely visualized since the Korean War and through other conflicts and crises on the Korean Peninsula.

## THE RISE OF CHINA

Since Deng Xiaoping, the Chinese leader who had experienced Western democratic and capitalist prosperity in his early childhood in France, opened up China's economy in the late 1970s, China has grown in wealth, power, and military sophistication and has established cooperative relations with many other nations (Vogel, 2011). Vogel (2011) emphasizes that Deng's character is straightforward and highly disciplined and that he speaks through actions. Additionally, and importantly, Vogel stresses that Deng's youthful experience in France brought him close to the Western world compared to Mao Zedong. Deng played a significant role in shaping social and economic developments in China. Consequently, the rise of China has become one of the most significant events in international politics in the post-Cold War era (Yang, 2009) and is undoubtedly one of the great dramas of the twenty-first century (Ikenberry, 2008). In addition, China has embraced new social, political, and economic agendas in its rise as a new superpower and has been viewed as one of the most essential subjects of foreign policy, as well as international security, since the 1990s (Christensen, 2006; Cooney & Sato, 2009; Kristof, 1993).

A vast amount of academic research has been conducted on the impact of a new superpower on the world. Nye (2003) strongly emphasizes that China's growing soft power is never neglectful and that the United States is losing its place in East Asia; thus, the United States should pay more attention to East Asia, considering the declining poll results regarding its positive influence compared to that of China. However, the East Asia Summit does not have a place for Washington.

In terms of the media discourse, the rise of China seems to have become a hot topic. For instance, in January 2012, Jeremy Paxman of the BBC's "Newsnight" commented on China's growing influence in the world and its grand ambition to become a superpower in the twenty-first century. Moreover, "Inside Out London," hosted by Matthew Wright, examined how high-spending Chinese visitors to London are helping to revive the city's economy; he interviewed the staff at one of the major department stores in London regarding how they should treat Chinese customers. For example, a member of Selfridges' sales team says, "They don't like sales to be pushy— very important to hand with both hands." Department stores such as Selfridges employ dozens of Mandarin-speaking staff because 150,000 Chinese tourists come to the UK every year and spend five times more than American visitors (February 4, 2013). Similarly, advertising companies in the United States must now consider what style of cars Chinese people prefer. GDP per capita is gross domestic product divided by midyear population. GDP is the sum of gross value added by all resident producers in the economy plus any product taxes and minus any subsidies not included in the value of the products. It is calculated without deductions for the depreciation of fabricated assets or for the depletion and degradation of natural resources. The data are in current U.S. dollars. I modified data from the World Bank.[4] The comparison of GDP per capita and exports of goods and services for China and the United States from 2007 to 2016 are as follows (Fig. 1.1 and Table 1.1).

According to the analysis by the World Bank,[5] in 2011, China's gross national income per capita of $4940 ranked 114th in the world, and over 170 million Chinese people still lived below the international poverty line, which was the second-highest number of poor in the world after India. However, with a population of 1.3 billion, China has recently become the world's second-largest economy and is increasingly playing a strongly influential role in the global economy. Moreover, it has been said that U.S. leaders should be aware that China could overtake the United States as the largest state in terms of purchasing by 2020, although the dominance of the Western world will likely continue (Ikenberry, 2008: 36). As shown above, China's extraordinarily rapid economic growth has been causing the United States concern because the United States itself is heavily economically invested in China. In other words, the two countries influence each other through already existing economic ties

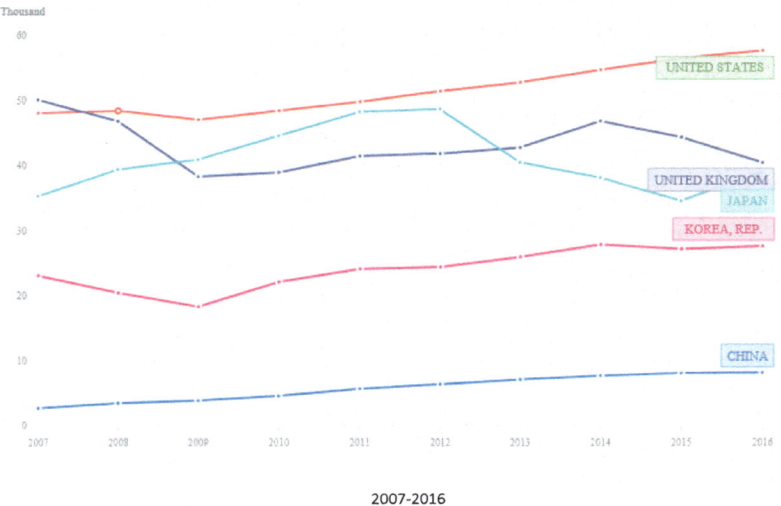

2007-2016

**Fig. 1.1** GDP per capita, 2007–2016 (current US$) (https://data.worldbank. org/, [The World Bank Data])

(Cooney & Sato, 2009). Despite the low GDP per capita in China, the United States. and China dominate the global list of billionaires (*CNN*, March 2, 2013), although the gap between rich and poor is extremely wide in China. However, some argue that it will take China 25 years to become a proper geopolitical actor capable of rivaling the United States in East Asia and in the Western Pacific. Some say that to close the gap with the United States, more sophisticated Chinese military forces and enormous technological advances will be required (David & Grondin, 2006). Apart from China's rapid economic growth, it appears that the United States perceives China as a threat to American security. According to a report to Congress on the Military Power of the People's Republic of China in 2006, the Department of Defense questioned China's intentions, noting that Chinese leaders had not provided an adequate rationale for a great number of recent arms purchases (Cooney & Sato, 2009). Moreover, analysts and experts have anticipated for more than a decade that China could eventually counter American hegemony (Zhang, 2004). Military and economic power do not necessarily mean that a nation will

Table 1.1  GDP per capita, 2007–2016

| | 2007 | 2008 | 2009 | 2010 | 2011 | 2012 | 2013 | 2014 | 2015 | 2016 |
|---|---|---|---|---|---|---|---|---|---|---|
| China | 2695.37 | 3471.248 | 3838.43 | 4560.51 | 5633.80 | 6337.88 | 7077.77 | 7683.50 | 8069.21 | 8123.18 |
| US | 48,061.54 | 48,401.43 | 47,001.56 | 48,373.88 | 49,790.67 | 51,450.12 | 52,787.03 | 54,706.82 | 56,469.01 | 57,638.16 |
| UK | 50,134.32 | 46,767.59 | 38,262.18 | 38,893.02 | 41,412.35 | 41,790.78 | 42,724.07 | 46,783.47 | 44,305.56 | 40,412.03 |
| S.KOREA | 23,060.71 | 20,430.64 | 18,291.92 | 22,086.95 | 24,079.79 | 24,358.78 | 25,890.02 | 27,811.37 | 27,105.08 | 27,538.81 |
| Japan | 35,275.23 | 39,339.30 | 40,855.18 | 44,507.68 | 48,168.00 | 48,603.48 | 40,454.45 | 38,109.41 | 34,567.75 | 38,972.34 |

gain great influence over the neoliberal international order, as seen in the case of the E.U., which has already surpassed the U.S. GDP. Hence, there is growing concern that the United States should modify its foreign policy strategies to retain its international influence (Farley, 2018).

## TERRITORIAL DISPUTES IN THE SOUTH CHINA SEA

The United States fears of China and perceptions of it as a threat are currently based mostly on economic and hegemonic concerns. However, neighboring countries in the Asia-Pacific region, such as Korea, are concerned not only about the economic perspective but also about security. For instance, there have been territorial conflicts between China and Japan and China and neighboring Southeast Asian countries, such as Malaysia, Indonesia, the Philippines, and Vietnam, regarding sovereignty over several groups of islands. Sovereignty over two island chains, the Paracels and the Spratlys, is claimed by China, Vietnam, the Philippines, Taiwan, and Malaysia. Another major island chain of the South China Sea, called "Senkaku" in Japanese or "Diaoyu" in Chinese, is a subject of dispute between China and Japan.

Tension over the sovereignty disputes in the region has intensified since 2015. To attempt to assure its control over the contested areas, China started building airstrips on the islands and established air defense zones, causing the United States to confront China (*The Bloomberg*, May 8, 2015). In the same year, on April 27, 2015, the United States and Japan unveiled new guidelines for defense cooperation that acknowledged Japan's right to "collective self-defense" and enabled greater United States-Japanese coordination of Japan's security in the South China Sea (*Reuters Online*, April 28, 2015).[6] Moreover, regarding China's recent reclamation of disputed South China Sea reefs, John Kerry reaffirmed the U.S. military commitment to cover all territories under Japanese administration, including the Senkaku islands, known as Diaoyu in China (*The Guardian Online*, April 27, 2015).[7] It has been argued that the contemporary idea of security, which was largely defined in militarized terms during the Cold War period, has been expanded (Baylis, Smith & Owens, 2014). However, through the conflict over the Southeast Asian islands, a new Cold War has emerged. Therefore, amid these recent tensions in the Far Eastern Asian region, exacerbated by the maritime conflicts between countries in the region, the U.S. role as a long-time ally of Japan, as well as South Korea since the end of the Second World War, has become even more significant in the post-Cold War era.

China has an open market similar to those in democratic countries, but information and policy decisions tend to be concealed and tightly controlled under the Communist Party system, and access to certain internet browsers such as Google is blocked in China. Hence, a number of Chinese policies and strategies initiated by Xi Jinping, General Secretary of the Communist Party of China, are likely to be clandestine. In addition, as will be discussed later but briefly mentioned here, the current acceptance of English as the universal language plays a crucial role in information exchange and flow as China announces its plans and policies in English through the news media.

Therefore, there are deep-rooted fears of the unpredictability of the veiled nation. That is why the world, including the United States, continually endeavors to interpret China through its actions, various indices and any kind of engagement with other nations. Thus, it is vital for countries in the region, in particular, to keep the eyes of the world, along with those of the United States, on Chinese affairs and foreign policy in terms of international security and to understand the directions of the Chinese power game. In addition, to maintain world order, geopolitics has become even more important in efforts to balance the power in the region against China's rise as a superpower (Baylis et al., 2014).

## THE OBAMA ADMINISTRATION'S PIVOT TO ASIA

The former U.S. President, Barack Obama, announced that the United States was "rebalancing" power in the Asia-Pacific region, a movement that is known as the pivot to Asia. President Obama saw the "opportunity, the obligation, the new challenges and opportunities that will define our future." According to his speech:

> The Pacific region has enjoyed peace and stability for over 60 years, and in that climate, first Japan, then Korea, and even, yes, now today China have had an environment in which they could develop economically and politically without war or conflict. That's not a birthright. That is something that was guaranteed, reinforced by the pivotal military power of the United States in that region.[8]

Thus, the United States would continue to play a pivotal military role in that region "to keep on with that good thing." In addition, the United States was shifting its naval presence to the Pacific with carriers, destroyers, attack submarines, and the new littoral combat ship all moving into the Pacific theater, and there would be a reduction in U.S. Marine Corps end strength, reflecting the wind-downs in Iraq and Afghanistan, but more Marines in East Asia. Finally, "we sustained or launched new capabilities specifically for the Asia-Pacific region – the new bomber, the Virginia payload module for the Virginia-class submarines conventional prompt strike and a host of upgrades in radar, electronic protection, electronic warfare, new munitions of various kinds and on, and on, and on, all not only protected but enhanced going forward" (Deputy Secretary of Defense Ashton B. Carter's speech, May 30, 2012).[9]

Schuman and Scott (1989) say that the Korean War might be hard to resurrect in the American collective memory. They asked a national sample of adult Americans to report "national or world events or changes over the past 50 years." Their findings show that while 21.3% reported the Second World War and 11.6% the Vietnam War, only 1% mentioned the Korean War. Choi (2009) notes that the Korean War has been unpopular both in mass media and among scholars, and a large portion of Korean War images have remained exclusively in communist countries. While the Vietnam War has been discussed frequently among critical scholars and exploited by photography, films and other media, the Korean War has been hidden behind the aura of the Cold War. Why, then, more than 60 years after the Korean War, is the United States shedding new light on the conflict? What does the "magnificent" permanent display in the Pentagon to honor veterans of the Korean War, dedicated by Defense Secretary Chuck Hagel tell us (U.S. Department of Defense, June 18, 2013)?[10] Since the end of the Cold War, in particular in the early 1990s, when the Soviet Union collapsed, partly because of the "glasnost" policy, several former North Korean officers involved in the Korean War published their memoirs about the war. Furthermore, newly released information about the Soviet and Chinese roles in the war introduced enlightened views into the study of the Korean War (Pierpaoli, 2001; Weathersby, 1993). These changes not only indicate new attitudes among the old Communists but also demonstrate that the U.S. pivot policy to the Asia-Pacific region is, in practice, a military shift to the East, "rebalancing" power in U.S. terms. The reason is perhaps Beijing's angry protests against United States and South Korean joint military exercises in the Yellow Sea.

Obama's pivot policy to Asia also shows the shifts of the U.S. military and diplomatic standpoints from a traditional European base to a Pacific base and demonstrates U.S. support for both Japan and the Republic of

Korea, a long-standing military alliance to reassure people in both countries. These countries will be protected under the U.S. nuclear umbrella because the United States and other nations might not want Japan or South Korea to pursue their own nuclear weapons program. Hence, it is important to send a clear message that the regions of South Korea and Japan will be protected by the United States against any North Korean nuclear threat.

## THE TRUMP ADMINISTRATION'S INDO-PACIFIC STRATEGIES

Feng at Beijing University maintains that "Beijing's paramount goal in Northeast Asia is to prevent any neighbour from evolving into a rival" (2008: 69–70). Feng (2008) argues that this policy is not in compliance with the Chinese "good neighbor policy" but is firmly within the Chinese "merchantalist" grand strategy. This means that China is concerned with its rivals in peripheral countries. Grave instability on the Korean peninsula could lead to Chinese domestic insecurity. However, Feng explains that regarding the Korean peninsula, China's greatest concern is how Korean strategies toward China would change after Korean reunification. For China, one of the most important geopolitical considerations related to the Korean Peninsula is whether Seoul will tilt toward the United States and become hostile to China. Some believe that Chinese military intervention in the Korean War will rebound against China with hostility if the two Koreas unify. Feng's arguments imply two key themes. One is concern about the aftermath of Korean reunification, which means that China does not wish to take any risks by playing an active role in persuading North Korea to come to the table. The other is the possibility that because South Korea is a strong ally of the United States, Korean reunification would mean that Korea would be pro-U.S. and anti-China because of Chinese intervention in the Korean War, and subsequently, the United States would have even greater power in the region. It appears that Beijing is concerned about these issues.

Beijing might not want U.S. forces to approach the Chinese border after Korean reunification. In addition, because economic sanctions imposed on North Korea by the United States would increase the North's economic dependence on China, Beijing wants stability within North Korea, not a collapsed North Korean state, which would bring a large number of refugees to China (McGlynn, 2010; Rich, 2010; Thompson, 2010). Moreover, China has been criticized, mainly by the

United States, for not reacting to North Korea's provocations in a timely manner. It is difficult not to receive the impression that these reactions by China have been strategic (Doran, 2012).

North Korea has been called a Chinese "puppet regime" because China has been a key partner for trade and aid with North Korea; thus, it does not want to, or have to, worry about a North Korean collapse (Feng, 2008; Thompson, 2010). However, North Korea does not seem to act as a Chinese puppet regime, although it might do so in the future. China has failed to influence Pyongyang. China's failure to persuade North Korea to cease its provocative actions is caused not by changes in Beijing's policy toward North Korea but by economic logic. It is argued that China has been skeptical about North Korean escalation tactics and unwillingness to participate in the international community (Feng, 2008; Snyder & Wit, 2007). North Korea has watched China's rising power in the social and economic sectors and must have sought ways to preserve its regime. China would not want North Korea to have nuclear weapons, but it might seek even greater power in the world, and Beijing has discovered that increased power is possible through economic growth. This economic logic has brought China power in international relations, empowered its military forces and helped it gain territory for which it hoped. Therefore, the North Korean issue is a complex one for Beijing.

It has been said that North Korea's nuclear provocations and skirmishes with South Korea were intended to bring the United States to the table for negotiations (He & Feng, 2013). However, although this view is still controversial, some believe that Trump's hardline policy of strict economic sanctions toward North Korea might have pressured it to come to the table for a dialogue. It may have led the North Korean leader, who has remained behind a veil, to decide to talk to South Korean President Moon Jae In, the President of the People's Republic of China and President of the United States Donald Trump directly and actively by convincing North Korea to give up its nuclear ambitions. The historic Singapore summit between Donald Trump and Kim Jong Un, who was unveiled on June 12, 2018, showed the world what North Korea ultimately wants. Its goal was to guarantee the nation's security and maintain its monopolistic state system. It seems that people, including journalists, as shown by the press conference immediately after the Singapore summit between Trump and Kim Jong Un, are interested in what was discussed in the summit and the human rights issue. American journalists are interested in what benefits the United States could obtain from the meeting. For South Koreans, the main interests are the economic benefit that South Korea could obtain in the future, reunification for elderly people and the peace treaty that could end the armistice.

However, I wish to note the importance of the process leading up to the summit. First, there was the inter-Korean summit between Kim Jong Un and Moon Jae In. The first-ever meeting since the Korean War between the North and the South in South Korea at the border was a historic moment. However, before the next inter-Korean meeting, Kim Jong Un secretly visited Xi Jinping by train on Monday, May 26 (*The New York Times*, March 28, 2018).[11] It was the first time that Kim Jong Un had visited the Chinese President since taking over the leadership of North Korea in 2011. South Korean President Moon Jae In also visited President Trump ahead of the inter-Korean meeting. In addition, President Moon met President Trump in the White House to discuss the Singapore summit between President Trump and Kim Jong Un in the hope of a successful meeting. A few days after their meeting, however, President Trump canceled the Singapore summit in a formal letter to Kim Jong Un on May 24, 2018. The reason to cancel the long-planned meeting was the anger and hostility displayed in North Korea's statement (*CNN*, May 2018).[12] A few days later, it was reported that Kim Jong Un had secretly met again with Xi Jinping. These roller-coaster-like meetings between South Korea and the United States and China and North Korea prior to the Singapore summit imply that the division and reunification of the two Koreas are dependent on the two superpowers, stemming from the history of the end of the Second World War and the end of the Korean War. In other words, China and the United States played pivotal roles in the process leading up to the summit.

U.S. Secretary of State Pompeo announced details of Washington's Indo-Pacific strategy: "After World War II, we worked with Japan to forge a great alliance and stimulate an economic boom. South Korea in the 50s was ravaged by conflict. American assistance and investment in railways, ports, and other infrastructure helped create a foundation for our South Korean friends to recover, thrive, and build one of the world's most prosperous economies." Then, he explained that the ASEAN states, such as South Korea, Japan, Australia, and Taiwan, including China and India, have interests that emphasize "free" and "open." The United States certainly wishes to include India with other core Asia-Pacific countries and seems to strive not to exclude China so that its strategy will not be perceived as countering China's one belt one road policy.

## FOREIGN POLICY AND NATIONAL INTERESTS

Condoleezza Rice (2000) suggests in her article "Promoting the National Interest" that American foreign policy in a Republican administration should refocus on the national interest and the pursuit of key priorities. These tasks are as follows:

- to ensure that America's military can deter war, project power, and fight in defense of U.S. interests if deterrence fails;
- to promote economic growth and political openness by extending free trade and a stable international monetary system to all committed to these principles, including in the western hemisphere, which has too often been neglected as a vital area of U.S. national interest;
- to renew strong and intimate relationships with allies who share American values and can thus share the burden of promoting peace, prosperity, and freedom;
- to focus U.S. energies on comprehensive relationships with the great powers, particularly Russia and China, that can, and will, mold the character of the international political system; and
- to deal decisively with the threat of rogue regimes and hostile powers, which is increasingly taking the forms of the potential for terrorism and the development of weapons of mass destruction (WMD).

At that time, she had been appointed national security adviser after George W. Bush was elected President. In 2008, she reflects on U.S. foreign policy over the past eight years in her article "Rethinking the National Interest." She states that the U.S. national interest is democratic state building and restoring an American world leadership role. However, after 9/11, she maintains that there should be some changes in foreign policy, such as maintaining good strategic ties with nations such as India and Brazil, a newly emerging great power (2008: 5). In accordance with U.S. national interests and foreign policy in the framework of globalized U.S. security, North Korea continues to be a threat and a potential terrorist regime. As Rice (2008) states, if significant transitions in U.S. foreign policy need to be made, what should those be? Considering the Iraq War, no one can guarantee that there will not be a war on the Korean peninsula based on the U.S. national interests and foreign policy described above.

As President Bush defined the "Axis of Evil," its members are Iraq, Iran, and North Korea. Prior to the U.S. invasion of Iraq, it was revealed that North Korea had the largest military force as well as the most advanced WMD program of the three. For instance, its numbers of active troops, active main battle tanks, and self-propelled artillery were more than twice what could be found in Iraq or Iran (Howard, 2004). Despite the fact that North Korea had a greater material capability than Iraq or Iran, the United States chose to negotiate with North Korea in lieu of a war at that time. Howard (2004) argues that the reason that the United States did not invade but negotiated with the North was based on American foreign policy toward South Korea. On the other hand, according to Victor Cha[13] (2002), who was President Bush's top adviser on North Korean affairs, the Bush administration resisted any dialogue with North Korea until it resolved and ceased its uranium enrichment activities. Additionally, he said that "Kim Jong-Il's credibility in Washington is not at zero, it is less than zero." Cha said that Kim Jong Un is not a reformer and that economic sanctions would not make any difference, as they never have (*AP*, March 8, 2013). Importantly, Victor Cha said that U.S. foreign policy toward the North would be dependent on the Korean President's policy. North Korean issues cannot be separate from politics, U.S. foreign policy and U.S. national interests under the umbrella of globalized security (*YTN*, February 26, 2013). In addition, Guy Sorman, a renowned French scholar and philosopher, said that China and North Korea are unpredictable and unstable. Thus, a good relationship and cooperation between Japan and South Korea are important (*The KyungHyang Shinmun*, September 18, 2012).

## North Korean Denuclearization

As I have outlined above, the issues related to North Korea are not only conflicts between South Korea and North Korea but also U.S. foreign policy issues as well as Japanese, Chinese, and South Korean policy and power relations. In particular, Mandelbaum (1997) states that the deployment of American military power near the border of Russia and China, together with post-Cold War American foreign policy and U.S. decisions and peaceful policies that it believes other countries will not fail to agree to, can be so sensitive that they may bring serious consequences. He explains that each country regards its actions as legitimate even when they can be perceived as a threat by opponents. For example, the American admission of Taiwanese President Lee Teng-hui to the United States in June 1995 caused China to view the United States as promoting Taiwanese independence, even though China believes that Taiwan is historically Chinese territory (1997: 87–88). Furthermore, Livingston emphasizes that "Of the presumed media effects on foreign policy…the U.S. foreign policy agenda itself is at times merely a reflection of news content" (1997: 6). He adds that the media content does not necessarily create issues from nothing but that foreign policy agendas are reiterated by news (1997: 6). Despite Livingston's stress on television news, such as *CNN*, due to its dramatic visuals, he shows how the news media impact the operation of foreign policy and the dynamic interaction between news coverage and U.S. foreign policy making that could lead to military intervention. In a country such as South Korea, which is confronting North Korea and was once occupied by Japan, and whose current wartime operational capacity is controlled by the United States, national policy making can be affected by U.S. foreign policy and peripheral countries' foreign policies. Thus, under the circumstances, it is imperative to study the ways in which international media report on international conflicts, specifically how the media set an agenda, how they frame news agendas, and how they interact with foreign policies, given that the media are influenced by U.S. foreign policy (Graber & Dunaway, 2018).

## NOTES

1. Japanese Prime Minister Noda claimed that there is no evidence that Japan forcefully recruited young Korean girls as sex slaves. These women, now elderly, protest regularly in front of the Japanese Embassy in Seoul, asking for an apology. Japan's brutal and repressive colonization and its denial of the recruitment of sex slaves have engendered strong feelings of animosity toward Japan and exacerbated the conflict between the two countries that continues to this day. In addition, Korean organizations continue to seek legal measures to force Japan to accept responsibility for this unresolved issue (Cho, 2011; Kim, 2011).
2. The 60th Anniversary of the Korean War Commemoration Committee, www.koreanwar60.go.kr.
3. The 60th Anniversary of the Korean War Commemoration Committee, www.koreanwar60.go.kr.
4. https://data.worldbank.org/indicator/NY.GDP.PCAP.CD?end=2016&locations=CN-US-GB-KR-JP&start=2007&view=chart.

5. http://webcache.googleusercontent.com/search?q=cache: KYQUrN6qolYJ:www.worldbank.org/en/country/china/overview+ &cd=6&hl=en&ct=clnk&gl=uk.
6. http://www.reuters.com/article/2015/04/28/us-usa-japan-defense-idUSKBN0NI08O20150428.
7. http://www.theguardian.com/us-news/2015/apr/27/us-japan-defense-deal-broadens-role-chinese-might.
8. http://www.defense.gov/news/newsarticle.aspx?id=116550.
9. U.S. Department of Defense, News Transcript. http://www.defense.gov/transcripts/transcript.aspx?transcriptid=5044.
10. http://www.defense.gov/news/newsarticle.aspx?id=120317.
11. https://www.nytimes.com/2018/03/27/world/asia/kim-jong-un-china-north-korea.html.
12. https://edition.cnn.com/2018/05/24/politics/trump-north-korea/index.html.
13. Victor Cha joined the Center for Strategic and International Studies (CSIS) as a senior advisor and professor at George Washington University in the U.S.

## REFERENCES

Baylis, J., Smith, S., & Owens, P. (2014). *The Globalization of World Politics: An Introduction to International Relations.* New York, NY: Oxford University Press.

Cha, V. (2002). Korea's Place in the Axis. *Foreign Affairs, 81*(3), 79–92.

Cho, S. (2011). Special Issue: National Humiliation, One Hundred Years; History and Legal Responsibility in the Japanese Military "Comfort Women" Issue. *Democratic Legal Studies, 45*(0), 81–112.

Choi, S. (2009). The New History and the Old Present: Archival Images in PBS Documentary Battle for Korea. *Media, Culture and Society, 31*(1), 59–77.

Christensen, T. (2006). Fostering Stability or Creating a Monster? The Rise of China and U.S. Policy toward East Asia. *International Security, 31*(1), 81–126.

Cooney, J. K., & Sato, Y. (2009). *The Rise of China and International Security: American and Asia Respond.* London and New York: Routledge.

Cumings, B. (1983). *Child of Conflict: The Korean-American Relationship, 1943–1953.* Seattle: University of Washington Press.

Cumings, B. (2010). *The Korean War: A History.* New York: Modern Library.

David, C.-P., & Grondin, D. (2006). *Hegemony or Empire?: The Redefinition of US Power Under George W. Bush.* Aldershot, UK and USA: Ashgate.

Doran, F. C. (2012). Power Cycle Theory and the Ascendance of China: Peaceful or Stormy? *SAIS Review of International Affairs, 32*(1), 73–87.

Farley, R. (2018, February 27). How Can the US Manage a Rising China? *The Diplomat*. https://thediplomat.com/2018/02/how-can-the-us-manage-a-rising-china/.

Feng, Z. (2008). The Russia-Georgia Military Conflict: For China, Does It Mean Scrambling Between a "Strategic Partnership" and Being a "Responsible Stakeholder"? *Korean Journal of Defense Analysis, 20*(4), 305–318.

Graber, A. D., & Dunaway, J. (2018). *Mass Media and American Politics* (10th ed.). Washington, DC: CQ Press.

Halberstam, D. (2007). *The Coldest Winter: America and the Korean War*. London: Pan Macmillan.

He, K., & Feng, H. (2013). Xi Jinping's Operational Code Beliefs and China's Foreign Policy. *The Chinese Journal of International Politics, 6*(3), 209–231.

Howard. (2004). Why Not Invade North Korea? Threats, Language Games, and U.S. Foreign Policy. *International Studies Quarterly, 48*, 805–828.

Ikenberry, G. J. (2008). The Rise of China and the Future of the West. *Foreign Affairs, 87*(1), 23–37.

Johnson, C. (2000). *Blowback, Sphere: The Costs and Consequences of American Empire*. Little, London: Time Warner Paperbacks.

Jung, J.-H., Kim, A.-K., Shin, S.-J., Shin, K.-J., & Cho, Y.-N. (2011). *The Dilemma and Solution of the Relationship Between Korea and China*. Samsung Economy Research Institute.

Kim, H.-K. (2011). *The Problems and Responsibilities for Comfort Woman*. ASEA Research, Korea University.

Kristof, N. D. (1993, November/December). The Rise of China. *Foreign Affairs, 72*(5).

Leckie, R. (1962). *Conflict: The History of the Korean War*. Canada: Longmans.

Lee, S. H. (2001). *The Korean War*. London: Pearson Education.

Livingston, S. (1997, June). *Clarifying the CNN Effect: An Examination of Media Effects According to Type of Military Intervention* (Research Paper R-18). Cambridge, MA: The Joan Shorenstein Barone Center on the Press, Politics and Public Policy at Harvard University. Retrieved from http://genocidewatch.info/images/1997ClarifyingtheCNNEffect-Livingston.pdf.

Lowe, P. (1997). *The Origins of the Korean War* (2nd ed.). London: Longman.

Mandelbaum, M. (1997). Westernizing Russia and China. *Foreign Affairs, 76*, 80–95.

McGlynn, J. (2010). Politics in Command: The "International" Investigation into the Sinking of the Cheonan. *The Asia-Pacific Journal: Japan Focus*. http://www.japanfocus.org/-john-mcglynn/3372.

Moon, M. (2018). Manufacturing Consent? The Role of the International News on the Korean Peninsula. *Global Media and Communication, 14*(3), 265–281.

Nye, J. S., Jr. (2003). US Power and Strategy After Iraq. *Foreign Affairs, 82*(60), Heinonline.

Perry, W. J. (2006). Proliferation on the Peninsula: Five North Korean Nuclear Crises. *The ANNALS of the American Academy of Political and Social Science, 607*, 78–86.

Pierpaoli, G. P. (2001). Beyond Collective Amnesia: A Korean War Retrospective. *International Social Science Review, 76*(3/4), 92–102.

Rice, C. (2000). Promoting National Interest. *Foreign Affairs, 79*, 46–62, HeinOnline.

Rice, C. (2008). Rethinking National Interest: American Realism for a New World. *Foreign Affairs, 87*, 2–26, HeinOnline.

Rich, S. T. (2010, Autumn/Winter). Engaging North Korea After the Cheonan Sinking. *The Newsletter, 55*.

Schuman, H., & Scott, J. (1989). Generations and Collective Memories. *American Sociological Review, 54*(3), 359–381.

Sheen, S.-H. (2009). Out of America, into the Dragon's Arms: South Korea, a Northeast Asian Balancer? In J. K. Cooney & Y. Sato (Eds.), *The Rise of China and International Security*. New York: Routledge.

Snyder, S., & Wit, J. (2007, February). *Chinese Views: Breaking the Stalemate on the Korean Peninsula* (Special Report 183). United States Institute of Peace. Retrieved from https://www.usip.org/sites/default/files/sr183.pdf.

Stueck, W. (2002). *Rethinking the Korean War: A New Diplomatic and Strategic History*. Princeton, NJ: Princeton University Press.

Thompson, D. (2010, August 13). *China's Perspective of Post-Cheonan Regional Security*. Presented at the Asan Institute for Policy Studies Symposium, Seoul, Korea.

Vogel, F. E. (2011). *Deng Xiaoping and the Transformation of China*. Cambridge, MA and London, UK: The Belknap Press of Harvard University Press.

Weathersby, K. (1993). The Soviet Role in the Early Phase of the Korean War: New Documentary Evidence. *Journal of American-East Asian Relations, 2*(4), 425–458.

Whiting, S. A. (1960). *China Crosses the Yalu: The Decision to Enter the Korean War*. Stanford, CA: Stanford University Press.

Williams, D. (2004). *Defending Japan's Pacific War: The Kyoto School Philosophers and Post-White Power*. London: RoutledgeCurzon.

Yang, J. (2009). The Rise of China: Chinese Perspectives. In K. Cooney & Y. Sato (Eds.), *The Rise of China and International Security: American and Asia Respond* (pp. 13–37). London and New York: Routledge.

Zhang, B. (2004). American Hegemony and China's U.S. Policy. *Asian Perspective, 28*(3), 87–113.

# CHAPTER 2

# Journalism Theories in Media Studies

This chapter discusses the current media literature and journalism theories to clarify the rationale for the framework of my research within the sociological field of news production. At the same time, given the conflict between the two Koreas, whether the major theoretical approaches can be applied to the examination of Korean news production will be discussed. By exploring the role of news in democratic countries, Bourdieu's concept of 'a field' and the factors that influence news frames will be construed. In addition, this chapter discusses the necessity of a paradigm shift in journalism studies in the wake of the end of the Cold War, as Hallin and Mancini (2004) state.

## The Role of the Media: Media and Democracy

Public opinion is said to be the great engine of democracy, shaping what governments do. In fact, public opinion does influence policy making (Page & Shapiro, 1983; Petry & Mendelsohn, 2004). Hence, various measurements have been used by politicians and the media as indicators or indexes of public opinion. The proliferation of polls seems to show that they provide accurate assessments of the popular sentiments of the public and are very important in a democratic society. In particular, the latest presidential poll results become an everyday news topic when elections are imminent, although the accuracy of public preelection polls during presidential campaigns and how they are reported in political communication have been criticized. Research on media effects on

© The Author(s) 2019
M. Moon, *International News Coverage and the Korean Conflict*,
https://doi.org/10.1007/978-981-13-6291-0_2

public opinion has appeared for decades in the literature of the media and public opinion. In particular, a great body of studies has explored the relationship between media coverage based on polls and its effects on voters in political communication (Blais & Bodet, 2006; Gunther & Christen, 1999; Irwin & van Holsteyn, 2002). The findings show that the media are able to reflect social issues in ways that indicate that they intend to influence and shape public opinion (Henry & Tator, 2000). In other words, in its impact on public opinion, the media representation of a subject plays a significant role in affecting citizens' interpretations of the issue. In the same vein, Curran asserts that news media "facilitate the formation of public opinion by providing an independent forum of debate, and they enable people to shape the conduct of government... The media are thus the principal institutions of the public sphere" (1991: 29).

In Entman's (1993) definition, news frames indicate to the public what to think about, what to look at and what not to look at, and how to think about an issue. In other words, journalists and editors decide what the public will think about and how they will think about it. Thus, a few judgments have already been made before a media audience makes contact with the news; the media "make moral judgments – evaluate causal agents and their effects and suggest remedies – offer and justify treatments for the problems and even predict or forecast their likely effects" (Entman, 1993: 52). However, Castells (2009) contends that information per se is unlikely to change public attitudes because they tend to obtain information according to set frames in their minds; thus, stimuli are needed to change public emotions and influence people's decision-making.

## WHAT IS NEWS?

Social science scholars say that journalists make news, or "news is constructed by reporters." According to Walter Lippmann (1922), one of the pioneers in attempting to explore the nature of news, news is a product of a series of selections by journalists—not through an objective process but through conventions.

To say that a news report is a story, no more, but no less, is not to demean
news, nor to accuse it of being fictitious. Rather, it alerts us that news, like
all public documents, is a constructed reality possessing its own internal
validity. (Tuchman, 1976: 97)

Tuchman defines news as a window on the world. Like Lippmann, she
maintains that news not only reflects a reality but also constructs a reality. "Even journalists who are critical of the daily practices of their colleagues and their own organizations find this talk offensive" (Schudson,
1989: 263). Schudson (1989) argues that journalists act as gatekeepers
in constructing news to "pass" their news item. In other words, news
items are selected by journalists and constructed by them in terms
of the ways that they perceive events. Hence, cultural, as well as sociological, perspectives in context must be considered because through
that window, the news delivered to the world is defined by the ways in
which people who hold power wish to construct it. In a similar vein,
Shoemaker (2006) states that news is a social construct—a thing, a commodity—whereas newsworthiness is a cognitive construction, a mental
judgment.

Allan approached the definition of news from the structuralist perspective, stating that "'news' does not reflect a reality, rather it provides a codified definition of what should count as the reality of an
event" (2004: 4). He argues that it is crucial to consider the process
of news selection because market-based impartiality leads to the objectivity of the practices of the newsroom based on the needs of the news
market and independence from political control. There are a myriad of
factors that affect the shaping of news content, including journalistic
practices of sourcing and narrative writing (Allan, 2004), in the same
vein as what Hall, Critcher, Jefferson, Clarke, and Roberts (1978)
stressed; the process of constructing a news story or topic is significant because it is involved in the ways in which a news article is presented and disseminated to the assumed audience, which is affected by
the media representation. In other words, the process of identification
and contextualization of a news event, meaning the ways in which a
news story is encoded within a context of social and cultural frames, is
important in terms that not only make the news event comprehensible

but also map its meaning—making the media message understood by the audience; these messages are structured through the procedures (Hall et al., 1978). Thus, these authors assert that the media's mapping is performed through the ways in which the media define and interpret an event (1978: 54–58). Therefore, it is worth noting that the news is not a simple reflection of reality, as in a mirror theory; instead, it has been argued that the news structures not only the public's perceptions but also the frame of social reality (Bennett, 1982; Hartley, 1982).

The concept of the social construct of reality has been embodied in more recent studies. In the process, scholars have tended to find operational frames in news texts. In particular, for studies related to ideological aspects of the mass media, the news frames have become conceptualized and used as a mechanism or a device. The concept of a frame has been adopted by researchers who study the characteristics of media messages and the process of media production. McQuail states that "there can be little doubt that the media, whether moulders or mirrors of society, are the main messengers about society" (2010: 82). Todd Gitlin defines a frame as follows: "what makes the world beyond direct experience look natural is a media frame" (1980: 6). He argues that in a corporate capitalistic society, the media play a pivotal role in forming and disseminating hegemonic ideology. In addition, he asserts that "frames are principles of selection, emphasis, and presentation constituted of little tacit theories about what exists, what happens and what matters" (1980: 6). He analyzes how the American mainstream news media, *The New York Times* and CBS News, covered Students for a Democratic Society in late 1965. In the beginning, the media selected a positive frame for the group, the New Left. However, as the group grew in size and power as part of the anti-Vietnam War movement and became a threat to dominant elite ideologies, Gitlin found that the news media depicted the students as a terrorist group, selecting negative news frames for the protesters in the news discourse and relying on government officials as news sources. Furthermore, Hallin examines American media coverage of the Vietnam War in the 1960s and the Civil War in El Salvador and demonstrates how news media coverage of the war in Vietnam, until 1968, was largely supportive of the war, which was the view of Washington, and rarely published criticisms of official U.S. policy (1989: 25).

## THE MEDIA IN POLITICS

Castells explains that "media politics is a composite social practice made of media and politics" (2009: 228). He notes that "While politicians feed the media, the media often feast on raw politics, either to cook it for the audience or let it rot, so that the feeders become exposed, thus attracting the interest of the public in both cases" (2009: 227–228). Along the same lines, Keane argues that journalists need politicians and governing officials for the raw material that is constantly required to fill space and program gaps. The relationship between officials and journalists is geared toward attracting public attention, which means constant announcements made by governing officials as a news source. However, Keane is critical of the way that these actors are likely to be in search of mutual favors rather than acting as detectors or triggers of political scandals. Therefore, a mediacracy in which accredited journalists and politicians mutually favor each other hampers the circulation or coexistence of other, different pictures of reality, such as democracy, and does not render the powerful accountable to the citizenry (Keane, 2011).

A substantial amount of work has been carried out to propose models that explain the factors that influence how journalists cover certain news events in attempts to enhance our understanding of the production of news stories (Kepplinger, Donsbach, Brosius, & Staab, 1989; Schudson, 1991; Shoemaker & Reese, 1996). Shoemaker and Reese (1996) classified the factors influencing journalists' news decisions in five levels: the individual level, media-routine level, organizational level, social-institution level, and social system level. The individual level of analysis involves the characteristics of individual people; the routine level is concerned with general patterns of communication; the organizational level looks at the characteristics of organizations; the social and institutional level examines forces outside media organizations, such as governments and advertisers; and the social system level accounts for social structures, ideologies, and cultures. For the individual-level perspective, Bennett (2012) contends that a journalist's ideology and partisan biases do not seem to be a concern. Nevertheless, a poll conducted by the Pew Research Center for the People & the Press finds that the majority of people believe that their political views have an effect on journalists' objective news reporting. Taking these survey results into account, he argues that many journalists are more liberal even than the general public but that they have difficulty remaining consistent with their news organizations, for example, with editors who "enforce norms of balance and fairness" (2012: 39).

In the same vein, Patterson and Donsbach explicitly address the idea that journalists are partisan actors, and the press and political parties were once closely linked (1996: 455). However, they conclude that partisan news organizations nearly disappeared in the modern society of the United States in the late 1990s, and there has been a gradual decline over a long period in Europe as well. They compare and contrast partisanship in Europe and in the United States. For example, their study shows that a journalist's partisanship has little relation to that of news organizations in the United States. Bennett (2012: 41–42) concludes that in reality, journalists write a story to draw the public's attention to an issue. In his view, this role is much more important than infusing political biases into the news. In addition, he argues that the influence of the Hutchins Commission report on the American press, which emphasized that various opinions should be exchanged face to face and the "truth" should be discovered through local market competition, seems to have failed because dominant views are the results of government publicity and interests, and it is difficult to bring together the views of diverse communities that usually lack face-to-face deliberation. Therefore, American news is highly dramatized, with little information and the narrowest possible choices of various views when the media cover events in mainstream news reporting, although American journalists are considered the freest in the world.

In contrast, in Europe, including Great Britain, there is a correlation between journalists' political partisanship and their perception of the editorial position of the news organization for which they work. The extent of partisanship is associated with the employment pattern of journalists in different countries. For instance, compared to news organizations in other European countries such as Germany and Sweden, only a few British national daily papers are on the political left, while *The Daily Telegraph*, *Times*, *Daily Mail*, *Sun*, *Daily Express*, *Star*, and *Today* (which ceased publication on Friday, November 17, 1995) are on the right (see Patterson & Donsbach, 1996).

Journalists have a responsibility to provide an abundant "pluralistic spectrum of information sources" to ensure that the public can be placed in an arena where they are exposed to miscellaneous ideas and opinions, as Allan argues (2004: 7). For journalists to be able to perform this mission, Curran (2010: 14) proposes that more public service regulation, as in Finland, leads to a higher level of public affairs knowledge than the market-driven media systems in Britain; consequently, a public broadcasting system better serves the public good.

## JOURNALISM THEORIES

Earlier theoretical approaches to journalism have been concerned with the role of journalism in a Western democratic society and questions of press freedom in the twentieth century (McQuail, 2010). The first media were newspapers. Hence, the original press theory refers to the political power of the press as the "fourth estate" (McQuail, 2010: 168). The Hutchins Commission of Inquiry, which emphasized the social responsibility of the press by stating that news reporting should be objective, was established in 1942 in response to American newspapers' commercialism and sensationalism. (Social responsibility was adopted by Siebert, Peterson, and Schramm (1956) as the third of the Four Theories). Although the Hutchins Commission examined free expression of the press in the United States and was critical of the press, its limitations were apparent, and there was a growing necessity for theoretical and practical treatments of journalism and democracy (Christians, Glasser, McQuail, Nordenstreng, & Whilte, 2009). Moreover, according to McQuail, journalists' ethics and professionalism were other practical principles to apply in sublating the commercial press and enhancing political independence. However, the codes of journalism are of limited Western value and do not embrace a variety of cultures (2010: 172–174). Thus, as Christians et al. (2009) state, what is needed is a general theoretical approach based on the foundations of normative and political theory. Amid the growing scholarly pursuit of a normative theoretical approach to the media (at that time more commonly known as the press) and democracy, the Four Theories were introduced (McQuail, 2010).

The Four Theories are described by Siebert et al. (1956) in "Four Theories of the Press." They introduce the key typological concepts: "The Authoritarian, Libertarian, Social Responsibility and Soviet Communist Concepts of What the Press Should Be and Do." They argue that the press reflects the role of journalism in society and the system of social control associated with sociopolitical systems and social values (Christians et al., 2009: 3–4). These theories overlap conceptually. In brief, the authoritarian theory refers to the media as a function of an elite group's propagandistic social control. The media under the libertarian theory play a role in presenting "the truth," although this presentation may contain pluralistic viewpoints. The communist theory refers to the media as a government instrument. Lastly, the social responsibility theory stems from the Hutchins Commission and is similar to the libertarian theory but stresses the media's responsibility to society. Petley notes that the Four Theories of the Press underline the role of the press as a "fourth estate." He argues that the purpose of the press is to "help discover truth, to assist in the process of solving political and social problems by presenting all manner of evidence and opinion as the basis for decisions" (2004: 68). Hence, he emphasizes the significance of the role of the media as a watchdog, which is a central component of creating democracy in the media and in the field of journalism. Next, I explore the key work, the Four Theories, which concerns the functioning of the press.

The Four Theories provide models to map different media systems in different countries and attempts to reflect the role of the media in society in a sociopolitical context. However, as Christians et al. (2004) state, the collapse of the Soviet Union increased the global South's independence, and criticism of these theories has increased because contemporary society is more fragmented and complex. Additionally, the classic Four Theories tend to fall into patterns of overgeneralization and conceptual narrowness. Others have argued that there should be a shift from the theories to a new reflection of the press (Christians et al., 2009; Hallin & Mancini, 2004; Stromback, 2005). As Hallin and Mancini (2004) say, "Four Theories of the Press has stalked the landscape of media studies like a horror-movie zombie for decades beyond its natural lifetime. We think it is time to give it a decent burial and move on to the development of more sophisticated models based on real comparative analysis" (2004: 10).

Hallin and Mancini (2004) stress the importance of comparative analysis in social investigation, which can contribute to forming a concept and refining the conceptual apparatus. They contend that most of the literature concerning the media is highly ethnocentric in the sense that it refers only to the experience of a dominant Western country—mainly Britain, the United States, France, and Germany—yet is written in general terms, as though the models are universal (2004: 279). In other words, especially for less developed countries, whether the theories developed in the West can be applied to them is an open question. Hallin and Mancini introduce three media system models: the liberal model, which is dominant in Britain, Ireland, and North America; the democratic corporatist model, which is dominant in northern continental Europe; and the polarized pluralist model, which prevails in the Mediterranean countries of southern Europe (2004: 67–70).

Hallin and Mancini emphasize that the classification relates to "ideal types" but could be a useful concept for organizing media and political systems in a comparative perspective (2004: 69). According to their explanations, the liberal model is a system of market-dominated mechanisms resulting in a market-driven commercial media, and the democratic corporatist model refers to the historical coexistence of commercial media and the media associated with social and political groups, which can limit state power. Finally, the polarized pluralist model evidences a strong bond between the media and party politics; thus, the role of the state is very strong. Newspaper sales and readership, the relationship between the media and political orientation/parallelism, journalists' professionalism and the role of the state are taken into account as components of the media system models in these models. However, they have been criticized on the grounds that models rooted in the Four Theories lack the context of media systems. The models do not consider the size of a state or its political context, both of which influence media systems (McQuail, 2005; Potschka, 2012; El Richani, 2012). For example, the liberal model has been applied to the role of the press in the UK by Hallin and Mancini (Petley, 2013: 131). However, in broadcasting, the model has limitations. For example, Britain has different political structures and television systems than the United States, which falls in the same category as the UK. Additionally, compared to America, Britain has a strong public service model of television and imposes strict regulations on commercial television channels. Furthermore, Hallin and Mancini exclude media production and distribution from global market perspectives (Curran, 2011: 44–45). Critically speaking, some of the elements of the components of each model overlap. For instance, journalists' professionalism has several definitional dimensions. One is the degree of journalistic autonomy. It is worth discussing these factors; therefore, I now explore the concepts of journalism practices.

## Journalism as "A Field"

Bourdieu (2005) explains the notion of a field before he addresses the question of degree of autonomy:

> A field is a field of forces within which the agents occupy positions that statistically determine the positions they take with respect to the field, these position-takings being aimed either at conserving or transforming the structure of relations of forces that is constitutive of the field. (2005: 30)

The quotation above is originally from a lecture delivered in Lyons, France, in November 1995 entitled "Champ politique, champ des sciences sociales, champ journalistique" (Benson & Neveu, 2005). A field is a sphere of actions and reactions executed by social agents and how they react to relations of the pressures from "heteronomous" and "autonomous" poles, which are economic and cultural forces, respectively, by constructing, perceiving, forming, and representing those relations. What Bourdieu meant by "social agents" is journalists, politicians, and television journalists. In the lecture, he notes that the field that he analyzes is an expanded form that is the political world, the political "microcosm," which is a social universe equipped with a "relative autonomy." He stresses that the "relative autonomy" must be taken into account to understand the nature of the social universe. In other words, a journalist's autonomy must be considered to comprehend a journalist's practice. Hence, as he states, it is significant to know "who wrote them, when they wrote them, how they wrote them, in which language, who defined the canon" (Benson & Neveu, 2005: 32) to understand texts and to analyze laws, literature, science, art, philosophy, or cultural productions.

Couldry and Curran (2003) contends that economic pressures and cultural forces have increasingly influenced the journalistic field and reduced journalistic autonomy, while the field plays an important role in cultural productions that are distributed to an audience. Hence, he argues that the field implies not a general concept of ideology but the struggle between journalists and other pressures in the process of constructing social objects under the increasing influence of other socioeconomic and political forces. However, Bourdieu stresses that among the three fields—the social sciences field, the journalistic field, and the political field—the journalistic field is a very weak autonomous field. Therefore, "to understand what happens in journalism, it is not sufficient to know who finances the publications, who the advertisers are, who pays for the advertising, where the subsidies come from, and so on … unless one conceptualizes this microcosm as such and endeavours to understand the effects that the people engaged in this microcosm exert on one another"

(Benson & Neveu, 2005: 33). Thus, in developing the concept of a "field," Bourdieu indicates that the producers of the works, the universe of writers, and the ideological background of the writers, such as education, are important elements and emphasizes the importance of journalistic autonomy within this field.

According to Patterson and Donsbach (1996), while only 7% of German journalists said that pressure from management was important, 27% of Italian journalists answered that it is "very" or "quite" important. In South Korea, when journalists based in Seoul were asked about freedom of the press, 20% of them said that it does not exist. In addition, the younger a journalist was, the stronger the journalist's belief that there is no freedom of the press. Those aged between 30 and 39 said that "it is impossible" (Sa, 2009). According to this survey of South Korean journalists, the internal factors that most influence the restriction of press freedom are media ownership, media managers, and media editors. Outside factors that influence journalists' autonomy are advertisers and the government. Sa quoted some Korean journalists who participated in the survey: "The press cannot be free from the government's pressure. Some media do not report the truth in order to protect power groups, and also they release information in favour of them" (2009: 5). As discussed earlier, the state and the conglomerates, also known as "Chaebol," provide the media with large amounts of advertising revenue.

As shown earlier, the degree of journalistic autonomy and heteronomy can be useful in measuring the forces that influence journalism and gauging their effects on society. More specifically, Willnat, Weaver, and Choi (2013) conducted surveys of more than 29,000 journalists in 31 countries or territories between 1996 and 2011. The study shows journalists' job satisfaction and perceived job autonomy. The journalists' demographics—age, education, working conditions, professional values, opinions, and attitudes, including new media technology skills, were all taken into account. Compared to journalists in other countries, Korean journalists had very low job satisfaction and autonomy. The authors conclude that the self-reported competencies of reporters in each nation are correlated with the quality of the news products they create (2013: 1).

However, Hallin and Mancini (2004) criticize two elements of Bourdieu's concept of a field. First, as in contemporary France, an evolutionary process of fields is already happening through the struggle of agents who are working within the field of economics rather than politics. This indicates that the nature of fields is not predetermined; thus, they can change. Second, Bourdieu does not pay attention to power. Hallin and Mancini (2004: 83) emphasize inequality in access to the media and distribution of power. In other words, media systems compete with each other for voice and power. However, in his concept of a field, Bourdieu does not consider comparing systems in terms of their ability to exert power and influence others. It is important to compare media systems because a structural imbalance could mean unfair competition between media systems in addition to the competition between media institutions with different media systems. Therefore, these issues definitely need to be taken into account.

## THE ROLE OF JOURNALISM IN THE NEW MEDIA ERA

One of the most important and emerging issues is whether the internet is revitalizing democracy. On the one hand, in lieu of merely sending messages in one direction, from media producers to the audience, the internet has brought two-way communication online by posting audience members' opinions and comments. On the other hand, the internet has led to the widespread reduction of paid jobs in journalism, and the current crisis of journalism has undermined the quality and depth of the news because constraints on time mean there is less time for investigative field work (Curran, 2011).

Chantal Mouffe says in an interview (Carpentier & Cammaerts, 2006) that many people believe that through the new media, especially the internet, they can realize democracy, but this idea probably stems from a very limited interpretation of democracy. Mouffe comments:

In fact, it (the new media – the internet) perversely allows people to just live in their little worlds, and not being exposed anymore to the conflicting ideas that characterize the agonistic public space. Old and new media are making it possible to only read and listen to things that completely reinforce what you believe in. (2006: 968)

As far as I understand her interpretation of democracy, deliberative democracy is important, but ideally, the participants should be exposed to different opinions and ideas. Through discussions that involve talking and listening to others with an open mind, "agonies" will occur. In the wake of those "agonies" and struggles, a consensus will be achieved.

However, the new media will attract or mobilize people who are in favor of similar ideologies and attributes; consequently, instead of facing different, opposing opinions and thoughts, users seek more possibilities of discussing issues with like-minded people online.

Given that confrontation with agonistic pluralism for deliberative democracy is essential, Dahlgren (2009: 164–165) argues that internet users (netizens) who live in (visit) a particular fragmented "network society" can play a role such as consolidating a collective identity, and in the process, they risk promoting a one-dimensional mentality. He also points out that such mechanisms do not foster the internet's positive potential for promoting agonistic civic cultures featuring citizens' vigorous participatory performances. Ettema (2007: 144–146) stresses that deliberative discussions must be analyzed at the interorganizational and interinstitutional levels, suggesting a definition of journalists' mission as reason-giving actors who enable mutual responsiveness between institutions or a democratic polity and informed citizens. In particular, he emphasizes the procedural principle in the process of finding common ground, together with publicity, because journalism plays a significant role in seeking and offering reasons that neither citizens nor their representatives can resist in order to achieve reciprocal cooperation. The concept of accountability in the realization of deliberative democracy is significant. Curran (2011: 80–82) states that "media doing different kinds of journalism can make different contributions to the functioning of democracy" and introduced four perspectives of democracy—the liberal-pluralist perspective, the rational-choice perspective, the deliberative model of democracy and radical democracy. Radical democracy emphasizes the need for the media to scrutinize not only the government but also social and economic institutions and stresses the role of partisan media in encouraging people to identify themselves and to make the voice of the marginalized heard. He also concludes that combining the two roles for contrast within a media system would be ideal to foster democratic media practices, thus adopting Baker's synthesized "complex" model of democracy.

A pioneer in the alternative media field, John Downing, approached alternative media as radical social actors that attempt to advance social movements in his classic 1984 book "Radical Media." In addition, Downey and Fenton (2003: 187) reinterpret Habermas's revised notion of the public sphere and say that Habermas recognizes both the existence of alternative public spheres and their capacity for challenging domination, highlighting the radical political potential of the internet. Media power might be part of what is at stake, as Couldry and Curran (2003: 7) state, and the mainstream media may be challenged and disrupted by amateur media practices in alternative media. Hence, the "symbolic power" described by Pierre Bourdieu, that is, participatory alternative media, could contest the concentration of institutional and professional mainstream media power and challenge the media monopoly on producing symbolic forms (Atton, 2007). In other words, considering alternative media means examining the relationship between dominant, mainstream media performances and marginal, subordinated alternative practices. The conflict between them is a struggle to dominate in the arena of media power.

Couldry states that "the media themselves are a social process organised in space" (2000: 25) and therefore may be challenged "by other kinds of social processes of media practice, which might lead to more inclusive and democratic forms of media production" (Atton, 2015: 6). In particular, the borders between producers and their audiences are fading, and currently, user-generated media content impacts the mainstream media as well as the media consumers (Couldry, 2010). Arguably, as Bennett (2003) shows, with the advent of interactive communication and information systems, the distributed property of web sites makes it difficult for journalists to work in a routinized manner in a newsroom. Reporters should incorporate the content of alternative media into their stories, and empowerment may then become widely shared, guaranteeing an important adjustment to media hegemony theories. The dynamics of the new media are hard to project because the new processes of technological communication proceed quickly and change immensely over short periods. Bennett points out that the importance of the new digital media in contesting power involves more than just their mere existence as new communication tools from an ontological perspective. Rather, the political impact of the emerging new technology media reflects the changing social, psychological, and economic conditions experienced by the citizens who use them. Therefore, it is significant to explore what political impact the new media have on news journalism and on society— the public.

The "monitorial role of journalism" is still the core task of delivering information to the public, and that role should not be challenged in our news media environment (Christians et al., 2009). The new online media reflect the diverse needs and uses of the audience. However, in the news media landscape, the lack of authoritative news sources and in-depth investigation by the online media is problematic in terms of credibility and uncertainty. In addition, the factors of the competitive market and media institutional pressures that still influence the news are still subject to debate. Thus, Christians et al. conclude that the "facilitative role of journalism, in our account, has been associated largely with encouragement of deliberative democracy at the grassroots level and with encouraging debate and circulation of ideas and information in the public arena" (2009: 238). In addition, they emphasize that independent criticism and comments are important and that the internet media cannot possibly represent critical viewpoints in the media spectrum because they perceive that the internet, "personal media" in their term, cannot play a facilitative role in the mainstream media over the long term. However, it could be argued that some of their views are contradictory. They say that rapid innovation in the use of computers and the internet for communication was already challenging the dominance of the old media. Then, in contrast, they argue that the internet is not good enough to challenge the mainstream media. It is interesting that they say that the structures of media ownership, political-economic critiques, and patterns in the media discourse include a persistent bias toward the strong role of the state, racism, ethnocentrism, the Cold War framework and reliance on the threat of nuclear war. Fundamentally, they argue that a whole new branch of communication law and governance should be created. As shown above, scholars maintain that it is necessary to find a new approach to examining journalistic practices as a new media era arrives with new media systems as well as a global culture (Christians et al., 2009; Hallin & Mancini, 2004). Multiplatform media and user-generated media provoke a series of questions and challenges for those seeking to develop an analysis of media patterns.

## AGENDA SETTING AND FRAMING

The agenda-setting theory was introduced in 1972 by Maxwell McCombs and Donald Shaw in their ground-breaking study of the role of the media in the 1968 presidential campaign in Chapel Hill, North Carolina. The most cited description of agenda-setting effects is "telling people not what to think but what to think about." The agenda-setting theory posits that media attention to a particular issue makes the public aware of the issue. Additionally, in the agenda-setting concept, the media make a particular issue prominent based on the level of coverage;

thus, the importance attributed to the issue is created for the audience (McCombs & Shaw, 1972). In other words, the media make a certain issue salient in the public's mind, so the media agenda influences the public agenda (McCombs & Estrada, 1997). The first level of agenda setting, which is "traditional agenda-setting effects," focuses on relative salience and implies the ability to influence the formation of the public agenda (McCombs, 2004: 13). Although agenda setting has been prevalent in communication research over the past three decades, there appears to be growing criticism of the theory.

Takeshita (2006) notes that the agenda-setting theory has three major problems: "process, identity, and environment" (2006: 276). The problem of process concerns the nature of the agenda-setting process, particularly the degree to which it is automatic and unthinking; the identity problem concerns the blurred concept between agenda setting and framing; and the environment problem is a concern that as communicational technologies develop and the media become multichannel, the public agenda will become fragmented (Takeshita, 2006). For the problem of process, Scheufele (2000) points out that the transfer from the media agenda to the public agenda can be problematic in terms of measurement because the public agenda is measured by a specific media audience's self-report of their schema/perceived recall (Shoemaker & Reese, 1996), while the media agenda is measured by word counts on a computer screen (Scheufele, 2000; Scheufele & Tewksbury, 2007). The agenda-setting theory has been further developed, and McCombs, Llamas, Lopez-Escobar, and Rey (1998) introduce second-level agenda setting, which pays more attention to attributing salience to an issue. First-level agenda setting highlights the salience attributed by the media to a topic, while second-level agenda setting emphasizes the media's influence on attributing salience to a particular issue. Thus, it is debatable that there are blurred lines between second-level agenda setting, and framing theory. Finally, as the technologies develop and the media becomes multichannel, the public agenda will be fragmented accordingly. Despite the criticisms, a concept of agenda setting is a useful research tool that is widely adopted for examining public opinion processes as well as media effects, particularly in a political communication area such as electoral campaigns.

A media frame is "the central organizing idea for news content that supplies a context and suggests what the issue is through the use of selection, emphasis, exclusion, and elaboration" (Tankard, Handerson, Sillberman, Bliss, & Ghanem, 1991: 3).

Framing is a process of organizing ideas or systematizing messages in media content to transfer a media producer's interpretation of a particular issue. Entman states that to frame is to select certain facets of a perceived reality and make them more salient to promote the definition that is created within the selector's framework (1993). Thus, according to Scheufele and Tewksbury, "an integral part of the agenda-setting story is how news reports portray, and how people understand, issues. Research in framing may certainly inform how those processes work and how they influence agenda setting" (2007: 17). In political communication, in particular, the agenda-setting theory supports the effects of a media campaign. For instance, the media set a specific agenda or attributes in favor of a presidential candidate that they support, and the voters will be influenced by the attributes promoted by the media. Although agenda-setting theory has limitations and has received criticism, it has become one of the most influential paradigms from the aspect of media effects on the public in media and communications research for over three decades (Bennett & Iyengar, 2008; Bryant & Miron, 2004; Walgrave & Van Aelst, 2006). In addition, both first- and second-level agenda-setting theory and framing theory play important roles in understanding the relationship between the media message and its impact on public perception. The core issue is that, as Song argues, while the media play a role in forming the public agenda, as explicated in the agenda-setting theory, "Who sets the media agenda to begin with?" is a question to be answered (2007: 75). Likewise, the most significant fact to be addressed in framing theory is that media producers, such as journalists and news institutions, set the agenda and use frames in the media messages that they produce. Hence, it is worthwhile to reconsider the reasons that the subject (i.e., journalists) sets an agenda and frames the agenda, as well as what the agenda is and why they set the frame, because "setting an agenda" connotes that the subject might have a particular intention.

As discussed above, according to agenda-setting theory, the media tell the public what to think about—a topic or issue. In framing theory, the media or journalist frames the agenda or issue based on his/her ideological or psychological context along with other influential factors (Shoemaker & Reese, 1991). Thus, a news agenda can be highlighted with attributes, which is the process of making an issue or attribute salient, while framing it, which is a generalized interpretation of a subject or an issue being constructed in the news by journalists. In other words, the difference between the two is that an agenda or attribute can be a component of the issue, while framing is the integration of the frames as a whole. Thus, framing denotes perspective as an overall view, "the substance of a particular issue," as Pan and Kosicki (1993: 58–59) point out. Through the process of gatekeeping and news selection, news values are determined and constructed by making some aspects salient (Entman, 1993; Gamson & Modigliani, 1989; Gitlin, 1980). To define an issue and make it comprehensible or to promote a certain value and message, frames are constructed by making some aspects salient, a process known as "scattered conceptualization." Entman (1993) stresses that framing has important implications for political communication because it can exert great social power and can lead the audience to have different reactions. Moreover, he says that the public is not well informed and cognitively active. Hence, framing heavily influences public responses to communications (Entman, 1993: 55–56).

Framing theory is an interpretive paradigm enabling an investigative understanding of a text of many texts. Borah (2011) points out that although framing theory has been widely criticized by many scholars, very few systematic examinations have appeared in the published literature. Thus, Borah examines 93 peer-reviewed journals identified as communication journals for a decade using text analysis. The findings show that the most common type of framing analysis method was content analysis (61.5%), followed by experiments (19.8%), which concentrated mostly on the examination of a message design. The important point is that framing studies should pay attention to various aspects, such as "interaction of organizational and ideological factors, gender of the reporters, or cultural repertoires" (Borah, 2011: 256), that influence media frames rather than examining only the media content, although the fundamental concept of framing is to examine the media message. Thus, this book aims to examine not only the news content but also the dominant factors that influence it.

## THE HIERARCHY OF INFLUENCES MODEL

According to Shoemaker and Reese (1996), several factors influence the ways in which news stories are framed and shaped by journalists. These factors can be divided into internal and external factors. In addition, Shoemaker and Reese established five dimensions. The external factors are individuals, media routines, news organizations, and extra-media and ideological dimensions. The internal factors that influence journalistic news content can decide the ways in which the news institution that a journalist belongs to frames the news. Of the five dimensions, the first dimension is the individual journalist himself/herself. This individual aspect includes, first, the individual's occupational background and education; second, the individual's experience, political and religious beliefs and attitudes, social values and faith; and third, the value that a journalist places on the profession, whether as a mere neutral deliverer or as an activist who plays a significant role in society—what role he or she is playing and what role he or she should play. However, these factors do not influence the news directly. In fact, their influence would be quite limited (Weaver & Wilhoit, 1996). Journalists' attitudes toward their occupation, however, are very important elements that can help them make decisions regarding a news story and how to develop it in terms of journalistic roles and ethics. The second dimension is media routines. This refers to routine daily work, meaning repetitive, routine work patterns. These patterns can create a certain context for a particular issue. Media routines have some positive aspects; for example, the media product is produced efficiently without any uncertainty because the journalists know what to do with it (Tuchman, 1973). For instance, news routines can help journalists distinguish good, professional information in order to write about cancer or diabetes based on low-quality materials. Moreover, they know what the audience is interested in and perceives as important news. However, this situation leads to the reason that we should focus on the relationship between news sources and journalists.

When journalists report breaking news, they are the ones who contact the news source for the initial process of framing (Entman, 1991). For instance, when flight KAL 007 was shot down in 1983, from the very first description by U.S. government officials and their stereotypical schematic understandings of international issues related to the Soviet Union, journalists quickly wrote headlines such as "KAL attacked," thus creating an event-specific schema. Such a schema requires that a journalist interpret, perceive and understand the event in a government-supportive way and eventually make the news and report it. In other words, through the interaction between news sources—U.S. government officials—and journalists, most framing is begun and the frames made; the process of framing the event is a so-called event-specific schema. Within those frames, journalists interpret and report the news (Kuypers, 2002, 2009). De Vreese (2005: 52) explains that there are also interactions between media frames and the frames that individuals maintain in their own minds.

Hence, news organizations try to report with the goal of attracting as much of the audience's attention and support as possible. Consequently, news stories are likely to conform to what the audience wants or wishes to see (Gamson & Modigliani, 1989; Schudson, 1978). This interaction results in a close relationship with advertisers (Vliegenthart & Zoonen, 2011). Therefore, media routines have a very close relationship with the goal of news organizations to attract the audience with an end goal of increasing advertising revenues.

From a slightly different perspective on media routines, a journalist is unlikely to pursue more information. Additionally, a journalist tends to maintain consistency with other news institutions. As journalists work more in a web-based work environment, and given their tendency to pursue topics similar to those of other news organizations, they approach and interview the same people. Consequently, they depend on newswire services, such as the Associated Press (Crouse, 1972; Hansen, Ward, & McLeod, 1987). According to Sigal (1973), two-thirds of the total news sources in *The New York Times* and the *Washington Post* that he analyzed were official news sources. Apart from those sources, the findings show that the news reports of American elite newspapers, particularly about wars or military conflicts, are heavily dependent on official government announcements, press conferences, and press releases (Hayes & Guardino, 2010; Schudson, 2011; Waisbord, 2002). This dependence on controlled official news sources discourages the interchange of dissenting opinions, disrupts a journalist's ability to gather news from a wide range of sources, and is likely to strengthen the relationship between the state and the press (Hallin & Mancini, 2004).

One of the most important elements in routinizing news sources is "the expert." Because journalists' personal views are supposed to be hidden in objective reporting, it is necessary for them to find an expert who can interpret an event well. However, the findings show that the total number of experts who appear in broadcast news is very low, and they are from the same elite group (Soley, 1992). No matter how objective and nonpartisan they are, they are from this group, which includes conservative think tanks in Washington, former Republican Party members, and people from elite universities in the eastern United States. For instance, news reporting on the Gulf War depended on a very limited number of experts. Most of them were retired military officials from think tanks in New York and Washington, and they clearly expressed strong political partisanship (Reese, Grant, & Danielian, 1994; Steele,

1995). Shoemaker and Reese (1996) say that except for briefings and pool journalists, general journalists' access is denied, and news reports are censored by military information experts; military officials' control creates source-oriented media routines. These routines are implemented in the name of national security and military policies (Kellner, 1992). Consequently, news organizations can do nothing but depend on military officials and their announcements (Carpenter, 2007).

The next dimension is news organizations. News organizations determine the role of the institution and news frames based on their politics and economics. The owners, news editors, producers, and higher management make up a news organization. According to Shoemaker and Reese (1996), regardless of the kinds of media, the most powerful force is ownership. It is said that ownership functions in favor of the conglomerates and results in media bias. Hence, this stage is very closely related to the effects of ideology. The most powerful ownership influences, indeed determines, company policy, and editors are likely to be influenced by owners' policies and ideology. As a result, the ideological preferences of editors influence the direction and ideology of journalists' news reports. Gulati, Just, and Crigler (2004: 239) state that structural bias means that "norms of journalism or reporter behaviour favour news about some topics over others and that this news emphasis is advantageous for some candidates and disadvantageous for others." In other words, the news is biased against candidates whom the news organization does not support, "not because of their policy positions, but because of reporters' decisions about what is 'news'." However, the reality is that reporters' decisions cannot be viewed as separate from the institution that they work for or from other factors. We first examined the role of frames in the social construction of reality and then discussed one of the factors that influence the media frames in a reporter's news selection. In a broader sense, Goffman (1974) notes that journalistic framing is shaped by the frames sponsored by other actors, such as politicians and organizations, in a heuristic way that involves experiencing broader structural and ideological processes. In other words, a journalist who selects issues and frames issues is challenged by other social, political, and economical actors, such as elites and politicians, and the framing contests one of the actors sponsored by other actors.

In studies in political communication regarding journalists' as well as citizens' partisanship, much research has been conducted, particularly on the effects of news coverage of a particular candidate in an election on public behaviors, such as decision-making in voting and voter turnout. Although Bennett and Iyengar claim minimal media effects on persuasion and attitude change (2008: 15–34), there are heated debates over whether a negative campaign or news coverage also influences public attitudes and turnout. The findings show that despite the great volume of debates and studies on negative political campaigns, attack campaigns do not significantly affect voters' attitudes and candidate preferences. However, notably, news content does influence political participation and public attitudes (Min, 2004). Therefore, the news media influence the public perception directly or indirectly, as the findings show. Consequently, the ways in which a news story is framed are very important in terms of public perception and political attitudes. In other words, the news frame is a highly influential factor that influences the public and its political participation and attitudes.

Finally, of the external factors that influence news coverage, previous studies have considered U.S. foreign policy an influential factor that affects media content. For instance, Chang (1989) analyzes news reports about China in *The New York Times* and the *Washington Post*. The findings show that the better the U.S. relationship with China is, the more positive the news reports are. In other words, foreign policy actually influences the content of the news. In the same vein, according to Lim and Seo (2009), the Bush administration denounced North Korea as part of an "Axis of Evil" and framed it as the greatest threat to existence. Consequently, the framing of the news influenced the perceptions of American citizens. Thus, the government's foreign policy plays a pivotal role in framing a news event because, through the President's and the government's foreign policy decisions, the flow of information from government officials to the news media can be controlled (Entman, 2004).

As discussed above, there are several factors that influence news reports and news frames. As foreign news media emphasize very often in their news reports, the Korean Peninsula is actually at war because the war, which lasted for three years and one month, ended with an armistice rather than a peace treaty. In this situation, what factors are most likely to influence foreign correspondents? How do they frame the news, and how do they report it? As discussed above, the factors that influence the news frame differ from country to country and depend on the media system, especially under circumstances such as those found on the Korean Peninsula, the only country in the world divided into two. First, to understand those influential factors in the Korean context, it is essential to examine the Korean media system along with Korean history.

There is a great body of critical literature discussing the relationship between the Korean media and the government (Choi, 2009; Park, Kim, & Sohn, 2000; Sa, 2009; 2004). However, the study of media–government relations in the Western Hemisphere does not seem to fit media–government relations in South Korea (Park & Curran, 2000). One reason may be that the Korean historical background is quite different from that of Western countries in its stress on "clientelism." In other words, Korean political systems and governments cannot be similar to those in developed countries. Park et al. (2000) describe clientelism as the give-and-take notion that the state provides a position to a political supporter in exchange for his or her support. In 2006, at the APSA annual meeting in Philadelphia, 31 August–3 September, Jonathan Hopkin (2006) unpacked the concept of "clientelism." "Clientelism" is "a way of describing the pattern of unequal, hierarchical exchange characteristic of feudal society, in which patrons and clients were tied to durable relationships by a powerful sense of obligation and duty." He explained that there are two major concepts of "clientelism" in the neoliberal era. The old and traditional clientelism is a form of social and political exchange in which a person does another a favor, and in return, the one who bestowed the favor is likely or expects to receive some benefit. In contrast, the new clientelism is rather a marketing idea in which the client seeks to exploit and maximize the available utility. In other words, economic dynamics have more influence on political relationships and on exchanges of action. Hallin and Mancini (2004) clearly explain this concept as follows:

> Clientelism is generally seen as destructive of 'horizontal' forms of organization such as mass parties and voluntary organizations, but it might be argued that forms of 'democratic clientelism' that aided the growth of such organizations did sometimes emerge in Southern Europe, as they also did when mass parties first developed in the United States in the nineteenth century. (2004: 136)

Hallin and Mancini (2004) point out that France is an exception to this pattern of clientelist relationships and weakened rational-legal authority. Thus, France is considered to be at the boundary between the polarized pluralist and democratic corporatist systems. Importantly, I would wish to stress their contention that "In Clientelist systems, information is treated as a private resource, not shared publicly, and this is one of the reasons journalism was slow to develop as an institution" (2004: 136–137). The traditional concept of "clientelism" might still prevail in Korean society in terms of domestic news production, but it would not be easy to apply it to the news-making of foreign journalists in Korea. Thus, I divide the discussion into two dimensions. First, I discuss the factors that influence news framing at a national level and explore the relationship between the United States and Britain in an international context. Briefly, it is not enough just to compare the media systems between countries because, for issues related to North Korea, several countries are involved, and their own goals and policies are intertwined. Therefore, it is significant to consider international communication theories to explore and expound the international news dynamics in the Korean Peninsula, which I will discuss in the following chapter.

> It is not enough for journalists to see themselves as mere messengers without understanding the hidden agendas of the message and myths surrounding it.—John Pilger[1]

"The War You Don't See" is a British documentary by John Pilger that was released in UK cinemas on Sunday, December 12, 2010. It was also broadcast on ITV in the UK. The documentary narrative describes the First World War, in which 16 million died and 21 million were wounded. At the height of the carnage, British Prime Minister David Lloyd George had a private chat with an editor of *The Guardian*, CP Scott. If people knew the truth, said the prime minister, the war would be stopped tomorrow. However, of course they did not know and could not know. The British public desperately wanted to know what was actually happening, the truth and the reality, so more than half of the British public gathered to watch an official propagandistic film "The Battle of the Somme." The camera showed marching young soldiers smiling, waving their caps, and saying, "Hello, Mum." However, the narrative adds, the horrifically injured, limbless, and decomposed bodies were never reported. This documentary was presented by Rageh Omaar, a *BBC* World Affairs reporter from 2000 to 2006, and Julian Assange, an Australian editor and journalist who is best known as the editor-in-chief and founder of WikiLeaks, which publishes secret information on a global scale. Omaar reported on location from Baghdad, Iraq, when

U.S. troops in tanks rolled into the main square, that "Iraqi people are welcoming the U.S. troops, and their arrival is liberation." In one scene, a boy was shown hitting the toppled statue of Saddam Hussein, and people were filmed kicking it. I recall the scene being reported repeatedly on television in Korea as well. The people pulling the Saddam statue to the ground symbolized the fall of the Saddam Hussein regime and represented the U.S. triumph.

This documentary does not accuse the great powers, such as the Obama administration or the Bush administration or even the British prime minister, but encourages an intellectual rationality in rethinking the value of journalism and the role of journalists. In the same vein, Susan Sontag (2004) also writes about a journalist's framing of war, in particular, how photojournalism can create perceptions and images of the war. She describes from her own sensitive viewpoint how photography, which she believes has a deeper impact on memory than "nonstop imagery," such as television, streaming video, and movies, impacts our memories of a particular frozen moment. Similar to the Pilger film, Sontag says that "the photographic image, even to the extent that it is a trace (not a construction made out of disparate photographic traces), cannot simply be a transparency of something that happened. It is always the image that someone chose: to photograph is to frame, and to frame is to exclude" (2004: 46). The production of a news story, a kind of news construction equivalent to this process that also creates an image, has an impact on the images that people perceive in photography and in documentaries. As Tuchman says (1978: 183–184), news constructs a reality and, in the process of doing so, defines and shapes an event; a journalist makes a story more salient by "highlighting bits of information through placement, repetition" (Entman, 1993: 51–58). Entman emphasizes that "what is excluded from a story or a text is equally as important as what was said." Thus, salience can be achieved through framing a certain aspect of a story (1993: 53).

Previous studies have adopted framing theory and focused on salient frames by analyzing what frames have been used in reporting the news. It might be equally important, however, to focus on investigating what was excluded from the news by a journalist and why. With news text analysis using framing theory, Carragee and Roefs (2004) criticize framing research, a current trend in media research, by maintaining that the relationship between media frames and issues of political and social power, which are frame sponsorship in a broader sense, are ignored. They note that framing theories should focus not only on reading media texts but also on how media frames are shaped. They integrate a media hegemony thesis that stems from Gramsci's framework, claiming that ideology and power relationships influence the process of framing. To determine what was excluded from news, it is crucial to explore news production and its processes—especially news about war—and how it operates. A certain issue may be excluded because a journalist cannot obtain information or because the journalist framed the story by giving salience to other matters "under different circumstances" (Carragee & Roefs, 2004). Hence, it is necessary to explore not only the news frames but also the framing process, which is influenced by a number of factors.

## POLITICAL ECONOMY IN INTERNATIONAL COMMUNICATION

Prior to specifically discussing international communication theories, it is essential to elucidate the concept of political economy and its evolution in mass communication research. As Thussu states, the political economy approach to communication, which examines the structures of political and economic power relations, stems from the critique of capitalism by Marx, Karl (2000: 41). Hence, Thussu notes that from the Marxian perspective, the role of international communication is construed as the exertion of power and control by the ruling classes. He further explains that, especially in the wake of the Second World War, communication theories used mapping to develop media technologies and an incorporated international economic and political system (2000: 41). The critical nature of political economy is also discussed by Murdock and Golding (1977). They mainly criticize media sociologists' "dominant paradigm." They argue that a media sociologist ignores class stratification by criticizing Marx's deterministic and static position; therefore, there is no need to reject Marx's connections between economics and cultural production, base and superstructure. However, as Hall asserts, the media reinforce dominant assumptions and ideas and exclude alternatives; broadcasting is the reproduction of power relations, and its ideological structure is far more central to those relations than "financial kickbacks" (Murdock & Golding, 1977: 9). Hence, news organization proprietors continue to maintain newspapers and analyze economics ceaselessly because it is one of the determinants of a newspaper's survival. It does not mean that the media directly transmit a ruling class's ideology to subordinate groups, but political economy theorists maintain that the role of the media and the imbalanced relationship between the two classes in a social order must be analyzed.

Murdock and Golding (1977) concentrate on the questions of ownership of the contemporary communications industry, control and production in their earlier work. They maintain that newspapers are part of a conglomerate's profitable assets because the operation of a national newspaper indirectly results in rewards of prestige and publicity. Therefore, it is important to understand the economic context of material-cultural production. They contend that it is significant to examine media ownership and the relationships among institutions. Within the territorial boundary of one state, this means focusing on the media relationship to the economic and political contexts by highlighting the role of the media in the "inegalitarian" market system and social structure. On a global macro level, it means that knowledge (news in this study) flows between developed countries, mainly the West and developing countries in the stratified global system, in particular in terms of the unequal transfer of technology and programs from developed countries to peripheral developing countries. Such an approach shows that the process of legitimation, which naturalizes the unequal structures of social relations as ordinary, seems to be inevitable. Hence, the processes of incorporation and legitimation entail discrepancies, gaps, and dissentience between what is to be perceived to be happening and what is actually taking place. Thus, based on the rediscovery of ideological perspectives in the critical paradigm, Hall is concerned with the reconceptualization of ideology and seeks to define the key framework of the paradigm. He states that in the structuralists' approach, the key issue lies in the question of "signification," meaning how a meaning is constructed (1982: 67). He argues that the first essential question that should be addressed is how the signification related to a dominant discourse is produced and legitimized and how alternative constructions around a particular event are marginalized. The second question is how the media successfully and systematically sustain a preferred meaning over dissentient meanings in the same event in the dominant systems of communication.

According to Garnham (1986), the purpose of a political economy of culture is to elucidate control of the means of mental production, which was never meant to be fixed in a simple dichotomous static state. He also says that without the base/superstructure relationship, it would be impossible to discuss a political economy of culture, while Raymond

Williams (1980) focuses on the widespread use of the base/superstructure model in Marxist cultural analysis. Garnham formulates a theory of cultural materialism and postulates that cultural form, what Marx called "nonmaterial production," is not always effective unless it is converted to social forms with material effectivity. For example, an individual may use their body not for cultural reproduction but merely for leisure and art because culture is a complex unity of ideas, institutions, distribution, technology, and audiences. Here, the role of the media is construed as the relatively autonomous ruling elite's ideologies, and as those ideologies become concentrated, cultural production is influenced by a few large corporations with increasingly concentrated power. As technologies develop and communication is digitized, due to the lower cost of media production, a few large corporations seem to have lost some of their power. However, digitization has helped conglomerates enhance globalization and sustain their power efficiently through privatization of the media and deregulation (Boyd-Barrett, 1995; De Beer & Merrill, 2009; Thussu, 2000). Then, how can we view media communications through the political economy lens? Media imperialism can be a useful concept for understanding social relations under the political economy in the neoliberal era (Boyd-Barrett, 1997, 1998). According to Boyd-Barrett, a Marxist analysis of imperialism helps us examine "the continuing dependence of post-colonial states on previous imperial powers within a context of post-Second World War U.S. dominance" (1998: 158).

> Political independence had to be judged within a context of continuing economic and cultural dependence, not simply on specific ex-imperial powers, but on a capitalist world order which was dominated by the prevailing US industrial-military-political coalition. (Boyd-Barrett, 1998: 158)

Classical scholar Herbert Schiller states that beginning after the end of World War II, the United States played a critical role in the development of "media imperialism" (1992). Schiller (1992) focuses largely on the U.S. dominance of the worldwide infrastructure and hardware systems, such as satellites, while other scholars, such as Tunstall and Boyd-Barrett, approach a position of "media imperialism" in media content (Boyd-Barrett, 2006; Tunstall, 1994). According to Boyd-Barrett, there are two main models of media imperialism. One is Schiller's model, and the other is an alternative, "generic" model that was developed in

Europe and is associated with the dependency/imperialism rooted in Marxist theory and the media history of colonialism. He contends that although both Schiller's model and the "generic" model were developed in the 1970s, they are still a useful approach to media practices, not only between developed and developing countries but also within nation-states, such as China, Hong Kong, Taiwan, Russia and other republics of the Russian Federation, Germany, and Austria (1998: 158–160), due to considerably unequal international media practices. Among the various positions that argue that the United States is a dominant media imperialist force, one major study is an international communication theory that is related to the flow of global news. It has been proposed that global news flows from the northwest, mainly from the United States, to the south—developing, peripheral countries (Boyd-Barrett & Thussu, 1992). Furthermore, the United States possesses geographical and infrastructural hegemonic power as well as framing "others" in media content.

## GLOBAL NEWS SYSTEM: GLOBAL NEWS AGENCIES

The dominant literature on global communication largely adopts a political economy perspective. International news agencies play a significant role in the globalization and commodification of international information (Boyd-Barrett, 1997; Thussu, 2000: 130). In addition, Western media, which dominate world news, set a news agenda and report news that reflects the West's global economic and strategic interests, such as the Israeli "good guy" and the Iranian "bad guy," depending on government statements (Thussu, 1997). Hence, global agencies are agenda setters for other media through selecting the allocation of their resources and how widely their stories should be distributed to national agencies, newspapers, magazines, and broadcasters (Boyd-Barrett & Rantanen, 1998; Paterson, 2005; Thussu, 1997, 2000). Boyd-Barrett (2000) explains that a modernized nation enters into a global hierarchical structure between states; then, the hegemonic order of industrialization, trade, and information maintains the global system structure. Thus, a news agency is a form of communication that stems from the necessity of disseminating information about state and capital in modern times, and it consolidates the status quo through the construction of global and national agendas. Global news agencies provide clients with global news through photos, videos, and texts because the elite media outlets have only a handful of reporters in major capitals or crisis locations (Boyd-Barrett, 1997). Hence, as Horvit (2010) states,

> more than 80% of the material in newspapers and other media worldwide emanates from global news agencies based in four of the world's major capitals – all of them in the West. (2010: 73)

She also notes that although influential nations, such as Russia, China, and France, are also home to global news agencies that sometimes function as propaganda tools for their own countries, the United States has the world's dominant news agency, *The Associated Press*, which is one of the largest suppliers of news to most U.S. daily newspapers (Horvit, 2010).

Traditionally, the principal "wholesale" suppliers of international television and print news are news agencies that indirectly represent a global hegemonic power in economy and politics (Boyd-Barrett, 1997). Additionally, a global manufacturer of hardware and software in computers is the dominant U.S. corporation Microsoft, and the manufacturing of parts for personal computers is also mostly under the control of another U.S. corporation, Intel (Boyd-Barrett, 1998). However, Rantanen says that global news agencies have already lost their power due to their financial difficulties and competition with other media (2004: 304). Hence, the world in the twenty-first century has three major global agencies—the British *Reuters*, the Associated Press (*AP*), and the French Agence France-Presse (*AFP*) (Rantanen & Boyd-Barrett, 2004: 39–40). The British Reuters is now Thomson Reuters because in 2008, the Thomson Corporation purchased the Reuters Group. Thomson started as a Canadian newspaper and once owned The Times, The Scotsman, and Scottish Television. Furthermore, the circulation of Thomson Newspapers was very high in the United States in the 1970s. After merging with the International Thomson Organization, it became the Thomson Corporation in 1989. The Thomson family owned 70% of the company and controlled it through the Woodbridge Company, based in Toronto, which also owned *The Globe and Mail* daily in Toronto and CTV, Canada's largest commercial television network.[2] According to Rantanen and Boyd-Barrett, the Thompson Corporation controlled approximately 53% of the new company, and Thompson and its rival business information supplier, Bloomberg, controlled 34 and

33% of the market for financial data, respectively. This situation shows not only the extension of sources of revenue but also the concentrated wealth in North America, where four of the wealthiest news agencies, AP, Bloomberg, Dow Jones, and Reuters, are located (2009: 43).

Rantanen (2004) notes that wholesale international news agencies compete with global broadcasting companies, such as *CNN* and *BBC World*, which operate both as wholesalers and retailers. Thus, western Europe faces competition with the United States to lead the world. She also stresses that news agencies are significant, even if they are not the only sources for foreign news, because they can afford to send costly foreign correspondents to locations where international conflicts occur and have the greatest resources for news gathering. Hence, all central and eastern European countries use Western sources (2004: 305). Furthermore, in a digitized and technological communication era, through the internet, an individual can access international newspapers and broadcast materials electronically in real time, offering alternative ways of consuming news services nationally and internationally (Boyd-Barrett, 2000). The proportion of the output produced by news agencies is very small because most material that can be accessed through the internet is limited compared to the proportion available to major retail clients. Thus, the dominance of wholesalers and retailers may appear to have weakened in the advent of new technologies in communication that have reduced the cost of media production and provided easy access to media products. However, the existing global media system—a large foreign correspondent network—has close affiliations with established media or nonmedia conglomerates (*CNN*, part of Time-Warner, Bloomberg with Merrill-Lynch and Yahoo with Reuters) and should still be taken into account (Boyd-Barrett, 2000: 302–304).

In sum, international news agencies, which are Western-dominated, act as global agenda setters, so their views are most likely to be presented as the norm (Paterson, 1998; Rantanen, 2004; Thussu, 2000). Rantanen (2004) argues that as more global news becomes easily accessible, the national media will tend to indigenize global news texts by translating them into their languages and reframing them to complement international news. Thus, it is imperative to examine news flows between national and international news media to reveal the current news production structures and the ways in which such news is constructed.

## NOTES

1. www.johnpilger.com.
2. http://en.wikipedia.org/wiki/The_Thomson_Corporation. Accessed on August 15, 2014.

## REFERENCES

Allan, S. (2004). *News Culture*. Maidenhead and New York: Open University Press.

Atton, C. (2007). Current Issues in Alternative Media Research. *Sociology Compass, 1*(1), 17–27.

Atton, C. (2015). *The Routledge Companion to Alternative and Community Media*. London and New York: Routledge.

Bennett, W. L. (1982). Rethinking Political Perception and Cognition. *Micropolitics, 2*, 175–202.

Bennett, W. L. (2003). New Media Power: The Internet and Global Activism. In N. Couldry & J. Curran (Eds.), *Contesting Media Power: Alternative Media in a Networked World* (pp. 13–37). Oxford, UK: Rowman & Littlefield.

Bennett, W. L. (2012). *News: The Politics of Illusion* (9th ed.). New York: Pearson Education.

Bennett, W. L., & Iyengar, S. (2008). A New Era of Minimal Effects? The Changing Foundations of Political Communication. *Journal of Communication, 58*, 707–731.

Benson, R., & Neveu, E. (2005). *Bourdieu and the Journalistic Field*. Cambridge: Polity Press.

Blais, A., & Bodet, M. A. (2006). How Do Voters Form Expectations About the Parties' Chances of Winning the Election? *Social Science Quarterly, 87*(3), 477–493.

Borah, P. (2011). Conceptual Issues in Framing Theory: A Systematic Examination of a Decade's Literature. *Journal of Communication, 61*(2), 246–263.

Bourdieu, P. (2005). The Political Field, the Social Science Field, and the Journalistic Field. In R. Benson & E. Neveu (Eds.), *Bourdieu and the Journalistic Field* (pp. 29–47). Cambridge: Polity Press.

Boyd-Barrett, O. (1995). The Political Economy Approaches. In O. Boyd-Barrett & C. Newbold (Eds.), *Approaches to Media: A Reader* (pp. 186–192). London: Arnold.

Boyd-Barrett, O. (1997). Global News Wholesalers as Agents of Globalization. In A. Sreberny-Mohammadi, D. A. Winseck, J. W. McKenna, & O. Boyd-Barrett (Eds.), *Media in the Global Context: A Reader*. London: Arnold.

Boyd-Barrett, O. (1998). Media Imperialism Reformulated. In D. Thussu (Ed.), *Electronic Empires, Global Media and Local Resistance* (pp. 157–176). Arnold: London.

Boyd-Barrett, O. (2000). National and International News Agencies: Issues of Crisis and Realignment. *Gazette, 62*(1), 5–18.

Boyd-Barrett, O. (2004). Judith Miller, *The New York Times*, and the Propaganda Model. *Journalism Studies, 5*(4), 435–449.

Boyd-Barrett, O. (2006). Cyberspace, Globalization and Empire. *Global Media and Communication, 2,* 21–41.

Boyd-Barrett, O., & Rantanen, T. (Eds.). (1998). *The Globalization of News.* London, Thousand Oaks, and New Delhi: Sage.

Boyd-Barrett, O., & Thussu, D. (1992). *Contra-Flow in Global News: International and Regional News Exchange Mechanisms.* London: John Libbey.

Bryant, J., & Miron, D. (2004). Theory and Research in Mass Communication. *Journal of Communication, 54*(4), 662–704.

Carpenter, S. (2007). U.S. Elite and Non-elite Newspapers' Portrayal of the Iraq War: A Comparison of Frames and Source Use. *Journalism and Mass Communication Quarterly, 84*(4), 761–776.

Carpentier, N., & Cammaerts, B. (2006). Hegemony, Democracy, Agonism and Journalism: An Interview with Chantal Mouffe. *Journalism Studies, 7*(6), 964–975 (http://eprints.lse.ac.uk/3020 in LSE Research Online).

Carragee, M. K., & Roefs, W. (2004). The Neglect of Power in Recent Framing Research. *Journal of Communication, 54*(2), 214–233.

Castells, M. (2009). *Communication Power.* Oxford and New York: Oxford University Press.

Chang, T. K. (1989). The Impact of Presidential Statements on Press Editorials Regarding U.S. China Policy, 1950–1984. *Communication Research, 16,* 486–509.

Choi, S. (2009). The New History and the Old Present: Archival Images in PBS Documentary Battle for Korea. *Media, Culture and Society, 31*(1), 59–77.

Christians, G. C., Glasser, L. T., McQuail, D., Nordenstreng, K., & Whilte A. R. (2009). *Normative Theories of the Media.* Champaign, IL: The University of Illinois.

Couldry, N. (2000). *The Place of Media Power: Pilgrims and Witnesses of the Media Age.* London: Routledge.

Couldry, N. (2010). *Why Voice Matters: Culture and Politics After Neoliberalism.* London, UK: Sage Publications.

Couldry, N., & Curran, J. (Eds.). (2003). *Contesting Media Power: Alternative Media in a Networked World.* Lanham, MD: Rowman & Littlefield.

Crouse, T. (1972). *The Boys on the Bus: Riding with the Campaign Press Corps.* New York: Random House.

Curran, J. (1991). Rethinking the Media as a Public Sphere. In P. Dahlgren & C. Sparks (Eds.), *Communication and Citizenship: Journalism and the Public Sphere.* New York: Routledge.

Curran, J. (Eds.). (2010). *Media and Society* (5th ed.). London and New York: Bloomsbury Academic.

Curran, J. (2011). *Media and Democracy*. Oxford: Routledge.

Dahlgren, P. (2009). *Media and Political Engagement: Citizens, Communication, and Democracy*. Cambridge: Cambridge University Press.

De Beer, S. A., & Merrill, C. J. (Eds.). (2009). *Global Journalism: Topical Issues and Media Systems* (5th ed.). Boston: Pearson Education.

De Vreese, H. C. (2005). News Framing: Theory and Typology. *Information Design Journal and Document Design, 13*(1), 51–62.

Downey, J., & Fenton, N. (2003). New Media, Counter Publicity and the Public Sphere. *New Media and Society, 5*(2), 185–202.

El Richani, S. (2012). Comparing Media Systems in the 'West' and Beyond. *Global Media Journal (German Edition), 2*(2), 1–7. Retrieved from https://www.db-thueringen.de/servlets/MCRFileNodeServlet/dbt_derivate_00026501/GMJ4_Richani_final.pdf.

Entman, R. M. (1991). Framing U.S. Coverage of International News: Contrasts in Narratives of KAL and Iran Air Incidents. *Journal of Communication, 41,* 6–27.

Entman, R. M. (1993). Framing, Towards Clarification of a Fractured Paradigm. *Journal of Communication, 414*(4), 51–58.

Entman, R. M. (2004). *Projections of Power: Framing News, Public Opinion, and U.S. Foreign Policy*. Chicago: University of Chicago Press.

Ettema, S. J. (2007). Journalism as Reason-Giving: Deliberative Democracy, Institutional Accountability, News Media's Mission. *Political Communication, 24*(2), 143–160.

Gamson, W. A., & Modigliani, A. (1989). Media Discourse and Public Opinion on Nuclear Power: A Constructionist Approach. *American Journal of Society, 95,* 1–37.

Garnham, N. (1986 [2001]). Contribution to a Political Economy of Mass Communication. In M. G. Durham & D. M. Kellner (Eds.), *Media and Cultural Studies: KeyWorks, Revised Edition* (pp. 201–229). Oxford: Blackwell Publishing Ltd.

Gitlin, T. (1980). *The Whole World is Watching: Mass Media in the Making and Unmaking of the New Left*. Berkely: University of California Press.

Goffman, E. (1974). *Frame Analysis: An Essay on the Organization of Experience*. Boston: Northeastern University Press.

Gulati, G. J., Just, M. R., & Crigler, A. N. (2004). News Coverage of Political Campaigns. In L. L. Kaid (Ed.), *The Handbook of Political Communication Research*. Mahwah: Lawrence Erlbaum.

Gunther, A., & Christen, C. (1999). Effects of News Slant and Base Rate Information on Perceived Public Opinion. *Journalism and Mass Communications Quarterly, 76*(2), 277–292.

Hall, S. (1982). The Rediscovery of 'Ideology'. In M. Gurevitch, T. Benneett, J. Curran, & J. Woollacott (Eds.), *Culture, Society and Media*. London: Methuen.

Hall, S., Critcher, C., Jefferson, T., Clarke, J., & Roberts, B. (1978). *Policing the Crisis: Mugging, the State and Law and Order.* London: Macmillan.

Hallin, D. C. (1989). *The "Uncensored War": The Media and Vietnam.* Berkeley and Los Angeles: University of California Press.

Hallin, D. C., & Mancini, P. (2004). *Comparing Media Systems: Three Models of Media and Politics.* Cambridge: Cambridge University Press.

Hansen, K., Ward, J., & McLeod, D. (1987). Role of the Newspaper Library in the Production of News. *Journalism Quarterly, 64,* 714–720.

Hartley, J. (1982). *Understanding News.* London and New York: Methuen.

Hayes, D., & Guardino, M. (2010). Whose Views Made the News? Media Coverage and the March to War in Iraq. *Political Communication, 27*(1), 59–87.

Henry, F., & Tator, C. (2000, March). *Racist Discourse in Canada's English Print Media.* Toronto: Canadian Race Relations Foundation. Retrieved from https://pdfs.semanticscholar.org/c66d/03d4d67c5978a349cefdf28bae5d-dee7975b.pdf.

Hopkin, J. (2006). Conceptualizing Political Clientelism: Political Exchange and Democratic Theory, APSA Annual Meeting, Philadelphia, 31 August–3 September, Panel 46-18 'Concept Analysis: Unpacking Clientelism, Governance and Neoliberalism'. (http://personal.lse.ac.uk/hopkin/apsahopkin2006.pdf).

Horvit, M. (2010). Global News Agencies and the Pre-war Debate: A Content Analysis. In R. D. Berenger (Ed.), *Global Media Go to War: Role of News and Entertainment Media During the 2003 Iraq War.* Spokane, WA: Marquette Books. Retrieved from http://www.marquettebooks.com/images/JGMC_Volume_3_2010.pdf#page=107.

Irwin, G. A., & van Holsteyn, J. J. M. (2002). According to the Polls: The Influence of Opinion Polls on Expectations. *Public Opinion Quarterly, 66*(1), 92–104.

Keane, J. (2011, September 1). The Hidden Media Powers that Undermine Democracy, *The Conversation.* Retrieved from http://theconversation.com/the-hidden-media-powers-that-undermine-democracy-3028.

Kellner, D. (1992). *The Persian Gulf TV War.* Boulder: Westview Press.

Kepplinger, H., Donsbach, W., Brosius, H.-B., & Staab, J. F. (1989). Media Tone and Public Opinion: A Longitudinal Study of Media Coverage and Public Opinion on Chancellor Kohl. *International Journal of Public Opinion Research, 1,* 327–342.

Kuypers, A. J. (2002). *Press Bias and Politics: How the Media Frame Controversial Issues.* Westport, CT: Praeger.

Kuypers, A. J. (Ed.). (2009). *Rhetorical Criticism: Perspectives in Action.* Lanham, MD: Lexington.

Lim, J., & Seo, H. (2009). Frame Flow Between Government and the News Media and Its Effects on the Public: Framing of North Korea. *International Journal of Public Opinion Research, 21*(2), 204–223.

Lippmann, W. (1922). *Public Opinion*. New York: The Free Press.

McCombs, M. (2004). *Setting the Agenda: The Mass Media and Public Opinion*. New York: Polity Press.

McCombs, M., & Estrada, G. (1997). The News Media and the Pictures in Our Heads. In S. Iyengar & R. Reeves (Eds.), *Do the Media Govern?: Politicians, Voters and Reporters in America*. Thousand Oaks, CA: Sage.

McCombs, M., & Shaw, D. L. (1972, Summer). The Agenda-Setting Function of Mass Media. *Public Opinion Quarterly, 36*, 176–185.

McCombs, M., Llamas, J., Lopez-Escobar, E., & Rey, F. (1998). Candidate Images in Spanish Elections: Second-Level Agenda-Setting Effects. *Journalism and Mass Communication Quarterly, 74*(4), 703–717.

McQuail, D. (2005). Daniel C. Hallin and Paolo Mancini, Comparing Media Systems Three Models of Media and Politics. *European Journal of Communication, 20*(2), 266–267.

McQuail, D. (2010). *McQuail's Mass Communication Theory* (6th ed.). London: Sage.

Min, Y. (2004). Campaign Agenda Formation in the 2000 U.S. Presidential Election-Issue Ownership and Tone of Issue Presentation. *Candidate Agenda Setting, Media & Society, 12*(3), 125–156.

Murdock, G., & Golding, P. (1977). Capitalism, Communication and Class Relations. In J. Curran, M. Gurevitch, & J. Woollacott (Eds.), *Mass Communication and Society*. London: Arnold.

Page, B. I., & Shapiro, R. Y. (1983). Effects of Public Opinion on Policy. *American Political Science Review, 77*(1), 175–190.

Pan, Z., & Kosicki, G. M. (1993). Framing Analysis: An Approach to News Discourse. *Political Communication, 10*(1), 55–75.

Park, M.-J., & Curran, J. (2000). *De-westernizing Media Studies*. London: Routledge.

Park, M.-J., Kim, C.-N., & Sohn, B.-W. (2000). Modernization, Globalization, and the Powerful State: The Korean Media. In M.-J. Park & J. Curran (Eds.), *De-westernizing Media Studies*. London: Routledge.

Paterson, C. (1998). Global News Agencies. In O. Boyd-Barrett & T. Rantanen (Eds.), *The Globalization of News*. London: Sage.

Paterson, C. (2005). News Agency Dominance in International News on the Internet. In D. Skinner, J. R. Compton, & M. Gasher (Eds.), *Converging Media, Diverging Politics: A Political Economy of News Media in the United States and Canada*. Lanham, MD: Lexington Books.

Patterson, E. T., & Donsbach, W. (1996). News Decisions: Journalists as Partisan Actors. *Political Communication, 13*, 455–468.

Petley, J. (2004). Fourth-Rate Estate. *Index on Censorship, 33*(2), 68–75.
Petley, J. (Eds.). (2013). *Media and Public Shaming: Drawing the Boundaries of Disclosure*. New York: Palgrave Macmillan.
Petry, F., & Mendelsohn, M. (2004). Public Opinion and Policy Making in Canada 1994–2001. *Canadian Journal of Political Science, 37*(3), 505–529.
Potschka, C. (2012). *Toward a Market in Broadcasting: Communications Policy in the UK and Germany*. Basingstoke, UK: Palgrave Macmillan.
Rantanen, T. (2004). European News Agencies and Their Sources in the Iraq War Coverage. In S. Allan & B. Zelizer (Eds.), *Reporting War: Journalism in Wartime*. London and New York: Routledge.
Rantanen, T., & Boyd-Barrett, O. (2009). Global and National News Agencies. In S. A. De Beer & C. J. Merrill (Eds.), *Global Journalism: Topical Issues and Media Systems* (5th ed.). Boston, MA: Pearson.
Reese, S., Grant, A., & Danielian, L. (1994). The Structure of News Sources on Television: A Network Analysis of *CBS News, Nightline, McNeil-Lehrer and This Week with David Brinkley*. *Journal of Communication, 44*(2), 84–107.
Sa, E.-S. (2009). Factors Influencing Freedom of the Press in South Korea. *Asian Social Science, 5*(3), 3–24.
Scheufele, A. D. (2000). Agenda-Setting, Priming and Framing Revisited: Another Look at Cognitive Effects of Political Communication. *Mass Communication and Society, 3*(2), 297–316.
Scheufele, A. D., & Tewksbury, D. (2007). Framing, Agenda-Setting, and Priming: The Evolution of Three Media Effects Models. *Journal of Communication, 57*(1), 9–20.
Schiller, H. I. (1992). *Mass Communications and American Empire* (2nd ed.). Boulder, CO: Westview.
Schudson, M. (1978). *Discovering the News: A Social History of American Newspapers*. New York: Basic Books.
Schudson, M. (1989). How Culture Works: Perspectives from Media Studies on the Efficacy of Symbols. *Theory and Society, 18*(2), 153–180.
Schudson, M. (1991, Spring). Delectable Materialism: Were the Critics of the Consumer Culture Wrong All Along? *The American Prospect, 5*, 26–35.
Schudson, M. (2011). *The Sociology of News* (2nd ed.). New York: W. W. Norton.
Shoemaker, J. (2006). News and Newsworthiness: A Commentary. *Communications, 31*(1), 105–111.
Shoemaker, J., & Reese, S. D. (1991). *Mediating the Message: Theories of Influence on Mass Media Content*. New York: Longman.
Shoemaker, J., & Reese, S. D. (1996). *Mediating the Message: Theories of Influence on Mass Media Content* (2nd ed.). White Plains, NY: Longman.
Siebert, F., Peterson, T., & Schramm, W. (1956). *Four Theories of the Press: The Authoritarian, Libertarian, Social Responsibility, and Soviet Communist Concepts of What the Press Should Be and Do*. Urbana: University of Illinois.

Sigal, V. L. (1973). *Reporters and Officials: The Organization and Politics of Newsmaking.* Lexington, MA: D. C. Heath.

Sohn, Y.-J. (2004). The Effects of Media Use on Conservative and Progressive Opinion. *The Korean Society for Journalism & Communication Studies, 8*(2), 240–267.

Soley, L. (1992). *The News Shapers: The Sources Who Explain the News.* New York: Praeger.

Song, Y. (2007). Internet News Media and Issue Development: A Case Study on the Roles of Independent Online News Services as Agenda-Builders for Anti-US Protests in South Korea. *New Media & Society, 9*(1), 71–92.

Sontag, S. (2004). *Regarding the Pain of Others.* London, UK: Penguin.

Steele, J. (1995, Winter). Experts and Opinion Bias of the Persian Gulf War. *Journalism and Mass Communication Quarterly, 72*(4), 799–812.

Stromback, J. (2005). In Search of a Standard: Four Models of Democracy and Their Normative Implications for Journalism. *Journalism Studies, 6*(3), 331–345.

Takeshita, T. (2006). Current Critical Problems in Agenda-Setting Research. *International Journal of Public Opinion Research, 18*(3), 275–296.

Tankard, J. W., Handerson, L., Sillberman, J., Bliss, K., & Ghanem, S. (1991, August 7–10). *Media Frames: Approaches to Conceptualization and Measurement.* Paper presented at the Association for Education in Journalism and Mass Communication, Boston, MA.

Thussu, D. K. (1997). How Media Manipulates Truth About Terrorism. *Economic and Political Weekly, 32*(6), 264–267.

Thussu, D. K. (2000). *International Communication: Continuity and Change.* London: Arnold.

Tuchman, G. (1973). Making News by Doing Work: Routinizing the Unexpected. *American Journal of Sociology, 79,* 110–131.

Tuchman, G. (1976). Telling Stories. *Journal of Communication, 26*(4), 93–97.

Tuchman, G. (1978). *Making News: A Study in the Construction of Reality.* New York: Free Press.

Tunstall, J. (1994). *The Media Are American: Anglo-American Media in the World* (2nd ed.). London, UK: Constable.

Vliegenthart, R., & Zoonen, L. (2011). Power to the Frame: Bringing Sociology Back to Frame Analysis. *European Journal of Communication, 26*(2), 101–115.

Waisbord, R. S. (2002). Journalism, Risk and Patriotism. In B. Zelizer & S. Allan (Eds.), *Journalism After September 11* (pp. 201–219). London: Routledge.

Walgrave, S., & Van Aelst, P. (2006). The Mass Media's Political Agenda-Setting Power: Toward a Preliminary Theory. *Journal of Communication, 56*(1), 88–109.

Weaver, D., & Wilhoit, G. (1996). *The American Journalist in the 1990s: U.S. News People at the End of an Era*. Mahwah, NJ: Lawrence Erlbaum Associates, Inc.

Williams, R. (1980). *Problems in Materialism and Culture*. London: Verso.

Willnat, L., Weaver, H., & Choi, J.-H. (2013). The Global Journalist in the Twenty-First Century. *Journalism Practice, 7*(2), 1–22.

# CHAPTER 3

# Historical Contexts of the Korean Press

As South Korea experienced a war, the consequent division, and political turmoil, the Korean media had to transform accordingly. Hence, this chapter seeks to provide the foundations of the sociopolitical and historical upheavals that have affected the Korean media and the severe restraints and censorship that existed prior to Korea becoming a stabilized liberal democratic country in 1987. This inquiry helps us understand the dynamics of the intermediation between the traditional media and the alternative media and the role of the new media in Korean society. Hence, through an understanding of Korea's sociopolitical context, this chapter explores journalistic challenges and provides context for the reporting of issues related to North Korea. First, this chapter begins with the Korean media's manifestations in the historical context of Korea since the beginning of the Korean War in 1950.

## A HISTORICAL OVERVIEW OF THE KOREAN MEDIA

Korean media systems transformed their ownership, as did other countries' media systems, but under the military regime, some media system mergers were forced by the state, and some changes occurred in the process of transforming the South Korean press during the transition from a military dictatorship to a functioning democracy. To aid in understanding each period of political rule in South Korea, I chronologically divided each administration and the major political changes associated with it, as well as the media changes corresponding to the political

© The Author(s) 2019
M. Moon, *International News Coverage and the Korean Conflict*,
https://doi.org/10.1007/978-981-13-6291-0_3

reforms in Korea. It is customary to separate each regime into five periods: American military government (1945–1948), the First Republic (1948–1960), the Second Republic (1960–1961), the Third and Fourth Republics (1962–1979), and the Fifth Republic (1980–1987). Han (2001) states that in reviewing the political or military regimes and Korean media systems, it is not difficult to observe that the Korean media system changes when a new President takes office. He does not think this linkage is coincidental. It means that the Korean media, particularly the Korean broadcasting system (KBS), were highly dependent upon the state due to the extremely brutal historical political turbulence that Korea experienced before democratization.

On September 11, 1945, Lieutenant General John R. Hodge, commanding general of the U.S. Army force in Korea, proclaimed that the American military government policy would not interfere with the Korean press at a news conference with Korean journalists. He said, "Since U.S. troops have entered Korea, freedom of the press comes into being in Korea now. The U.S. Army will not disturb or interfere with the thought and expression of the Korean people. Also we will not censor any of your publishing. Freedom of the media should stimulate public discussion and formulate public opinion. In this way, the U.S. Army will not tamper with the investigative activities of the Korean press." However, he added, "in case of disturbance of public security, those measures will be reconsidered. I hope I will not face such an occasion. Also I hope this opportunity will function appropriately for the Korean press" (Jung, 1985: 248).

Less than a month after the proclamation on press freedom, on October 10, Major General Archibald V. Arnold, the military governor, declared, "As long as freedom of speech and the press is permitted, it is possible that foolish and careless stories can be published by inexperienced editors. Nevertheless, these childish acts ... can be dismissed as a matter of nature unless they disrupt law and order and interfere with the orderly administration of the Korean government. South Korea below 38 degrees north latitude is directed, controlled, or managed only by the United States ..." (Song et al., The Korean Press 100 years, 2000: 128–129). However, in response to the Korean media's criticism of the statement by General Arnold, the U.S. military government suspended *Kyungsung Ilbo*, which was the controlled newspaper of the Japanese government general of Korea, issued in Japan, on September 25, 1945. Furthermore, it also tried to suspend *Maeil Shinbo*, which was printed in Korean (not in Japanese) in Korea, but failed because approximately six hundred staff members resisted. Eventually, on 10 November of the same year, General Arnold ordered the discontinuance of *Maeil Shinbo* issues, justifying the action by claiming that the suspension was due to the results of a *Maeil Shinbo* financial probe. A British journalist and missionary, Ernest Thomas Bethell, who was born in Bristol, England, and was a foreign correspondent for the London Daily News, founded the newspaper *Daehan Maeil Shinbo* in 1904 (*The Koreanjoongang daily*, June 30, 2008).[1] According to the paper, Tom Warwick, head of the Public Affairs Division at the British Embassy in Korea, said that Bethell was a voice for the Korean independence movement. Under the Japanese colonial rule, *Maeil Shinbo* had practically been the Japanese regime's mouthpiece; after independence, the staff organized their own committee, consisting of anti-Japanese members. With the suspension measure, *Maeil Shinbo* disappeared, but its issues continued to be printed after November 23, 1945, when its name was changed to "*Seoul Shinmun*" (Song et al., 2000: 115–116).

Kang (2007: 302) notes that, as seen in the case of *Maeil Shinbo*, the U.S. military government suppressed left-wing newspapers in contrast to its assertion of "the guaranteed freedom of speech" (the press). He contends that, on the other hand, right-wing newspapers such as *Dong-A Ilbo* and *Chosun Ilbo*, which have remained among the top three dailies until the present day, received the benefits of the U.S. government's nurturance after the discontinuation of the left-wing newspaper. However, Song et al. (2000: 116) maintain that *Dong-A Ilbo* and *Chosun Ilbo* were conservative but were not influential newspapers at that time. Rather, *Haebang Ilbo*, which was a pro-Communist and radical newspaper, was equipped with better publishing facilities and offices. Kang (2000) contends that whether the papers were left wing or right wing, if they had any nuances in their reporting against the U.S. government, then they became the target of repression by the Americans. On the one hand, it is understandable that during the period when American authorities governed South Korea (1945–1948), the society was very poor and in political chaos after a brief moment of celebration of its sudden liberation from Japan's repressive colonial rule. Communist newspapers, as well as publishers, came into being and inundated South Korea. Choi states, "Posters, leaflets, and newspapers were flooding society … In particular, newspapers swept Seoul freely and in a lively manner after being shut down for six years" (1987: 338).

The Constitution of the First Republic under President Lee Seungman was promulgated on July 17, 1948, and South Korea was renamed "Dae Han Min Kook," a name Lee decided upon himself (Hickey, 2000). The freedom of speech (press) was supposed to be ensured and unrestricted, according to the basic constitutional rights of Koreans (Lim, 1998). However, in September, the Korean government under the Lee administration issued a decree prohibiting newspapers from promoting communist-inspired terrorism and subversive activities. The decree, which proscribed publications considered harmful to the state, was very similar to the official decree of the U.S. military government. The decree stated that the U.S. military government ruled the southern part of Chosun, the Korean Peninsula below the 38th parallel, and residents must obey all the commands of the U.S. military government (Kang, 2000: 326–327).

Under its uncompromising anti-communist policy, the Lee government systematically restricted newspapers that adhered to a left-wing ideology. The Lee regime closed or suspended approximately 56 newspapers, including *Seoul Shinmun* and *Segae Ilbo*, and two news agencies, claiming that they published positive frames of North Korea, and the government alleged that articles reported by these newspapers supported the North Korean formula for national unification (Lee, 2008: 130). In June 25, 1950, the Korean War broke out. The Korean press had to report it, but the Lee government imposed severe censorship on newspapers. According to Kang, when the North occupied Seoul on June 28, all the media disappeared and ceased. In contrast, the activities of the foreign media were vigorous (2000: 329). For example, at the beginning of the Korean War, 238 international journalists came to Korea (Lee, 2001: 83).

According to McDonald, General Douglas MacArthur, a UN military leader, provided films for free to a newsreel company and TV network and instructed that he was to be accompanied by a cameraman during the front-line inspection (1985: 32). He probably knew the impact of the media when used as a tool of propaganda. However, General MacArthur strictly repressed the investigative activities of independent war correspondents. For example, American authorities were furious over interviews with injured soldiers by journalists from the AP and UPI, and the journalists were expelled to Japan for retraining (Mott, 1962: 848). In addition, according to McFarland (1986), six war correspondents won Pulitzer Prizes in 1951 in the international section. This number was unprecedented. Moreover, all of the prizewinners were Korean War correspondents. This demonstrates that reporting and investigating were dangerous, and the situation was more serious than was presumed. In fact, in only one month, July, 6 journalists were killed and 14 injured. A total of 17 foreign journalists, including 10 Americans, had been killed by the end of 1950. The Lee government was replaced by a parliamentary system under Premier Jang Myun. The guarantee of press freedom in the 1960 Constitution seems to have differed from that of the First Republic. The new Constitution stated:

> Citizens shall not be subjected to any restriction on the freedom of speech and of the press... The liberties and rights of citizens may be restricted by the law only in cases deemed necessary for the maintenance of social order and public welfare. In case of such restriction, the essential substance of liberties and rights shall not be infringed. With regard to speeches, the press, assemblies, and associations, licensing, censorship or any kind of permission shall not be recognized. (Lee, 1999: 119)

Jang's government seemed to allow the Korean press broader freedom than before, replacing the old licensing system with a system of registration. These legal changes in favor of press freedom helped the Korean press enjoy the greatest freedom it had experienced in Korean history. The number of newspapers increased exponentially, to nearly 389 from 41 (dailies), to 476 from 136 (weeklies), to 470 from 400 (monthlies), and to 274 from 14 (news agencies) by December 30 in the first five months after the system of registration was activated. Additionally, 160,000 reporters were employed. Furthermore, the left-wing newspapers, such as *Minjok Ilbo*, which had been closed because of their promotion of North Korean unification policies, reappeared (Kim, 1996: 404–405). During the chaotic period, the numbers of press outlets rapidly increased, regardless of quality, and press freedom seemed to accompany this increase. However, this press freedom was not long-lived because Chang was overthrown in a military coup in 1961.

Park Jong Min, a KBS producer, testified that on May 16, 1961, at approximately 4.15 a.m., General Park occupied KBS with airborne troops equipped with machine guns. PD Park Jong Min and announcer Park Jong Sae, who were night-shift workers, hid under a desk. Suddenly, they heard, "Come out, announcer Park!" Mr. Park emerged and followed the troops to a common room. High-ranking officers, General Kim Dong Ha and General Park Jung Hee, were present. General Park asked him to broadcast that "the 5.16 revolution has just started now" (Yoo, 1998: 247).

From the very beginning, the military regime under Park proclaimed a suppressive policy toward the Korean press. In Decree No. 1, the regime first established the Military Revolutionary Committee, which was later renamed the Supreme Council for National Reconstruction (SCNR). It ordered the censorship of all newspaper and magazine feature articles, comics, cartoons, editorials, photographs, and foreign news prior to publication. Furthermore, in an effort to "purify" the Korean press, the SCNR drastically restructured the mass media of Korea. As a result, 15 major dailies survived of 64, 24 local newspapers of 51, 11 news agencies of 316 (local news agencies were all shut down), 31 major weeklies of 355, and only one local weekly of 130 (*Chosun Ilbo*, October 19, 1989: 24). In association with this ordeal suffered by the Korean press during the military regime period, the *Minjok Ilbo* case shows how far Park's regime went in controlling press freedom. The Revolutionary Court sentenced to death three executives (including Jo Yong Soo, the *Minjok Ilbo* publisher) of the *Minjok Ilbo* newspaper in August 1961 for advocating political and ideological doctrines similar to those of North Korea and promoting the neutrality of Korea. In addition, the newspaper was in favor of negotiations with the North Korean communists, exchanges of mail with North Korea, and student meetings between North and South Korea. It is said that hundreds of people, ranging from Korean writers and press societies to the Japanese Pen Club, International Pen Club, and International Press Association, submitted a petition to Park. However, Mr. Jo was executed in December 1961, while the other two were granted a commutation from a death sentence to life imprisonment on December 22 (Jung, 1985: 289–290; *Kyungnam Domin Ilbo*, December 11, 2012).

On the one hand, although President Park accomplished notably rapid economic growth in Korea by fostering the "Saemaul Undong" (New Town Movement), some people regard him as a strongman who controlled the Korean press to sustain his power (Chae, 2000). The Saemaul initiative was a state-initiated nationwide revolutionary economic improvement program, which was launched on April 22, 1970, and the Park regime vigorously implemented it for approximately 10 years. Although the military coup d'état led by Park Jung Hee and his brutal repression of the freedom of speech of the Korean media at that time have been roundly condemned, his strategic and systematic economic improvement movement, Saemaeul, has been praised by many (Jung, 2012). In fact, the movement, also known as "The Saemaul Undong," has been a good model for economic development in Africa, and South Korea has become an emerging player as a development partner in Africa for the sake of both national interests and African economic development (Seitz, 2017).[2] The Saemaul Undong centers on education and cooperation, so African countries feel that compared to neo-colonial investment by other core nations, such as the United States, the EU and Japan, including China by credit financing or nonlocalized globalization, South Korean investment is approached through human communication and activities that induce participation to equip the African countries with self-supporting economies, following the Saemaul initiatives together with aid from the Korean international cooperation agency (KOICA). This situation represents a Korean economic development wave (ChosunBiz, May 14, 2018).

Consequently, Park Geun Hye, President of the Republic of Korea, who is the first daughter of President Park, inherited blame that accumulated from the past suppression of the Korean people when her father ruled the country. However, the rapid economic growth under Park Jung Hee's regime has been understood as a formidable achievement nationally and internationally. Therefore, although the military rule had a dark side, perhaps because of the most significant issue, boosting the economy during an era of economic crisis, Park Geun Hye was supported by many Koreans who elected her as the first female President in Korean history in the 2012 presidential election. As it may prove, when she won the election, *Time* magazine placed President Park on the front cover with the title "The Strongman's Daughter" (*Time online*, December 17). During the campaign, the criticisms that she received were about her father's suppression and ruling power in the past, and Park Geun Hye seems to have tried hard to somehow compensate those who suffered under the military regime. The conflict between the press and the government had been an issue for some time. The Park government tried to place fetters on the press, but the Korean press often refused to yield to governmental pressures, both direct and indirect. The climax of the press–government battle occurred in August 1964. The Park administration enacted the Press Ethics Commission Act on 2 August despite strong opposition from both the press and the public. This act was not agreed upon by any political party but was enacted by Park's own decision. The Press Ethics Commission Act was aimed toward "enhancing the effectiveness of self-regulation by the press and broadcasting services" (Kang, 2000: 401).

When the act was promulgated, it was strongly criticized by the Korean press. The National Assembly and capitol hall journalists association refused to report any news about it. On 5 August, The Press Ethics Commission Act Lifting institution was created by the press associations. However, the government did not consider rejecting the code and instead took measures against the opposing newspapers, including *Dong-A Ilbo*, *Kyunghang Shinmum*, *Chosun Ilbo, and Daegu Maeil Shinmum*. One of the measures was that subscriptions would be stopped by governmental institutions (Joh, 2007: 66–67). As a result of the press campaign, the press–government crisis over the Press Ethics Commission Act ended when President Park agreed to withhold enforcement of the law (Park, 2014). On September 22, *JoongAng Ilbo*, one of the top three dailies in Korea, was founded by Samsung (Kim, 2000: 92–93). The Samsung Group owned practically all the media because it had already bought RSB (Radio Seoul) in 1964 and had launched the first private commercial TV broadcasting company, DTV, in the same year (Kang, 2000: 405).

In South Korea, the major news agency is *Yonhap*, launched on December 19, 1989. Before a private news agency, Newsis, was launched in September 2001, *Yonhap* was the only option. Furthermore, Newsis articles have not yet been published in the mainstream media. For the last few years, thanks to online journalism and the news box on a dominant Korean portal site, "Naver," news by Newsis has begun to receive some attention from internet users. As a source for international news, the contribution of Newsis is negligible to the point that Newsis articles cannot be found or used as a news source. On April 11, 2011, the economic newspaper "*Money Today*" launched a news agency, the so-called "News 1." As far as I understand, the English version of *Yonhap* news, which is quickly updated, and its native English language level have contributed to its prominence as an international news source. In addition, it has 550 journalists, which makes it the largest news agency in Korea. There are other English language news media, but they are not as frequently updated, the topics that they cover in English are very limited, and the language that they use is not sufficiently fluent for English-speaking people. Liberal newspapers, such as *Kyunghyang Shinmun* and *Hankyoreh Shinmun*, have claimed that Korea should implement a restructuring of the *Yonhap* news agency ownership, because it has become a government institution and an offspring of the military dictatorship, to enhance the nation's democratic status at a higher level and consolidate the aims and position of the agency as a public service (*Hankyoreh Shinmun*, June 12, 1999; *Kyunghyang Shinmun*, June 12, 1999). Ex-President Chun Doo Hwan forcefully merged three broadcasting companies—TBS (Dong Yang Broadcasting), DBS (Dong Ah Broadcasting), and KBS—into one company, KBS, in 1980 (Han, 2011: 161–167).

According to Han, in 1967, when certain financial incentives were offered, the normal loan interest rate was 25%, and newspaper companies were loaned money at 18%. Additionally, instead of a 30% tariff rate, they received a 4.5% rate on imported paper, and press companies were allowed to receive foreign loans (2010: 33). On the one hand, these kinds of benefits gave the Korean press opportunities to enrich their assets; it was a turning point for a few major newspaper companies to become a conglomerate. On the other hand, these policies hindered newspapers from functioning in their role as watchdogs because they sometimes had to act according to government directives to continue receiving benefits. On April 27, 1971, there was a presidential election. At that time, it could be seen how far the press went to protect themselves because most of the media were occupied with praising the government and campaigning to support Park's republican party (Kim, 1993: 348–349).

Michael Breen, a British analyst, says that university student protests against the military regime in power in the 1970s and 1980s became almost de rigueur for Korean students, although he adds that student protests were not effective in terms of expanding democracy in Korea (*The Korea Herald*, February 1, 2012). However, student and citizen movements contributed to journalists' and politicians' motives to try to read public opinion, such as what people think, or at least whether they support a particular issue, throughout Korea's modern history. Under severe repression by the state, there might have been cases where the press compromised between what the government wanted and what they had to say. However, university students played a pivotal role in Korea's democratization. The people who contributed the most to Korea's democratization were members of the so-called "386" generation, born in the 1960s, educated during the military regime, and participating in democratic movements (Fairclough, 2004; Kim, 2000). Castells (2008: 84) also stresses that "Student movements remain an influential source of social change in East Asia, particularly in South Korea."

For example, thirty representatives of universities in Seoul posted a placard with a written "warning to the press" in front of the building of *Dong-A Ilbo* and delivered a warning message with a megaphone. The content of the message was "You cannot write political matters for fear of violence, and do not report social problems because of the received bribes. Also, the culture section is rushing to lower standards—it is full of sexuality … newspapers are not for newspapers but for the public. Even if the money is tempting and violence is scary, is it right to forget what you should do? It's not a watcher preventing a robber but an outsider just wandering around…" Furthermore, over five hundred students at Yonsei University in Seoul held a demonstration to warn the press about its activities leaning toward the regime. Student rallies continued and influenced many journalists. Consequently, a great number of journalists from different newspapers declared their support for freedom of the press (Dong-A Ilbo Labour Union, Dong-A free press activities, 1989: 25–26, 150).

In October 17, 1972, Park initiated the "October Yooshin" (Reforms). This was an important turning point for Korean broadcasting because a new broadcasting law was issued. Hence, the broadcasting media were used to promote news, laws, and policies, such as the economy improvement program of the Saemaeul movement, as mentioned above. Moreover, other long-running TV programs had to add content promoting the Yooshin system (Han, 2011). In October 1979, the general-turned-President Park was suddenly assassinated. On December 12, 1979, another general, Chun Do-Hwan, seized power with the backing of the Military Corps. The Chun era was called the "biggest purge" in the history of the Korean press, as it forced a sweeping structural reorganization of the mass media.

According to Kim, the Chun regime fired approximately ten thousand journalists, including staff, and forced approximately two hundred kinds of publishing venues to close on 30–31 July 1980 (2012: 152). As the suppression continued, the demand for political democracy was seemingly growing stronger. The political activation of the student movement escalated greatly during April and May 1980. Students called for the withdrawal of martial law, quick modification toward a democratic constitution, and the release of Kim Dae-Jung. In early May, students started to stage street demonstrations to express their requests more strongly. They urged citizens' political activation and participation in the reformation movement. The movement reached its peak at rallies in front of Seoul Station on May 14 and 15. The demonstrations drew approximately 10,000 citizens to rise up. Paratroopers were deployed, and they attacked the demonstrators with clubs and rifle butts (Ahn & Ransberg, 1999: 111). It is difficult to calculate the number of people who were killed at Gwangju. It has been said that there was no United Nations investigation, as in the case of the Hungarian uprising. The South Korean government settled on a figure of at least 240 killed, but Gwangju sources claimed that more than 3000 were killed or injured (Johnson, 2000).

Television in South Korea had transformed dramatically in the 1990s. South Korea had three terrestrial television stations. They were *KBS1*, *KBS2* (Korean Broadcasting System—public broadcasting), and *MBC* (Munwha Broadcasting Corporation). *MBC* was originally Busan Broadcasting Corporation in 1959 and was later launched in Seoul in 1961. The government owned it at one time during the 1980s, when a military regime controlled all the media. Significantly, a commercial channel, Seoul Broadcasting System (SBS), was launched in December 1991 (Han, 2011). As I have shown above, there were decades—37 years—when military regimes ruled the people and controlled even individual behavior. For example, for 37 years, from 1945 to 1982, there was a curfew that stipulated that a person could not go outside after 12 p.m. (Doosan Encyclopedia).[3] The content of news, dramas, and songs was strictly censored and often prohibited. Former Presidents, both Chung-Hee Park and Doo-Hwan Chon, who was a former ROK Army general, kept South Korea under military dictatorship from 1961 to 1987. Immediately after Jeon Doo-Hwan, in October 1987, Tae-Woo Roh was elected President; he was also a former ROK Army general had joined the coup d'état led by former President Jeon Doo-Hwan. Finally, in 1992, Kim Young-Sam was elected President. He was the country's first Civilian President in 30 years. Consequently, the nineties are an important era because liberalization and democracy were emerging in society, and in the wake of social and political changes, the Korean media transformed accordingly.

Journalists were kidnapped by the militant government, and others were jailed if they talked about what was happened during the 1980s. Shin (2012) describes the process in detail when he writes about how he gathered information and reported about the death of Park Jong-Cheol, an undergraduate student at Seoul National University, one of the top universities in South Korea. Shin is a journalist at *Joongang Ilbo*. He is the first journalist who reported the incident. The police tortured

Park Jong-Chul to death, but the incident was not covered properly. Therefore, Shin started to investigate. In his thesis, he describes how, at that time, journalists were told by the government what to report and how to report it—for example, the length of an article or the size of a picture. His status was almost at the danger point after he reported the truth that Park had died of water torture. Initially, it was reported that the police had hit the desk, and the student had fainted and died. The death caused a stir throughout the nation, with feelings that the Chun Doo-Hwan regime had gone too far in killing a college student and trying to cover up the affair. Hence, the reason that we mark 1987 as the year when South Korea finally achieved a democratic society is that there were so many pro-democratic resistance movements in June 1987. In Seoul alone, there were large-scale demonstrations in approximately 30 places. The demonstrations developed as a nationwide movement of approximately 240,000 people in 22 cities. The police arrested approximately 3500 demonstrators. In the meantime, presidential candidate Roh Tae Woo announced a system of direct election of the President and the release on June 29, 1987 of Kim Dae-Jung, a former President who was in jail due to his democratic movement (Shin, 2012).

*Hankyoreh Shinmun* was established as a liberal alternative newspaper in the traditionally conservative dominant press circumstances. It was founded on May 15, 1988 by journalists who fought against the dictatorship and has more than 60,000 citizen shareholders, none of whom have more than 1% of the share. With a circulation of approximately 600,000, it is the fourth-largest newspaper after *Chosun Ilbo, JoongAng Ilbo,* and *Dong-A Ilbo.* It claimed to be independent from power, meaning the government. According to Han (1996: 160–161), one of the main reasons that the media cannot be as democratic as they should be is that the media have failed to achieve independence from media capital and the state. He emphasizes that *Hankyoreh Shinmun* raises its capital from the general public and sets the maximum shareholding rate at 1% of the total issued shares. The total number of shareholders has been as high as 61,866, and the largest shareholding proportion has been only 0.24%. Therefore, neither the state nor any individual shareholder can control the paper. However, since *Hankyoreh* came into being, it has been widely recognized as a left wing, independent newspaper and does not seem to be regarded as an affective news medium in Korea. Academically, the newspaper is often viewed as a counterpart of a conservative newspaper, such as *Chosun Ilbo, Joongang Ilbo, and Dong-A Ilbo.* It will be discussed further in later sections.

## FICTION: TELEVISION DRAMA AND FILM

We have examined historical sociopolitical changes alongside press oppression by the government in South Korea. Under the circumstances, and despite the radical newspaper, *Hankyoreh*, another affective communicator beyond the rational framework, such as the vehicle of television fiction, might have been needed. Affective communication is required to condition positive dissent and dialogic reasons for genuine democracy, and melodrama can function as entertainment but also as an education (Dahlgren, 1995; Gripsrud, 1992; McGuigan, 2005). Jostein Gripsrud (1992) has commented upon the historical role of melodrama in the public sphere and states that melodrama performs not only an entertainment but also an educational function, which is also true of tabloid journalism: "Today's popular press…teaches the audience a lesson, everyday" (1992: 87). From this perspective, *The Hourglass* was not only one of the most successful dramas, with phenomenal ratings (average 50%, highest 69%) (*Yonhap*, February 9, 1995) but also rekindled debates about the nature and role of the Gwangju uprising.

*The Hourglass* (1995), "*Moreshegye*" in Korean, is a Korean drama set in South Korea's politically turbulent recent past that aired on SBS in 1995. The series lasted for 24 episodes and is one of the highest-rated dramas in Korean history. It is the story of two men whose friendship is put to the test through the 1970s and 1980s, one of Korea's politically tumultuous periods. Park Tae-soo (Choi Min-soo), tough and loyal, grows up to become a gangster, and Kang Woo-suk (Park Sang-won), smart and with firm moral values, grows up to become a prosecutor. Yoon Hye-rin (Go Hyun-jung), the beautiful and spirited daughter of a wealthy casino owner, is a classmate of Woo-suk in college. Hye-rin is introduced to Tae-soo via Woo-suk, and they subsequently fall in love. One unforgettable subject that is addressed in the drama is the 1980 Gwangju democratization movement, when General and President Chun Doo Hwan sent paratroopers into Gwangju to suppress the rebellion, leading to the subsequent massacre of hundreds of innocent people. The horrific scenes based on true accounts of those people being murdered sparked a deep sense of shock and grief for Koreans at that time (in the mid-1990s, Korea still had not come to terms with what had happened after the government suppressed free speech).

The popularity of the drama implies that a number of issues need to be revisited. First, the broadcasting company that produced and aired the series was SBS. The company was launched in the same year as the first private broadcasting company in South Korea. Thus, unlike other companies, it was the first to be launched as a commercial broadcaster independent of the government and under private control. Second, TV dramas and soap operas in particular are constructed by commercial imperatives and advertisers (Henderson, 2007). Third, the breakdown of "hard news" and "soft news" occurred for the first time through this drama. The issue in this dramatization of the democratization movement under the militant government was different from the typical social and medical issues; the challenging representation of such an issue by a soap opera and the breakdown of what is meant by "news," whether "hard" or "soft," certainly engrossed laypeople, especially the 386 generation (who were university students in the 1980s). Thus, television fiction forms part of a wider approach to eliciting change in social attitudes and healthy behavior (Henderson, 2007: 19). After this drama aired, more films were made that addressed this very subject, such as The Petal (1996) and Peppermint Candy (2000).

Significantly, the drama about the Gwangju democratization movement represented the challenges naturally, which no newspapers or television documentaries could do. In the same year, in December, former President Chun Doo Hwan, who was responsible for the massacre, was jailed. Covering the same issue, the democratic movement in Gwangju in 1980, the film "A Taxi Driver" was released in 2017 and is the seventh-highest-grossing film of all time in the nation. Interestingly, the film depicts a German TV journalist (played by Thomas Kretschmann), Jürgen Hinzpeter, who reported the movement and told the world about the uprising. It is a political drama, but it moved many Korean viewers with humor and touching human dramatic elements. The story starts with Hinzpeter taking a taxi to cover the uprising in Gwangju, which is approximately 300 kilometers from Seoul, approximately three hours and a half by car. He persuades the taxi driver to drive him there and return before the curfew. Thus, he will pay a high taxi fare. Like this book that I am writing, in the movie, the tragic history has been viewed, depicted, and covered by a foreign correspondent, the East German-born reporter. He reports the bloody conflict between student protesters and the military. Unlike Korean reporters, his status as a foreigner protects him from arrest, torture, and repression. It is still difficult to believe that the inhumane massacre occurred not long ago in this country, which is now modernized and tech-savvy. When the film was released, Hinzpeter's wife made her ninth visit to Korea. He passed away in 2016, and his remains were buried in Gwangju according to the terms of his will.

A new President, Roh Tae Woo, was elected with 36.6% of the vote on December 16, 1987. The year 1987 marks the beginning of Korean democracy. During his era, a number of positive changes took place in the Korean press. First, President Roh abolished restrictions on the press in favor of greater freedom of information. In addition, according to Kim (1994), Roh revised the Constitution in October 1987 and prohibited censorship of speech and the press while guaranteeing freedom of expression. The government's view of the press in the era of democracy is apparent in the number of newspapers. In December 1987, the total number of daily newspapers increased from 30 to 65 within a year, reaching 85 in 1990 and 112 at the end of 1992. There were 226 weeklies in December 1987, and the number increased by more than 1000 in 1990. Furthermore, after the Roh government enacted the new press law in June 1987, 3728 periodicals were registered by the spring of 1989. This meant that periodicals increased by 1492.

It is noteworthy that on May 15, 1988, the radical newspaper *Hankyoreh Shinmun* was founded. A nationwide democratization movement allowed journalists to conduct a fund-raising campaign to found this newspaper. It is striking that the journalists quit their jobs and declared that *Hankyoreh* would be a progressive voice in comparison to the largely conservative newspapers that had (as they say) "refrained from criticizing authority" (Shim & Lee, 1998: 8–9). It can be controversial to argue that the *Hankyoreh* has been a counterpoint to the conservative news dailies; the aspects of journalism practices and its existence as a counterpoint of dominant conservative newspapers may imply its impact, but evaluating the role of a progressive newspaper in society is difficult in contemporary Korea. While the history of broadcast reformism in Britain could well be subtitled a study of success, Curran says that "the record of press reformism has been one of failure" (2000: 35). However, thanks to the internet, communication technologies have made it possible for the public to have better access to media sources where they can freely express their opinion. This situation implies that an alternative way of communicating with others has given rise to a rather open and democratic society.

## THE INTERNET AND PUBLIC PARTICIPATION

McChesney (2000: 159) maintains that digital broadcasters and many other media companies have indulged in the pursuit of internet riches in the new media era. He believes that many phenomena stem both from a desire for more profit and from fear of falling behind competitors on the internet if the media do not proceed aggressively, but he points out that the crucial factor for the internet to become dominant is the expansion of broadband capability to the bulk of the population. When this happens, the internet may well become a vast convergent communications machine, eliminating the traditional distinctions between communication and media sectors as all forms of communication become digital.

It is well known that South Korea is one of the most wired countries in the world, with more than 90% of households connected to broadband internet (The Associated Press online, July 6, 2012; *The Chicago Tribune* online, June 24, 2012). According to a survey by Millward Brown Media Research in 2009, 57.7% of South Koreans use TV to receive the news, and 19.8% of people use the internet. Only 14.8% read newspapers to access news stories. However, people in their twenties use the internet more than other methods to obtain the news. Korea's rate of internet news use was ranked number one among the OECD countries in 2008 (Maeil Broadcasting Network online, June 21, 2010). Korea was a leading country, with the greatest proportion of users in the world. Perhaps this ranking is due to a common characteristic among Korean people, which is to do many things "quickly, quickly (ppalli ppalli in Korean)". As the expansion of the internet has made computer-mediated communication increasingly popular, internet users (hereafter called netizens) have become an influential group of communicators. In particular, in the news media, netizens have played a critical role not only in consuming the media but also in producing media messages in society. Netizens gather specialized information and inform the public. Some news sources used on TV news programs every day, such as video and audio clips, have been recorded by netizens. It is common to watch video clips about citizens' deviant behavior in the subway, recorded by netizens, on terrestrial television news programs. According to previous studies conducted by many international scholars, OhmyNews is one of the most successful online journalism sites in the world. The CEO, Oh Yeon Ho, has become a world-famous inventor, and Google has online news links on the right-hand side of the window for international users, which are generally

Western views of events in Asia. For many reasons, the site has decreased in popularity (Curran, Fenton, & Freedman, 2012). It is well known that to make a convincing argument, it will be necessary to examine OhmyNews and its foundational background—how it came into being, its structure and, importantly, its impact on the media as a whole to the present. When it first started, the number of "news guerrillas," citizen journalists, was approximately 15,000 (I received the information from Ohmynews Company via email). If all of them worked in one company, it would be larger than "Chaebol."

As citizen participation increased, the interactivity of internet users led to the launch of the first successful online news medium, OhmyNews, in South Korea. As reported previously,

> With its 65,000 contributors, the Korean news organisation, OhmyNews, is not just one of the biggest in the world but also one of the most established, having been launched back in 2000. (*The Guardian* online, January 19, 2011)[4]

Moreover, as Kim and Lee (2006) show, the shocking controversy over fabricated stem cell research by a top human cloning scientist at Seoul National University, Professor Hwang Woo-suk, became part of the public agenda through the efforts of two ordinary young scientists who raised suspicion using communications on the internet. In other words, the alleged "fabrication" of papers on cloned embryonic stem cells was first investigated not by the media but by the public. According to Kim and Lee (2006), this example shows that agenda-setting theory can be challenged and that the public agenda can be proposed not only by the media but also by the general public, which is in opposition to the traditional agenda-setting theory. A good example of the concept of agenda rippling is the presidential election of 2002. Studies on the election show the influence of netizens on politics and their impact on Korean society. Oh Yeon Ho, the founder of OhmyNews, attended the Berkman Center Internet and Society Conference at Harvard University on December 11, 2004 and explained as follows:

> Let's look back to the last day of the 2002 Korean presidential election campaign. Just 8 hours before the start of voting, at around 10.30 pm on December 18th, Mr. Chung Mong Joon, Roh Moo Hyun's campaign partner, suddenly withdrew his support. This astonished the whole

nation. Because the competition between the reform candidate Roh Moo Hyun, and conservative candidate Lee Hae Chang was too close to call, Mr. Chung's withdrawal was a kind of atomic bomb. Interestingly enough, the news provoked a last-minute confrontation between old media and new media. The conservative mainstream newspaper *Chosun Daily* changed its editorial and posed a question to voters along the lines of "Mr. Chung withdrew his support for Roh; will you?" But reform-minded netizens, including OhmyNews readers, quickly mobilized overnight to fight Mr. Chung's atomic bomb. They visited many internet bulletin boards and posted urgent messages like 'Mr. Chung betrayed his party, Roh Moo Hyun is in danger. Save the country, please vote for Roh.' They even called their conservative parents to persuade them, crying 'If Roh Moo Hyun fails, I will die.' OhmyNews reported Mr. Chung's withdrawal and updated the story of netizen reactions every 30 minutes, all night long. The number of hits for that main breaking story was 720,000 in just 10 hours. Thanks to nonstop reporting through the night, OhmyNews was the epicentre of reform-minded netizens. On the night of December 19th, when Mr Roh's victory was confirmed, I wrote on OhmyNews: 'As of today, the long-lasting media power in Korea has changed. The power of media has shifted from conservative mainstream newspapers to netizens and internet media.'

*The Guardian* reported on the presidential election, with an article entitled "World's First Internet President Logs On." It covered the development of internet technology and services in South Korea, comparing the 70% broadband saturation in South Korea with the approximately 5% in Britain. Quoting diplomats in Seoul, who said that Korea is the most online country, *The Guardian* reported on the power of online communication such as OhmyNews in South Korea (*The Guardian* online, February 24, 2003).[5] Together with the rapid development of the broadband internet infrastructure, it has been questioned what aspects of the historical, socio-economic background of Korean society and politics might have given birth to successful alternative online journalism such as OhmyNews in South Korea.

## THE FALL OF "OHMYNEWS"

South Korea, which is often described as "the most wired country in the world" by major US and UK newspapers, offers a perfect example of the new media's impact on politics and journalism practices. OhmyNews, based upon citizen journalists, generated support for Korean former

President Roh Moo Hyun via e-campaigns—mainly emails and text messages—and eventually, Roh became President. Koreans regard his victory as a victory of netizens (Allan, 2006: 131). Previous studies have examined the effects of the mobilization of the online news medium "OhmyNews" on the 2002 Korean presidential election (Allan, 2006; Chang, 2005; Hauben, 2008; Joyce, 2007). However, in terms of news sources, news formats, and news content, scarcely any research has been done to compare and contrast the texts between the dominant news media and the alternative media. From a global public sphere perspective, openDemocracy is considered a space for posting news from all over the world, ensuring that "marginalized views and voices are heard, although social and global inequalities still exist in terms of the geographical and demographic distribution of its authors" (Fenton, 2010: 102–117). On the other hand, the internet could create a crisis of journalism.

According to Curran (2011: 116), British journalists are working under pressure to produce more stories in a shorter time than ever before due to the newly established system of the traditional news media, which demands that news be continually updated in a twenty-four-hour news cycle. Consequently, the quality of the product is reduced, sometimes by copying news from rival news companies' websites or forcing journalists to find alternative ways to generate stories as quickly as possible. Sunstein (2001: 387–397) maintains that the internet has the potential to be part of the public sphere but is not a blessing for democracy because in political discussion, in particular, we observe the phenomenon of group polarization, where groups with distinctive identities tend to engage only in within-group discussion.

However, for over a decade, OhmyNews, which is one of the most cited Korean citizen journalism arenas in communication studies, has represented the democratic role of the internet in journalism and has demonstrated all the celebrated positive facets of the internet in academic fields because the internet has been regarded as a virtual space where the public has the opportunity to express their own opinions and debate issues. One reason that OhmyNews was regarded as a public sphere is that any citizen could be a reporter. It enabled the viewers to participate and interact actively in creating commentary and engaging in public debates and discussions. What about the present day? Does OhmyNews still contribute to a Korean democracy in journalism? Is there any difference between domestic views and views from outside Korea on OhmyNews? As far as I am concerned, there have certainly been changes in public perceptions of the role of the news and its influence on society over the past decade. Additionally, there have been some changes in the influence of OhmyNews on both society and journalism in Korea as well as changes from the founding father of the first citizen journalism to. However, previous studies have highlighted only its positive aspects, and there are almost no examinations of how it has changed over time in terms of sociopolitical and cultural perspectives, including the media landscape.

Curran (2012) addresses OhmyNews extensively in terms of its ups and downs in the Korean context. He states that ever since the nonmilitary President, Young-Sam Kim, was elected in 1992, there has been a long-running campaign for greater media independence from government. Public attacks have been made on collusion between conglomerates and government, and the neoliberal policies pursued in the wake of the Asian 1997–1998 economic crisis, which is also known as the International Monetary Fund (IMF) crisis in South Korea. During the currency crisis of 1997, the sight of South Koreans standing in line for hours to donate their gold to the national treasury to help the country was unforgettable. South Korea exported the first 300 kilograms of gold collected at that time in a public campaign in a gesture of support for their country in its economic crisis. Additionally, public sentiment in opposition to the presence of the U.S. Army was growing. OhmyNews was launched in 2000 and differed from the big three dominant national dailies; for example, it became engaged in the political mobilization that led to the election of President Roh. In 2003, OhmyNews became profitable due to its substantial online advertising, and by 2004, OhmyNews had become a website "daily." According to Curran et al. (2012), this remarkable achievement of attracting volunteer reporters with professional skills and building a mass audience was possible only because there was "the ground-swell of progressive support" behind the website. However, he attributes the decline of the groundswell to growing disappointment with President Roh's government, a branch in Japan with low traffic and the international website that was set up in English in 2004.

Curran specifically points out the underperforming Korean economy under Roh and his suicide when faced with the prospect of criminal charges for bribery and corruption (2012: 23). Regarding Roh's underperformance in boosting the Korean economy, Korean media scholars have argued that the relationship between Mr. Roh and the dominant big three daily newspapers—*Chosun Ilbo, Joongang Ilbo, and Dong-A*

*Ilbo*—was problematic; it has been said in South Korea that the Korean media blamed former President Roh for everything. Lee and Park (2008) analyses the economic news in the periods of Roh Moo-Hyun and Kim Dae-Jung because he considers economic news a nonpartisan and impartial news selection compared to politics and social issues. Hence, They analyzed the economic news during the two different administrations to examine whether there were any differences in the tone of the news between the conservative and the liberal newspaper companies in terms of partisanship. Their findings show that during the Roh administration, more negative economic news was reported by the mainstream news media, although the economy was better because the social index, unemployment rates, and prices were better than during Kim's administration. Consequently, due to more asymmetrical negative economic reports in relation to the President's underperformance, the public's support for the President decreased. In other words, the news media made the negative news even more negative and did not make positive reports salient in the economic news during Roh's administration. Curran (2012) concludes that due to its close association with a "failed" President and the decline of the left, the proliferation of new websites, the heavy concentration of volunteers in Seoul with a disproportionate ratio of male and females (40 and 77%, respectively), and financial difficulty, OhmyNews ceased to be the natural home of cultural dissent. However, it is probable that the main causes of the decline of OhmyNews will be argued further because from the Korean perspective, it is likely that the political ideology of OhmyNews led readers to perceive it as merely another politically fragmented medium, similar to other existing Korean news media.

One-third of the Korean population, over 10 million people, lives in Seoul, the capital of South Korea. Regarding the decline of the left, *Dae Han Mail Shinbo* and the *Korea Daily News* in the English edition were founded on July 18, 1904. They are now *Seoul Shinmun*, which circulates approximately 780,000 copies per day in South Korea. The largest shareholder of Seoul Shinmun was formerly the government, with more than 64%. However, on January 15, 2002, the employees became the largest shareholder (www.seoul.co.kr). Another major daily newspaper in South Korea, *Kyunghyang Shinmun*, was founded in 1945 by the Catholic Church. Before the Korean War, it was edited by Fr. Peter Ryan, a refugee from the North, with a circulation of approximately 100,000. It was temporarily closed down in May 1959 by the Lee Seungman administration but revived after the prodemocracy revolution of April 19, 1960. It was owned by the Hanwha Chaebol, but it relinquished its control of the newspaper after the 1997 IMF crisis. Importantly, in 1998, *Kyunghyang Shinmun* became an independent newspaper with employee ownership at 96%.[6] The CEO is elected by the employees, and significantly, the editor-in-chief must be approved by a majority of the journalist-employees, although he or she is appointed by the CEO. It is well known that *Kyunghyang Shinmun* describes itself as moderately progressive, like *Hankyoreh Shinmun*. I wish to point out that the two major daily newspapers became independent of the Chaebol and government, respectively, during the Kim and Roh administrations; thus, more progressive newspapers came into being. Consequently, progressive newspapers were rather dominant at that time. Hence, the decline of OhmyNews could have been led by two consecutive presidencies from the Democratic Party and by its loss of objectivity as nonpartisan press.

In South Korea, OhmyNews has not been regarded as a major news outlet for over a decade. Just as *Hankyoreh Shinmun* was founded as a form of alternative media by fired journalists and citizens who voluntarily collected funds (Curran & Park, 2000: 106), resisting the military authorities' repression of the press on May 15, 1988 and with citizens as stock shareholders, OhmyNews appeared as another media reformer when it first started in 2000. However, as time passed, OhmyNews turned out to be somewhat partisan in favor of the Democratic Party, and young internet users seemed to lose their passion for reviving democracy in Korean journalism. That might have been the cause of the decline of OhmyNews at some point. Nevertheless, OhmyNews continues to publish exclusive interviews with scholars and researchers from abroad in the sociopolitical and economic fields amid its growing financial difficulties without incurring great costs because foreign audiences still perceive OhmyNews to be one of the most influential online media in Korea, with its own novel quality and democratic journalistic nature.

Raymond Williams defines "culture" in his essay "Culture is ordinary," written in 1958. The concept of "culture" that he discerned implies the transitory but collective nature of ideas and values that lead individuals to join in community. This concept emphasizes a nation being shaped through its own experience and for its own purposes (Szeman & Kaposy, 2010: 53–56). In the same vein, between 2002 and 2006, OhmyNews was the most influential of the online news media, but it has been experiencing a downturn for more than five years. However, as user-generated technologies have developed and become popular, social network systems (SNSs) have seemingly had a powerful impact on Korean society.

## THE PROLIFERATION OF SNSs

From 2010 until the beginning of 2012, the power of SNSs and the podcast *Naneun Ggomsuda*—known as "*Nakkomsu*," meaning "I am a weasel"—was very influential. *The New York Times* and the *LA Times* covered the widely popular podcast with articles entitled "By Lampooning Leaders, Talk Show Channels Young People's Anger," (November 1, 2011), and "South Korea's 'Weasel' Ferrets out the Funny," (November 18, 2011), respectively. The four hosts of the show are a politician, a former politician, a current journalist for a news and current affairs magazine, and a former online news organization President. Kim Ou-Joon is the main host, Kim Yong-Min is a former politician and a critic, Joo Jin-Woo is a reporter at *Sisa-In*, a weekly news and current affairs magazine, and Chung Bong-ju is a politician. Their main target for lampooning is the President, Lee Myung-Bak. On the program, they sarcastically call President Lee "His Highness," or Gaka in Korean. To provide more detail about the podcast, it is necessary to explain the background of one of the four hosts of the program, Kim Ou-Joon. Kim Ou-Joon, the leader of the show, had a close relationship with the CEO of *OhmyNews*. I wish to briefly introduce background information based on the book titled "South Korea's specialty, *OhmyNews*," Daehanminkook tteukssanpoom (meaning "national specialty product"), published in Korean in 2004 by Youn Ho Oh.

*OhmyNews* is very well known, as its CEO, Youn-Ho Oh, has been invited to symposiums and conferences, such as the symposium hosted by the World Association of Newspapers (WAN), which was attended by approximately 1400 Presidents of press companies from all over the world, to explicate the development of *OhmyNews*, one of the most successful online journalism sites in South Korea. However, a rarely known or mentioned fact is that before *OhmyNews* was launched, there was an equally popular online journalism site called "*DDanzi Ilbo*," and the CEO of "*DDanzi Ilbo*" was Kim Ou-Joon, the leading host of the popular radio podcast "*Naneun Ggomsuda*," or "I am a petty-minded creep" in English. "Ilbo" means newspaper in Korean, as in *Dong-A Ilbo, Chosun Ilbo,* and *Joongang Ilbo*. "DDanzi" is a colloquial term meaning "deviant behavior."

The site started in 1998, approximately a year earlier than *OhmyNews*. *DDanzi Ilbo* was a parody of news in traditional newspapers. Youn Ho Oh, the current CEO of *OhmyNews*, visited Kim Ou-Joon and discussed how to launch online news differently than traditional newspapers in pursuit of the goal of all citizens being journalists. Oh asked for advice about how to create successful online journalism. Oh even asked Kim to think of a name for online news. Kim advised him that "in order to make a successful online news site, you should make a site where netizens choose to go, as they will visit and share and spread information, and eventually, the website is successful." He meant that each of those netizens should become an honorary ambassador to let people know about the online news so that the online news company would not necessarily incur any advertising expenses for its website. It was an absolutely important point, according to Oh. He says that when a citizen reporter wrote a news article, and his or her article appeared on *OhmyNews*, they became excited about the fact that their story was on a web page where everybody could see it, so they told people about their publication online, saying, "I became a reporter," "my story went on the top news," or "news viewers love my story because so many people commented on my news." This process is exactly what Kim means when she says, "netizens become honorary ambassadors for promoting the website" (Oh, 2004).

The most popular podcast has been the top keyword for months, and it is currently omnipresent in the news and broadcasts in Korea due to its powerful influence. It arranged a talk performance in an auditorium on October 20 and 30, 2011; one minute after online ticket sales began, 1600 seats had been sold out. "*Naggomsu*"—an acronym for Naneun Ggomsuda—has been breaking records for Apple iTunes downloads each month, easily maintaining its top ranking. Its download numbers are much higher than those of NPR's "Planet Money" or HBO's "Real Time" (*Munwha Journal*, March 2, 2012). In particular, after Chung Bong-Joo was sentenced to one year in prison, charged with mentioning information related to President Lee's alleged stock fraud, the podcast became one of the world's most downloaded political podcasts. In the wake of Chung's imprisonment, citizens have been demonstrating for his release not by scuffles with the police, as was common in the past, but by using their SNSs. For instance, women, including a current journalist, have been demonstrating via SNSs by uploading photographs of themselves in bikinis with "Release him!" written on their chests. Again, freedom of speech has become a hot topic. People say that they feel catharsis when they listen to the podcast because it reveals issues directly. The audience feels that there is no hidden or behind-the-scenes story. The news seems to be frankly spoken. The public knows that not all of what is said on the show is true. However, the public continues to listen to it even though mainstream shows are available.

As I have described thus far, the new media craze has been sweeping the nation in many different ways. Hence, it is worth noting its popularity and its impact on society from the socioeconomic and political perspectives. Amid growing concerns about the new medium's power, one army unit designated "*Naggomsu*" a pro-North Korean app and ordered that it be deleted from soldiers' smartphones in January 2012; officials announced that they would check smartphones every Wednesday, and Defense Ministry spokesman Min Seok Kim said that "Korean soldiers are supposed to protect a nation from North Korea's threat, so it was appropriate measures" (*Yonhap*, February 6, 2012). Moreover, the Korea communications commission, a broadcasting watchdog, stated that it would soon censor podcasts that used to be exempt from scrutiny. The commission is independent and consists of nine members who were appointed by the President to the public broadcasting service, *KBS*. Why is the alternative form of journalism, such as the left-wing-centered "*Naneun Ggomsuda*," so popular and having such a great impact on Korean society? Does the phenomenon imply Korean democracy in the press and in politics? From the perspective of national security, what are the consequences of dissenting views and various opinions regarding the North and related issues in the already complicated situation?

## "Raw" Culture as Popular Culture

Picard states that "To survive and prosper, news and information media must provide better and different news and information than that provided by competitors, and news and information for users who value it" (2010: 374). The host of the radio show, Kim Ou Joon, started hosting a news and current affairs program on TBS, a Seoul city-owned public broadcasting network, on September 26, 2016 (*Yonhap*, September 19, 2016). The show received an unprecedented top rating among all radio shows and podcasts, including entertainment programs, in South Korea. Kim also became a host of a current affairs program at SBS, one of the three major terrestrial broadcasting companies in Korea, in January 2018. The impeachments of former President Park Geun Hye from a conservative party in December, 2016 and President Moon Jae In from the opposition party in the following year, May 2017, do not seem irrelevant to approximately 3800 employees of KBS and MBC, two public broadcasting companies, who participated in a massive labor union strike over 300 days in 2017; highly popular left-wing morning programs such as Kim Ou Joon's radio and podcast show and the news program at JTBC, a South Korean nationwide generalist cable TV network, featured investigative journalism on President Park's issue. However, why are nonmainstream news shows popular? As Picard (2010) states, the programs seek to provide different news and information to the audiences. I add that people, especially young people, like to tell it "as it is." In other words, they are often critical of setting up social constructions. Among them, "as it is" culture is popular. They prefer, or rather trust, restaurant rankings in blog posts rather than newspapers because their perceptions of mainstream media programs are that they are all about construction or are the same as the news on portal sites. They want "reality," the "real world," "not constructed." People love watching a little boy singing at home in front of a wobbly camera on YouTube, rather than in a professional studio, on TV. I call this phenomenon "raw" culture. One of the reasons that people become hooked on reality shows is that audiences are tired of watching "constructed" reality, so they want to see reality on TV that is closer to actual reality. In Korea, YouTube journalism is currently emerging and becoming popular. The very first person to investigate a particular issue to find the truth or the facts is usually a journalist at a mainstream news organization. Then, broadcast reporters or alternative media newscasts or YouTube videos reframe the newspaper report. Therefore, the ways that journalists, newscasts, and reporters frame a particular issue are significant.

The movie *Dogani* (2011)—*The Crucible* in English—showed the power of netizens once again. The film is about the revelations by former school staff of repeated rapes and sexual harassment that took place at Inhwa School in Gwangju in the southern part of South Korea and is based on a true story. A former teacher at the school, Kim Yeong-il, claimed that two students there had been abused, had subsequently died and had been secretly buried approximately 50 years ago. He claimed in a media briefing that in October 1964, when he was working at the school, the vice principal starved an orphan boy and beat him to death. In another incident, a six-year-old girl's death occurred approximately six months later. Kim said that a woman taking care of the girl threw her off a building. He reported this incident to the police but was ignored; they said that they could not find any evidence. Thousands of Korean netizens and bloggers started a petition demanding that the abuse case be reinvestigated. In an interview, the director of the film said that he had never expected that the movie release would gain such widespread public attention. Additionally, he said that netizens, especially those who used SNSs, played a key role in making the film successful, with a viewership of more than 4 million. Approximately two months after the film was released, the city of Gwanju officially announced that it would shut down Inhwa School, and the education office of the province said that it had notified Wuseok, the social welfare foundation that owned and ran the school, that its license would be canceled on November 14, 2011. Moreover, a city spokesman said that the 57 disabled students who were attending the school would be transferred to other schools in adjacent areas (*Yonhap*, November 18, 2011). There have been many cases in which internet users all over the country raised their voices to express their opinions and claimed further investigations and justice that finally affected policies. One notorious case is a murder in 1997, when a 22-year-old university student was stabbed to death in a Burger King bathroom in Itaewon, Seoul. Arthur Patterson and his friend Edward Lee were arrested as the main suspects; they were released by the Supreme Court in 1998 but were banned from traveling to South Korea. However, they were sent back to Korea with the cooperation of the authorities. Patterson was found guilty and sentenced to 20 years. It has been said that the film "The Case of the Itaewon Homicide," released in 2009, and internet users' condemnation of the prosecutors' poor investigation in online communities were not irrelevant to the reopening of the murder file (*Segye Ilbo*, October 13, 2011).[7] Examples of the power of collective identities (netizen) in network society could be endlessly added.

SNSs have become one of the most important social and political media in South Korea, as in many other countries. In contemporary news coverage of major incidents, such as crimes in a subway or a natural disaster in a region, video images captured by the mobile phones of the public, especially the young, often constitute an important part of the coverage in the news on TV as well as on the internet. Journalists also use user-generated content (UGC), such as YouTube or Facebook, in news coverage. As mentioned above, netizens have become a new powerful and influential social class in the media realm, both as encoders and decoders, and journalists use their comments and opinions as a news source. Previous studies on online journalism and the new media focus mainly on public participation in discussions and the creation of a public sphere in the pursuit of democracy. However, in the new media era, SNSs are not only the sole alternative news media forum in online discussions but also a powerful tool to affect social actors' policies in action. Netizens talk together, share opinions, and mobilize on a sociopolitical scale in a virtual space. Numerous postings and opinions in online communities do not mean mobilization.

What mobilizes the public? What makes people take action on a particular issue? Based on his and his colleagues' empirical observations, Castells (2009) says in a speech at Harvard University that they have identified the patterns of a new type of social movement. First, "they are networked in multiple forms. They start in the internet and in social communication networks." Due to mobile communication, society phases into an even broader networked society, which creates the powerful effect of the rapid diffusion of a movement, interactive debates, and communicative autonomy. Second, social movements symbolically occupy the urban space to become visible. They always exist on the internet. Thus, the connection between cyberspace and the urban space is what he calls the space of autonomy. In addition, they begin locally but immediately become global, and a spark of indignation, such as an unbearable image of violence or reports on corruption, can ignite a movement or a call to action. In particular, he emphasizes that images on YouTube rather than Twitter can be determiners of a social movement. He says that societies are based on fear, and fear is overwhelmed only by togetherness in sharing the fear, so they occupy the urban space. Importantly, major agents of social change, which are social movements, are triggered by emotions and shared collectively and become collective action through a process of communication. Therefore, internet users can be part of a collective group that shares powerful emotions. Hence, they can be part of social movements where what starts as emotion mobilizes citizens and shapes social movements, such as social movements in Brazil, Turkey, Arab, and Ukraine against social injustice and for dignity in the networked society (February 20, 2014).[8]

Donohue, Tichenor, and Olien (1995) address the controversial role of mass media as an independent and powerful force in society. The fourth estate role of the watchdog media should include autonomy for the media so that it can represent the interests of the public rather than the dominant groups. However, the concept of media autonomy is ideal. Thus, it seems hard to be independent from each other as well. Curran (2011) observed that the media are controlled by institutions, mainly governments, and authoritarian states, and said that in contrast with the independence of American journalism, the media are still controlled in overt ways in other parts of the world. Castells (2009: 282–283) notes that since the late 1990s, the Chinese government has attempted to control the internet by censoring words such as "porn, Tiananmen, Taiwan, or democracy," adopting surveillance technologies that can keep records and provide content upon the authoritarian government's request. Dozens of internet users have been tracked down, arrested, and jailed.

Local sociopolitical mobilization is organized by means of internet and mobile communication, as Castells (2009: 85–88) says, as in the Philippines, Spain, Ukraine, Ecuador, Nepal, and Thailand. He argues that it illustrates the new capacity of movements to organize and mobilize citizens in their country while calling for solidarity in the world at large. The first demonstrations were relatively small, but they soon became huge after participants filmed events with their own cellular phones and immediately uploaded the videos to YouTube, Twitter, and Facebook. He says that images of the determination of the demonstrators and the brutality of the military regime amplified the movements. The mainstream media rebroadcast and repackaged this citizen-produced content by reframing it to fit their individual institutional purposes. Castells (2009) emphasizes that global civil society has the technological means to exist independently of political institutions and the mass media. However, the question of whether social movements could change the public mind still depends, to a great extent, on their ability to shape the debate in the public sphere. The war has not ended; we have been at war for almost 60 years. There have been small and large incidents and events between the two Koreas since the ceasefire of the Korean War. Hence, it is highly complicated in that there coexist vestiges of the Cold War period and citizens' pursuit of democracy in Korean society. Under these circumstances, what roles do the media play in the divided Korea of an unfinished war?

Since 1987, conditions, both social and political, for freedom of expression have improved rapidly because the Basic Law of the Press was abolished in July 1987, and the mass media, including newspapers, magazines, and broadcasting stations, were regulated by the Act Concerning the Registration of Periodicals and the Broadcasting Act. With the removal of market barriers, many provincial newspapers were founded. Taking advantage of the new opportunities, the Council for Democratic Press Movement (CDPM) supported the establishment of the progressive daily, *Hankyoreh Shinmun*, in May 1988 as an alternative to the conservative mainstream press (Kern & Nam, 2008). The CDPM was literally aiming to plan social movements for press democracy; it later changed its name to Citizens' Coalition for Democratic Media on March 27, 1998. The coalition consists of 13,000 members who are dismissed journalists, radical publishers, and several hundred associated fellow members. In 1998, they organized seminars about journalism practices, such as video journalism; writing for the news by Oh Yeon Ho, founder of OhmyNews; making documentaries; and more.

According to Kern and Nam (2008), the Korea Federation of Press Union (KFPU), which was renamed the National Union of Media Workers (NUMW) in 2000, was established in November 1988. In 1989, the KFPU organized lay-offs to strengthen its rights to independent editorial work. They say that in the 1990s, the democratic media movement changed profoundly. First, many new social movement organizations were founded to promote the political liberalization of society. In contrast to the democracy movement of the 1980s, which broadly demanded democratization in terms of social justice and unification, the new groups quickly evolved to specialize in single issues, such as environmentalism, feminism, and labor activism. Following those strategic media movements for democracy, priority was given to specific media issues, such as the structural deficits of the press market. However, Kern and Nam (2008) emphasize that the top three major newspapers—*Dong-A Ilbo, Chosun Ilbo,* and *JoongAng Ilbo*—were still dominant in the newspaper market, although some political barriers to the establishment of media companies had been removed. In the past, most of the newspapers had repeatedly provoked public outrage with questionable management practices and frequent intrusions by the newspaper management upon editorial procedures. Furthermore, the campaigns of media activists continued to address the allegedly strong conservative, anti-communist, and neoliberal bias of the mainstream press. It may not be easy to conclude that those campaigns and social movements in Korea, have rarely been effective. However, as shown above, there are cases in which social movements, often instigated by citizens and the alternative media, are used as tools to express the opinions of the public.

Rhee (2010) maintains that Korea is a country in which political parallelism, which is the degree of connection between media systems and the party system, prevails. He also points out that Korean top daily newspapers routinely decided to side with major political parties, while public service broadcasters oscillated, depending on who was in power. In addition, as the ideology of the media has become heavily engaged, there has been a decline in public trust of the Korean press over time, and major national newspapers' coverage of the government policy regarding North Korea has significantly changed in such a way that the "ideological orientations of the conservative and liberal dailies became differentiated and aligned to ideological positions of conflicting parties over time between the Kim Young Sam and Kim Dae-Jung Governments" (2010: 351). Historically, this differentiation might not be between only those two administrations. As in Western democratic countries, the media are influenced by the highly competitive market-driven environment in South Korea. However, an ideological binary division, even in the post-Cold War era in politics, is still rooted in the media and society, which results in reduced trust by the public in the press. The war has not ended. There have been small and large incidents and events between the two Koreas since the ceasefire of the Korean War. Hence, it is highly complicated in that vestiges of the Cold War period coexist with citizens' pursuit of democracy in Korean society. Under these circumstances, what roles do the media play in the divided Korea of an unfinished war?

In this chapter, I have introduced the background of Korean politics and the Korean media since the Korean War to help readers understand the current Korean society and the media system. The overview described the role of the media in sociopolitical contexts, in particular, in the transitions of the Korean government. During the turbulent regimes, the media were suppressed, and there were instances of resistance for journalistic autonomy and independence. As Korea transformed into a democratic country, accompanied by the development of digital media, resistance in the new media and the vigorous social activity of netizens (internet users) have been demonstrated in this section through SNSs and the alternative media. Thus, I have discussed the role of the alternative media by examining the sociological, political, and cultural contexts of South Korea in this section.

In Chapters 2 and 3, I set up some of the necessary journalism frameworks and place them in Korean contexts to examine journalists' practices in covering the Korean conflict by applying them. Thus, contextual background to the Korean media and society in detail will be introduced. In addition, I attempted to shed new light on international relations, foreign policies, and national interests in the post-Cold war to proceed a better evaluation of the journalism theories in Korean contexts. This would provide a rationale for examining the news frames and the factors that influenced the news. Therefore, the following chapter explicitly states details of the procedures and the methodology employed in this research project.

## NOTES

1. http://koreajoongangdaily.joins.com/news/article/article. aspx?aid=2891703.
2. https://thediplomat.com/2017/10/south-koreas-saemaul-undong-in-africa/.
3. http://terms.naver.com/entry.nhn?docId=1216768&cid=40942&categoryId=31778.
4. http://www.theguardian.com/media/pda/2011/jan/19/ohmynews-korea-citizen-journalism.
5. http://www.theguardian.com/technology/2003/feb/24/newmedia. koreanews.
6. www.khan.co.kr.
7. http://www.segye.com/newsView/20111012005329.
8. https://www.youtube.com/watch?v=sGUAOyk58jo.

## REFERENCES

Ahn, B.-W., & Ransberg, Na, G. (1999). *Is 5.18 Finished?* Pureun Soop.
Allan, S. (2006). *Online News: Journalism and the Internet.* Maidenhead and New York: Open University Press.
Castells, M. (2008). The New Public Sphere: Global Civil Society, Communication Networks, and Global Governance. *The Annals of the American Academy of Political and Social Science, 616*(1), 78–93.

Castells, M. (2009). *Communication Power.* Oxford and New York: Oxford University Press.

Chae, B. (2000). Rapid Economic Development and Power: The Military Regime Era. *Newspaper and Broadcasting, 349,* 67–73.

Chang, W. (2005). Online Civic Participation, and Political Empowerment: Online Media and Public Opinion Formation in Korea. *Media, Culture and Society, 27*(6), 925–935.

Choi, J. (1987). The Korean Press History, Iljohgahk. In J.-M. Kang (Ed.), (2000). *Power Transition: The Korean Press History for 117 Years* (p. 298). Inmul & Sasangsa.

Curran, J. (2000). Press Reformism 1918–98: A Study of Failure. In H. Tumber (Ed.), *Media Power, Professionals and Policies.* London: Routledge.

Curran, J. (2011). *Media and Democracy.* Oxford: Routledge.

Curran, J. (2012). Reinterpreting the Internet, In J. Curran, N. Fenton & D. Freedman (Eds.), *Misunderstanding the internet* (pp. 3–33). London: Routledge.

Curran, J., & Park, M.-J. (2000). *De-westernizing Media Studies.* London: Routledge.

Curran, J., Fenton, N., & Freedman, D. (Eds.). (2012). *Misunderstanding the Internet.* London: Routledge.

Dahlgren, P. (1995). *Television and the Public Sphere: Citizenship, Democracy and the Media.* London: Sage.

Donohue, G. A., Tichenor, J., & Olien, C. N. (1995). A Guard Dog Perspective on the Role of Media. *Journal of Communication, 45*(2), 115–132.

Fairclough, G. (2004, April 14). Generation Why? The 386ers of Korea Question Old Rules. *Wall Street Journal,* A1.

Fenton, N. (2010). *New Media, Old News: Journalism & Democracy in the Digital Age.* London: Sage.

Gripsrud, J. (1992). The Aesthetics and Politics of Melodrama. In P. Dahlgren & C. Sparks (Eds.), *Journalism and Popular Culture.* London, Newbury Park, and New Delhi: Sage.

Han, D.-S. (1996). *Challenging Economic Barriers: A Case Study of a South Korean Newspaper* (Thesis). University of Westminster.

Han, J.-M. (2001). *Understanding Korean Broadcasting.* Hanwool Academy.

Han, Y.-H. (2010). *Anti-Chosun Movement History: Penetrating Modern Korean History* (Text).

Hauben, R. (2008). *Online Grassroots Journalism and Participatory Democracy in South Korea.* Columbia University, 22 April 2009. www.columbia.edu/~rh120/other/netizens_draft.pdf.

Henderson, L. (2007). *Social Issues in Television Fiction.* Edinburgh: Edinburgh University Press.

Hickey, M. (2000). *The Korean War: The West Confronts Communism.* Woodstock and New York: The Overlook Press.

Joh, H.-Y. (2007). Park Jung Hee and the Military Regime: From 5.16 to 10.26, YuksaBeepyungsa.

Johnson, C. (2000). *Blowback, Sphere: The Costs and Consequences of American Empire.* Little London: Time Warner Paperbacks.

Joyce, M. (2007, December). *The Citizen Journalism Web Site 'Ohmynews' and the 2002 South Korean Presidential Election: The Berkman Center for Internet and Society at Harvard University.* Retrieved from https://cyber.harvard.edu/sites/cyber.harvard.edu/files/Joyce_South_Korea_2007.pdf.

Jung, J.-S. (1985). Historical Theories of the Korean Modern Press, JeonYehWon.

Jung, G.-J. (2012). *Saemaeul Movement and Enlightenment, Report, Ministry of Strategy and Finance and KDI (Korea Development Institute).*

Kang, J.-M. (2000). *Power Transition: The Korean Press History for 117 Years.* Seoul: Inmul & Sasangsa.

Kang, J.-M. (2007). *The Korean Mass Media History.* Seoul: Inmul & Sasangsa.

Kern, T., & Nam, S.-H. (2008). *Social Movements as Agents of Innovation: Citizen Journalism in South Korea, April, GIGA (German Institute of Global and Area Studies).* Research Programme: Legitimacy and Efficiency of Political Systems. www.giga-hamburg.de/workingpapers.

Kim, M.-N. (1993). *The New Korean Press History.* Ahchim.

Kim, H.-S. (1994). *A Sociological Study on the Korean Press.* Seoul: Nanam.

Kim, M.-H. (1996). *The History of Korean Mass Media.* Sah Hoi Be Pyung Sa.

Kim, S. (2000). *The Politics of Democratization in Korea: The Role of Civil Society.* Pittsburgh: University of Pittsburgh Press.

Kim, D.-H. (2012). *The Economic History of South Korean Presidents.* Seoul: Ch'aekbat.

Kim, S.-T., & Lee, Y.-W. (2006). New Functions of Internet Mediated Agenda-Setting: Agenda-Rippling and Reversed Agenda-Setting. *Asian Communication Research, 50*(3), 175–204.

Lee, Y.-W. (1999). *The Second Republic and Jang Myun.* Beomwoosa.

Lee, S. H. (2001). *The Korean War.* Great Britain: Pearson Education.

Lee, S.-C. (2008). *North Korean Nationalism Research.* History Review Publishing.

Lee, W.-S., & Park, J. Y. (2008). The Tone of Economy News During the Kim Dae-jung and Roh Moo-hyun Government. *Korean Journal of Journalism and Communication Studies, 52*(4), 5–24.

Lim, D. (1998). *Choice and Distort of South North Korea in 1950s.* YukSaBeePyungSa.

MacDonald, J. F. (1985). *Television and the Red Menace: The Video Road to Vietnam.* New York: Praeger.

McChesney, R. W. (2000). *Rich Media, Poor Democracy.* New York and London: The New Press.

McFarland, D. K. (1986). *The Korean War: An Annotated Bibliography*. New York: Routledge.

McGuigan, J. (2005). The Cultural Public Sphere. *European Journal of Cultural Studies, 8*(4), 427–443.

Mott, F. L. (1962). *American Journalism*. New York: The Macmillan Company.

Oh, Y.-H. (2004). *Ohmynews—Korea's Unique Product*. Humanist.

Park, Y.-G. (2014). Changes in Professional Identity of Journalists During the Park Chung-Hee Regime. *Press Information Research, 51*(2), 34–76.

Picard, R. G. (2010). The Future of the News Industry. In J. Curran (Ed.), *Media and Society* (5th ed.). London and New York: Bloomsbury Academic.

Rhee, J.-W. (2010). The Rise of Internet News Media and the Emergence of Discursive Publics in South Korea. In J. Curran (Ed.), *Media and Society* (5th ed.). (pp. 348–364). London and New York: Bloomsbury Academic.

Seitz, M. (2017, October 20). South Korea's Saemaul Undong in Africa, The Diplomat. Retrieved from https://thediplomat.com/2017/10/south-koreas-saemaul-undong-in-africa/.

Shim, S., & Lee, I.-W. (1998). *People Who Want to Change the World*. Hankyoreh Shinmun Publishing.

Shin, S.-H. (2012). *An Investigative Report on Park Jong-Cheol and the Changes of Korea's Democratic Policies* (PhD thesis). Korea University, South Korea.

Song, G.-H, Choi, M.-J, Park, J.-D., Yoon, D.-H., Sohn, S.-C., & Kang, M.-K. (2000). *Looking at the Korean Press*. Dasudsooreh.

Sunstein, C. (2001). *Republic.com*. Princeton, NJ: Princeton University Press.

Szeman, I., & Kaposy, T. (2010). *Cultural Theory: An Anthology*. Malden, MA: Wiley-Blackwell.

Yoo, B.-G. (1998). *Episode in Broadcasting*. KBS MunHwa.

# CHAPTER 4

# News Framing and In-Depth Interviews

The research design is outlined and main methodological approaches are described in this chapter. The methods utilized in this study are twofold. First, a news framing analysis by comparing and contrasting the news narratives of news outlets in the United States, the UK, and South Korea were conducted. Second, semi-structured interviews with international journalists and Korean journalists were performed. This chapter explicates the methods employed for this research, the results of which is presented in Chapters 5 and 6.

## THE KOREAN CONFLICT

Since the end of the Korean War, there have been ongoing small- or large-scale conflicts between South and North Korea. In particular, there have been major naval battles between the South and the North in 1999, 2002, and 2009 near the Northern Limit Line (NLL) in the West Sea, which is a disputed area. South Korea calls the skirmishes "Seo Hae Kyo Jeon" in Korean (西海交戰 in Chinese). The first skirmish occurred in 1999 when patrolling ships from the South and the North confronted each other near the NLL. After five minutes of confrontation, twenty North Korean naval soldiers died, many were injured, a South Korean vessel was damaged, and seven South Koreans had minor injuries. Another deadly sea battle near the NLL in 2002 resulted in the loss of five South Korean sailors' lives and nineteen wounded. Not long after that battle, a clash occurred on November 10, 2009, when a North

M. Moon, *International News Coverage and the Korean Conflict*,
https://doi.org/10.1007/978-981-13-6291-0_4

Korean patrol boat infringed on the NLL near Daecheong Island. In the international news coverage of the Korean conflict, reports repeatedly referred to the NLL as "disputed," reflecting the status of the line, which was unilaterally promulgated by the United Nations Command when the Korean War ended. The NLL was drawn to protect South Korea, but the North refuses to accept the line as a maritime border (Kotch & Abbey, 2003; Van Dyke, Valencia, & Garmendia, 2003).

One of the most tragic Korean conflicts, the sinking of the South Korean corvette Cheonan, occurred near the contested maritime demarcation line, the NLL. On March 26, 2010, the Republic of Korea warship Cheonan (PCC-722) sank near Bakryeong Island in the Yellow Sea (or West Sea) at approximately 9:22 p.m., killing 46 sailors. South Korea faced judgment following a probe by a multinational investigation team, and the reports were rife with speculation about the cause of the disaster. Furthermore, the discrepancies between competing versions of the cause of the sinking in the national news brought more speculation and rumors in Korea. The South Korean government and the joint international investigation team from the United States, Britain, Australia, and Sweden concluded that the corvette had been torpedoed by North Korea on May 20, 2010 (*Yonhap*, May 20, 2010). A number of major national and international news agencies reported the results of the probe at that time. However, North Korea denied its involvement in the disaster, and the UN Security Council condemned North Korea "but avoided blaming Pyongyang" (*BBC*, July 9, 2010).[1]

The issue of who was responsible for this tragedy has become an ongoing, controversial debate throughout the nation. It may be a surprise to non-Koreans that when even when naval battles or North Korean nuclear tests have occurred, the Korean public seems to fear a war much less than a summer typhoon, especially during the monsoon season. Expatriates who have resided in South Korea for some time also seem to have little fear of war, although foreign visitors are prone to worry and want to leave the country when they are exposed to news about Korean conflicts or a North Korean satellite launch. For example, when I worked in public broadcasting, there was an all-English radio station in the network. The Korean staff did not appear to prepare for any emergency, while the English radio production team seemed extremely concerned about what to do in the case of a war. Thus, the American hosts at the English radio station said that they would leave their shows behind and return home when they heard the news about the South

Korean warship sinking. In contrast, hosts who had lived in Korea for years explained that there would not be a war despite the news that tensions were escalating. Within South Korea, North Korea's nuclear tests and satellite launch are not a threat because the military apparatus is largely out-of-date, and Koreans perceive these incidents as part of the ongoing brinkmanship of the past sixty years.

Based on the report by the joint international investigation team, the South Korean government announced that North Korea had attacked the Cheonan warship on May 20, 2018. Until the international joint investigation team's conclusion, which was released about two months after the attack, the cause of the sinking was unknown. Therefore, I thought, as in reporting a war, that international news articles pertaining to the Cheonan incident would constitute good case study data to analyze the ways in which journalists produce a news story on a conflict and to examine the processes of news production under war conditions of inaccessibility and lack of sources.

Practical military drills by the public were more strictly enforced than usual. For example, on the 15th of each month, South Korea has a civil defense drill. According to the National Disaster Information Center, the drill is to defend and protect the public from enemy attacks and all kinds of disasters.[2] On that day, if a siren goes off, people are expected to go indoors wherever they are. If they are in an office building, they should go downstairs to the basement. Enforcement of this practice had slackened, so members of the public and institutions did not follow it very diligently. However, in 2010 after the incident, government officials became much stricter about the drills. In the broadcasting company where I worked, all staff, including the President of the company, went to the basement and waited until the siren stopped.

Furthermore, South Korean men must complete their 26-month military service when they are in their 20s. Even after finishing their service, they become reserve soldiers who participate in military drills three to four times a year until they reach the age of forty. During 2010, reserve soldiers received letters informing them that, in the case of a war, they would have to participate.[3] In a similar manner, every year during the four days from 20 August to 23 August, public officers or civil servants have what is called a "Eul Ji" drill during which they must come to work in the very early morning and stay up working all night. During the night duty, they receive and send faxes to other institutions, such as nearby police stations or fire stations, to simulate a state of war. After the sinking of the Cheonan, the country went into a state of high alert, and public officers had to perform the Eul Ji drill twice that year. Additionally, if the government issued a draft for all public officers, they had to go to work within one hour, wherever they were. In Gangwon Province, which is nearest to the North, the government issued an emergency alert.

As described above, after the incident, it appeared to many that the government was preparing for a war. However, although practicing and experiencing the stricter drills required by the government, the public seemed to have no fear of a new war. There were criticisms of the government's untimely and weak reaction to the North, and at the same time, the public were eager to know more about the incident, especially after watching news reports about the families of the sailors killed. National newspapers conducted opinion polls asking whether people believed that North Korea had attacked the Cheonan warship, but public opinion on the issue was divided. It seems that this incident represented a watershed that was different from past news of the clashes between South Korea and North Korea due to the unknown cause, particularly before the international investigative team's conclusion. Hence, by examining as a case study the ways in which news about the sinking of the Cheonan warship was constructed, mainly by international journalists, I explore the role of journalism and its impact on Korean society and the region as well as international communities, considering the limited access and news sources when journalists cover news about North Korea. In addition, this analysis takes a critical view of the warship sinking in a domestic and global context because the two superpowers, China and the United States, play a key role in dealing with North Korean issues even in the post-Cold War era.

A great body of media and communication studies employs framing theory to analyze news content, adopting the theory that the media shape public perceptions, and the news media, in particular, are one of the most significant sources for comprehending the world. Journalism studies concentrate on media systems, with comparisons between countries, in particular, Western countries and developing countries, and news text analysis by predominantly applying framing theory to a news topic (i.e., a news framing analysis of nuclear tests, six-party talks and North Korea in general). However, I intend to explore the processes of news production and discuss the role of the news media within the study of journalism and communication. In particular, I concentrate on the nature of news production in covering the Korean conflicts by interviewing mainly international correspondents in Seoul in addition to Korean journalists to investigate the circumstances in which journalism practices and major factors affect their news frames. Thus, I sought to investigate journalism practices by Seoul correspondents as well as Korean journalists, with a particular focus on discussing reporting of those who have covered North Korea. As very limited information and news sources are available, the public cannot help but depend on the news regarding issues related to North Korea. North Korea is the most reclusive country in the world, and there is no access to any original information about the nation. Hence, this study intends to explore the factors that influenced the journalists who covered the Cheonan issue, and news framing, by comparing three nations: South Korea, the UK, and the United States. It is necessary to investigate how the news was reported in various nations and why it was framed the way it was to fully understand news as a social construction of reality by a journalist in a sociopolitical and economic context.

## Quantitative and Qualitative Research Methods

Quantitative and qualitative methods are two major paradigms in social science. Since my study examines news frames and explores the factors that influenced those frames, quantitative and qualitative research methods were combined. For news content analysis, I will adopt news framing analysis. Framing analysis can be divided into two approaches: inductive and deductive. An inductive approach is to analyze news texts with "a priori defined frames in mind" (De Vreese, 2005: 53). This approach has been criticized for its typically small sample size and the difficulty of replicating results. The other approach is deductive framing analysis, which is more widely used by scholars (De Vreese, 2005; Semetko & Valkenburg, 2000). This approach is utilized to investigate frames by applying operationally defined frames in content analysis adopted from previous studies, such as the conflict frame or the attribution of responsibility or human interest frames. In contrast to the former approach, the latter is easy to replicate and works better with large samples (Semetko & Valkenburg, 2000). Since my news data are not a large sample, I will conduct an inductive framing analysis.

A large volume of framing studies have been conducted on cross-national news coverage of various issues, highlighting the relationship between news media frames and public perceptions (Altheide & Grimes, 2005; Castells, 2009; Dimitrova & Stromback, 2005; Freedman & Thussu, 2012; Moeller, 2004a; Norris, Kern, & Just, 2003). In addition, some studies show that the U.S. news media frames of North Korea were terrorism, weapons, and a global threat, and the public perception was that it is a terrorist state (Moeller, 2004a, b). Considering the impact of news frames on public perceptions discussed in previous studies, it would be significant to investigate news frames employed in the news coverage of the Cheonan episode. Thus, for this study, I analyzed news texts to investigate the comparative news frames in news coverage of the Cheonan in the United States, the UK and South Korea, focusing on elite newspapers and news agencies. Entman (1991) states that analyzing news narratives is one of the critical and reliable ways of detecting frames (1991: 6). In addition, Zelizer (1997) emphasizes how the study of news narratives leads to a deeper understanding of journalism and its practice. Adopting Entman's categories in the news framing analysis, I compared and contrasted news narratives from mainstream news outlets to investigate the dominant news frames. The size of news articles is an essential element in a news framing analysis because it can show whether the media were making the issue salient (Entman, 1991). In addition, identifying news sources cited in news stories is one of the most significant ways of examining the main determinants that influence news frames (Entman, 1991; Herman & Chomsky, 2002). Hence, I examined what form of news sources were employed in the news coverage of the Cheonan.

## DATA COLLECTION: SAMPLING AND CODING

The three main news agencies in the twenty-first century are Reuters, the Associated Press (AP), and Agence France-Presse (AFP), and these global news agencies have a significant impact on shaping the news content of the mainstream media worldwide (De Beer & Merrill, 2009). In particular, "global and regional news agencies are all the more crucial due to their potentially substantial agenda-setting influence on other media" (Paterson, 2003: 2). Do major news agencies influence elite and international mainstream news media in this case? Do we observe an information flow from "the North" to "the South," or does it appear to be a contra-information flow in the case of the Cheonan (Thussu, 2000, 2002)? I selected the AP, one of the three large news agencies, and obtained the news articles reported by the AP from the LexisNexis database.

In terms of each country's mainstream media, for the UK, the *BBC* news was selected because the *BBC* is a public broadcasting corporation in the UK and is the most influential television news broadcaster in the world as well (McPhail, 2016; Thussu, 2000). In addition, Koreans can watch the *BBC* World News, just as they can watch *CNN*, and the *BBC* entertainment TV channel, *BBC* Prime, on cable and satellite. Hence, I chose the *BBC* for this research. For the U.S. news media, *CNN* was selected because it is a pioneering example of a global television news network (McPhail, 2016; Thussu, 2000). For the U.S. daily newspaper, I selected *The New York Times*, an elite and influential newspaper, based on its crucial role as an agenda setter for other news media (Boyd-Barrett & Rantanen, 1998; Meraz, 2009; Thussu, 2000). *The Guardian*, London, was selected for the UK daily newspaper. According to Bantimaroudis and Ban (2001: 176), *The Guardian* and *The New York Times* are "major gatekeepers in the United States and Europe respectively," and their news articles are redistributed by other local media. Therefore, examining the two elite newspapers' news coverage patterns and trends is a very useful tool to understand various perspectives and views on the two continents (2001: 175–176).

For domestic news media news analysis, in terms of international news flow, I examined news coverage by the largest Korean news agency, *Yonhap*. Additionally, for domestic daily newspapers, I chose *Dong-A Ilbo*, which is one of the major three conservative newspapers, and *Hankyoreh*, which is one of the top progressive newspapers in South Korea (Jeong, 2011). Moreover, according to the Rankey.com website ranking software, the largest three conservative newspapers' online versions, Chosun.com, Joins.com, and Donga.com, have the highest traffic rates.[4] In short, for international news, I chose *BBC*, *The Guardian* in the UK and *CNN* and *The New York Times* in the United States. For news agencies, the news coverage of the AP will be examined and compared. If necessary, news excerpts from other news media companies will be presented to explicate the detailed information and background. I included only standard news reports and excluded opinion pieces and editorial items because this study explores the ways in which a journalist constructed a reality and framed the issue.

For actual news gathering, I used the LexisNexis database for the AP, *The New York Times*, and *The Guardian* (London) using a keyword search. The word "Cheonan" in English does not overlap with any other word, unless it indicates the name of a city in the southern part of the metropolitan area of South Korea. However, during the period of my data collection, there was no international news about the city Cheonan, so overlapping was avoidable. Other than that, the word "Cheonan" has no other meaning. To retrieve Korean news articles, I used the two words "CheonanHahm" as the pronoun to avoid obtaining news about "Cheonan"-related news ("Hahm" can mean "warship," "corvette" or any other ship-related words in Korean). To collect domestic news articles from *Yonhap*, Dong-A Ilbo and Hankyoreh, I retrieved news from the news archives of the largest portal, "Naver," with the keyword "CheonanHahm." Korean researchers formerly obtained news data from the "KINDS" archives, but the three major newspapers, Chosun Ilbo, Joongang Ilbo, and Dong-A Ilbo, no longer provide news data to those archives, so researchers use the largest portal, "Naver," which is equivalent to Google in South Korea (Moon, 2015). For the *BBC* and *CNN*—for which the LexisNexis database does not provide data—I used their company websites. While all other international news outlets displayed their news with the keyword "Cheonan," for Guardian news articles, if I typed "Cheonan," no news text was found. However, if I typed "the Cheonan," a list of news articles pertaining to the Cheonan incident was shown. For data sampling, Riffe, Lacy, and Fico (1993: 139) state that one constructed week for a six-month population and two constructed weeks for an entire year are reliable. Therefore, my data cover the period from March 26, 2010 to May 31, 2010; the unit of analysis was an individual news story; and for data sampling, I used one constructed week, March 26, 2010–April 1, 2010. For Korean news data sampling, I used random sampling. The first news item of each day was used for data analysis.

## IN-DEPTH INTERVIEWS

Shoemaker and Reese (1996: 28) argue, "A study of content alone is not sufficient ... to understand either the force that produced that content or the nature or extent of its effects." Furthermore, according to Wengraf (2001: 37), 90% of all social science research involves interviews, and as Kvale (1996: 14) asserts, through interviews, a researcher collects data and obtains knowledge. In addition, interviews are a way of gaining the views, opinions, and perceptions of interviewees through their confessional responses or "biographic" narratives. Additionally, as for in-depth interviews, Wengraf (2001: 6) states that interviews function "to get a sense of how the apparently straightforward is actually more complicated, of how the 'surface appearances' may be quite misleading about 'depth realities.'" In lieu of finding patterned norms and common characteristic conceptions of narrative knowledge, he points out that the detailed quality of the narratives precludes the failure that might be a consequence of generalization. Thus, Wengraf (2001: 333) contends that a well-designed interview is planned in advance, and the role of the interviewer in facilitating the informants' storytelling is very important.

Semi-structured, individual, in-depth interviews with 18 journalists (fourteen international and four Korean journalists) were conducted to gain knowledge about how journalists operate and the nature of news production. In particular, this thesis concentrates on investigating what influences their practices and how they collect information since a comparative news analysis alone could not provide detailed background information about the processes of news production and the nature of news production (Shoemaker & Reese, 1996: 28), especially in covering news about a sensitive issue such as the Cheonan. I approached the interviews not with a specific hypothesis (David & Sutton, 2004: 87) but rather with prepared questions and issues to be addressed. In the format of a semi-structured interview, the interviewer has discretion. Therefore, depending on the journalists' answers and directions, the order of questions varied. In addition, if further questions and explanations were needed, I could ask the interviewee to elucidate at any stage without interrupting the flow of the interview. The list of the interviewees with details— name and media organization—follows. To provide references for the quotations by each journalist in this study, each one was assigned an ID number (under the interviewee name); thus, when the interviewees are quoted hereafter, they will be referred to by the ID (Table 4.1).

Seale and Silverman (1997) contend that verbatim transcription is only one method of capturing verbal data content; hence, it should be treated as central to qualitative data collection in terms of reliability. In addition, the requirements for transcribing an interview are a proper recording without any technical defects or human errors and audible recordings in which the voices do not blend with background noise (Kvale, 1996: 93–94). Based on my work experience as an editor at a public broadcasting network, I double-checked the background noise and a recorder battery as I asked my reporters for vox pops. I also

**Table 4.1** Interviewee details

| ID | News organization | Ownership | Nationality | Position |
|---|---|---|---|---|
| 1 | AP | US | American | Correspondent |
| 2 | CNN | US | British | Correspondent |
| 3 | The New York Times | US | Korean | Correspondent |
| 4 | The Wall Street Journal/ The Dow Jones Newswire | US | American | Asia Bureau Chief |
| 5 | The Washington Times | US | British | Analyst, former correspondent |
| 6 | The Christian Science Monitor | US | American | Correspondent |
| 7 | The Voice of America | US | American | Asia Bureau Chief |
| 8 | Reuters | Canada/UK | British | News editor, Asia Bureau Chief |
| 9 | BBC | UK | Anonymous | News producer, editor |
| 10 | The Financial Times | UK | British | Correspondent |
| 11 | The Financial Times | UK | American | Analyst, former Correspondent |
| 12 | AFP | France | British | Senior editor |
| 13 | Le Figaro | France | French | Correspondent |
| 14 | The Mainichi Shimbun | Japan | Japanese | Bureau Chief, correspondent |
| 15 | KBS | Korea | Korean | TV news reporter |
| 16 | KBS | Korea | Korean | TV news reporter |
| 17 | Dong-A Ilbo | Korea | Korean | Journalist |
| 18 | The Hankyoreh | Korea | Korean | News editor |

arranged a place for an interview in advance to ensure that it was suitable and met the requirements. For the transcription, I ensured that I wrote the words as they were and did not "clean up" by removing any language even if the interviewees used slang, grammatically incorrect language or even profanities (McLellan, MacQueen, & Neidig, 2003: 73).

## ANALYZING THE INTERVIEW DATA

For the interpretation of the interview materials, a thematic analysis was used. According to Arksey and Knight (1999: 162), "In grounded theory, analysis is interwoven with data collection, a process of finding, analyzing and theorizing...the discovery of theory from data is a crucial process." This means that the data and research processes are integrated. Thematic analysis is a qualitative research methodological framework for identifying, analyzing, and reporting within research, but it is nuanced and constructed so that patterns of meanings in data that tend to be latent can be identified. Hence, defining themes from the data and coding and analyzing the identified key themes are important. As Braun and Clarke (2006: 77) point out, thematic analysis is a "deliberate and rigorous" method that finds patterns "in relation to different epistemological and ontological positions." Therefore, through transparent thematic analysis, key themes and patterns will be discovered and refined to understand the data in the following chapter.

## NOTES

1. http://www.BBC.co.uk/news/10565560.
2. For more information, www.safekorea.go.kr.
3. For more information, www.yebigun1.mil.kr.
4. http://www.rankey.com/blog/blog.php?type=W_Report&sub_type=&writer=&no=12679.

## REFERENCES

Altheide, D. L., & Grimes, J. N. (2005). War Programming: The Propaganda Project and the Iraq War. *Sociological Quarterly, 46*, 617–643.

Arksey, H., & Knight, P. (1999). *Interviewing for Social Scientists: An Introductory Resource with Examples*. London: Sage.

Bantimaroudis, P., & Ban, H. (2001). Covering the Crisis in Somalia: Framing Choices by *The New York Times* and *The Manchester Guardian*. In S. D. Reese, O. H. Gandy Jr, & A. E. Grant (Eds.), *Framing Public Life: Perspectives on Media and Our Understanding of the Social World* (pp.175–184). Mahwah, NJ: Erlbaum.

Boyd-Barrett, O., & Rantanen, T. (Eds.). (1998). *The Globalization of News*. London, Thousand Oaks, and New Delhi: Sage.

Braun, V., & Clarke, V. (2006). Using Thematic Analysis in Psychology. *Qualitative Research in Psychology, 3*(2), 77–101.

Castells, M. (2009). *Communication Power*. Oxford and New York: Oxford University Press.

David, M., & Sutton, C. D. (2004). *Social Research: The Basics*. London: Sage.

De Beer, S. A., & Merrill, C. J. (Eds.). (2009). *Global Journalism: Topical Issues and Media Systems* (5th ed.). Boston: Pearson Education.

De Vreese, H. C. (2005). News Framing: Theory and Typology. *Information Design Journal and Document Design, 13*(1), 51–62.

Dimitrova, D. V., & Stromback, J. (2005). Mission Accomplished? Framing of the Iraq War in the Elite Newspapers in Sweden and the United States. *Gazette: The International Journal for Communication Studies, 67*(5), 399–417.

Entman, R. M. (1991). Framing U.S. Coverage of International News: Contrasts in Narratives of KAL and Iran Air Incidents. *Journal of communication, 41,* 6–27.

Freedman, D., & Thussu, K. D. (2012). *Media and Terrorism: Global Perspectives.* London, Thousand Oaks, New Delhi, and Singapore: Sage.

Herman, S. E., & Chomsky, N. (2002). *Manufacturing Consent: The Political Economy of the Mass Media.* New York: Pantheon Books.

Jeong, J.-C. (2011). A Critical Study on Korean Newspaper's Social Welfare Populism Discourse. *Media Science Research, 11*(1), 371–398.

Kotch, B. J., & Abbey, M. (2003). Ending Naval Clashes on the Northern Limit Line and the Quest for a West Sea Peace Regime. *Asian Perspective, 27*(2), 175–204.

Kvale, S. (1996). *Interviews: An Introduction to Qualitative Research Interviewing.* Thousand Oaks, CA: Sage.

McLellan, E., MacQueen, K., & Neidig, J. (2003). Beyond the Qualitative Interview: Data Preparation and Transcription. *Filed Methods, 15,* 63–84.

McPhail, T. (2016). *Global Communication: Theories, Stakeholders, and Trends.* Malden, MA: Wiley.

Meraz, S. (2009). Is There an Elite Hold? Traditional Media to Social Media Agenda Setting Influence in Blog Networks. *Journal of Computer-Mediated Communication, 14*(3), 682–707.

Moeller, S. (2004a). A Moral Imagination—The Media's Response to the War on Terrorism. In S. Allen & B. Zelizer (Eds.), *Reporting War—Journalism in Wartime* (pp. 59–76). London and New York: Routledge.

Moeller, S. (2004b). *Media Coverage of Weapons of Mass Destruction: Anatomy of a Failure.* Retrieved from http://www.cissm.umd.edu/documents/ WMDstudy_short.pdf. September 7, 2005.

Moon, M. (2015). Cosmetic Surgery as a Commodity for 'Sale' in Online News, *Asian Journal of Communication, 25*(1), 102–113.

Norris, P., Kern, M., & Just, M. (Eds.) (2003). *Framing Terrorism: The News Media, the Government and the Public.* New York and London: Routledge.

Paterson, C. (2003, April 23–26). *Prospects for a Democratic Information Society: The News Agency Stranglehold on Global Political Discourse, New Media, Technology and Everyday Life in Europe Conference,* London.

Riffe, D., Lacy, S., & Fico, F. (1993). *Analyzing Media Messages: Using Quantitative Content Analysis in Research.* Mahwah, NJ: Lawrence Erlbaum Associates.

Seale, C., & Silverman, D. (1997). Ensuring Rigour in Qualitative Research. *European Journal of Public Health, 7*(4), 379–384.

Semetko, H. A., & Valkenburg, M. (2000). Framing European Politics: A Content Analysis of Press and Television News. *Journal of Communication, 50*(2), 93–109.

Shoemaker, J., & Reese, S. D. (1996). *Mediating the Message: Theories of Influence on Mass Media Content* (2nd ed.). White Plains, NY: Longman.

Thussu, D. K. (2000). *International Communication: Continuity and Change.* London: Arnold.

Thussu, D. K. (2002). Managing the Media in an Era of Round-the-Clock News: Notes From India's First Tele-War. *Journalism Studies, 3*(2), 203–212.

Van Dyke, J. M., Valencia, M. J., & Garmendia, J. M. (2003). The North/South Korea Boundary Dispute in the Yellow (West) Sea. *Marine Policy, 27*(2), 143–158.

Wengraf, T. (2001). *Qualitative Research Interviewing: Biographic Narrative and Semi-Structured Method.* London: Sage.

Zelizer, B. (1997). Has Communication Explained Journalism? In D. Berkowitz (Ed.), *Social Meanings of News: A Text-Reader* (pp. 23–30). London: Sage.

# CHAPTER 5

# International News Coverage of the Korean Conflict

This chapter presents the findings concerning what frames were prominent in the sampled news data. First, the frequency of news articles and the narrative analysis of the news coverage of the incident in national and international news outlets will be examined. The combined size of all related news texts is an important element in news framing analysis, and it is significant to interpret the media representation of the conflict by analyzing the employed news frames. In addition, this chapter analyzes the dominant news sources used in news articles since a news source is an effective element in news framing analysis. Moreover, to examine the international news flow, I attempted to determine the best way to visibly track the news flow and to compare and contrast the national and international news texts, together with the time that they were reported.

## The Frequency of News Articles

As discussed in an earlier chapter, to investigate news frames, it is essential to examine the prominence of an issue through the measurement of the size of the news data. News data for news framing analysis were collected between March 26, 2010 and April 1, 2010. The dates may differ by a day before or after these dates due to the time differences between the UK, the United States, and Korea. For instance, the incident occurred on March 26, 2010 at approximately 9 p.m.

© The Author(s) 2019

M. Moon, *International News Coverage and the Korean Conflict*,
https://doi.org/10.1007/978-981-13-6291-0_5

local time (Korea time), but the date when it first appeared in news reports was March 27, 2010 on *CNN*. Considering the time differences, I included all the news texts of the first full week from the day when the incident happened.

By contrasting the number of news stories and the volume of the news reportage of the KAL and Iran Air incidents, Entman (1991) determines that the KAL incident had more air time in news broadcasts and more news text and was considered a far more prominent and politically important news event. He adds that the more the media cover a story, the more the audience is likely to be exposed to the media content (1991: 10). The findings show that the size of news articles of the sinking of the Cheonan and comparisons between national and international media (Moon, 2018: 271). The amount of coverage from the Korean news agency, *Yonhap*, was 14,123. The two Korean national newspapers reported a far greater number of news articles, with 1236 for *Dong-A Ilbo* and 890 for *Hankyoreh Shinmun*. In contrast, *The New York Times* and *The Guardian* covered the Cheonan relatively little, 29 and 19, respectively. The *BBC* reported 23, and *CNN* reported the event twice as much as the *BBC* at 57. The number of news stories by the AP global news agency was 80. Compared to the global news agency, *Yonhap* reported far more news about the Cheonan. Additionally, both the UK newspaper and network reported the news topic far more than the U.S. news media did. This finding does not generalize the volume of news data about the issue in all the UK and U.S. media, as the validity of the results is limited to the media measured for this study. Despite a news report calling it one of the South's "worst sea disasters" since the Korean War (*BBC*, May 27, 2010, May 28, 2010) and considering that the number of news stories in *The New York Times* about the KAL 007 and Iran Air incidents over two weeks were 286 and 102, respectively (Entman, 1991), the Cheonan incident, which killed 46 young sailors, did not appear to be treated as a critical event by international media in terms of sizing in framing.

Entman explicates that frames in news narratives consist of "a series of idea clusters." He says that ideas are established in the process of formulating familiar cultural components to make a topic comprehensible (1991: 11). Entman analyzed both words and images that were used repeatedly in news. However, in this study, I will focus on the words used in news stories because the cause of the incident was unknown, and not all news retrieved from the LexisNexis database contained images. First, the number of news articles in the AP, *BBC*, *CNN*, *The New York Times* and *The Guardian* during the week between March 26, 2010 and April 1, 2010 was 9, 6, 9, 3, and 4, respectively. In contrast, the number in the Korean media in *Yonhap*, *Dong-A Ilbo*, and *Hankyoreh Shinmun* was 2040, 114, and 109, respectively. In examining the news data, it is very noticeable that the news content in the international news media, including the AP, was almost identical, and the news source patterns and background information were also almost the same.

From day one, the words "North Korea" were used more than five times each day, "a disputed naval border, the NLL" and "three bloody skirmishes"—referring to past battles between North Korean fishing boats and the South Korean marine police, who are prevented from crossing the Northern Limit Line (NLL)—were routinely used in news texts. In the first report on the Cheonan, the AP reported that "North Korea's military had threatened 'unpredictable strikes' against the U.S. and South Korea in anger over a report that the two countries planned to prepare for possible instability..." This wording was repeated on the second day after the incident. Emphasizing the situation that the two Koreas are technically at war and that the sinking happened near the disputed naval border, the NLL, the reports stated that North Korea was likely to be involved despite news citing a Korean official who said that there was no sign of North Korean movement. In Korean news, the news content detailed the history of the warship and included many interviews with the families of the sailors who had been on board. Both the national and international news media waited to hear what steps were being taken rather than trying to determine what happened and how, presumably due to the sensitive security issue. For example, news reports using the words "a state of war," "the disputed sea border (NLL)," "nuclear program," "tension," "threat," and "three bloody skirmishes," reflecting a conflict in the coverage of the sinking of the Cheonan, are shown in Table 5.1.

**Table 5.1**   News narratives and news sources

| News narratives | News sources |
|---|---|
| "North and South Korea are still in an official state of war" | *BBC*, March 27, 2010 |
| "North and South Korea are still in an official state of war" | *BBC*, March 28, 2010 |
| "The two Koreas remain locked in a state of war because their three-year conflict ended in a truce, not a peace treaty, in 1953" | AP, March 27, 2010 |
| "The ship went down near a disputed maritime border that has been the site of three bloody skirmishes between the Koreas, which remain in a state of war" | AP, March 28, 2010 |
| "North and South Korea are still in an official state of war" | *The New York Times*, March 28, 2010 |
| "Military accidents get special scrutiny here, since North and South Korea are still in an official state of war" | *The New York Times*, March 29, 2010 |
| "If North Korea is ultimately found culpable, it will amount to one of the most serious military provocations since the Korean War ended in a truce, leaving the peninsula technically in a state of war" | *The New York Times*, April 9, 2010 |
| "South Korea is scrambling to determine why a naval ship patrolling the disputed sea border with the North sank last night, leaving scores of sailors missing and several reported dead" | *The Guardian*, March 27, 2010 |
| "A North Korean mine may have caused the explosion that sank a South Korean naval ship near a disputed sea border on Friday night, the south's defence minister said yesterday" | *The Guardian*, March 30, 2010 |
| "Dozens of sailors died when the Cheonan split in two and sank while on a routine patrol along a disputed sea border" | *The Guardian*, April 20, 2010 |
| "South Korea has lifted the stern of the 1200-tonne Cheonan, which went down near a sea area disputed with North Korea" | *The Guardian*, April 23, 2010 |
| "Naval clashes in the West Sea between the two Koreas are no new development. Not only is there a disputed maritime boundary" | *The Guardian*, May 21, 2010 |

(continued)

**Table 5.1**   (continued)

| News narratives | News sources |
| --- | --- |
| "The two sides have argued over – and from time to time skirmished over – the precise location of the 'Northern Limit Line', which divides their territorial waters. That was where the naval patrol ship Cheonan was sunk" | *The New York Times*, May 20, 2010 |
| "The sinking of the ship near the disputed sea border, where the navies of the two Koreas have fought bloody skirmishes, raised the possibility of a North Korean torpedo attack or sabotage" | *The New York Times*, March 28, 2010 |
| "The fragility of peace on the divided Korean Peninsula is most evident along the disputed western maritime border…where the two navies fought skirmishes in 1999 and 2002" | *The New York Times*, March 30, 2010 |
| "Tensions simmered after the Cheonan went down off Baengnyeong, a Seoul-administered island in a flashpoint maritime border area between the Koreas" | *CNN*, March 27, 2010 |

## DOMINANT NEWS FRAMES: SALIENT WORDS IN NEWS

According to Semetko and Valkenburg (2000), the literature of framing studies has detected common frames that are employed in the media. They are the conflict, economic consequences, human interests, morality, and responsibility frames. The five news frames investigated by Semetko and Valkenburg are as follows (2000: 95–96):

*Conflict frame.* This frame stresses conflict between two opponents to catch the audience's attention.

*Human interest frame.* This frame, which usually accompanies the conflict frame in the news, again arouses emotional and humanized emotion to attract the audience's interest.

*Economic consequences frame.* This frame, which is commonly employed, reports an event from the perspective of economic consequences.

*Morality frame.* The news reports an event by prominently featuring moral attribution, usually utilizing the views of other parties through quotation or inference.

*Responsibility frame.* This frame attributes responsibility for the cause or solution of an issue to either the government or an individual. For social problems, the news tends to attribute responsibility to individuals. For example, responsibility for poverty can be attributed to individuals rather than to social systems or the government.

Based on the identified frames above, the dominant frame in international news outlets was the conflict frame. The prominent messages of the news narratives from the selected news outlets were disagreements between the two Koreas about the disputed sea border, the NLL, North Korea's threat, tension, warfare, North Korea (presented as a totalitarian country), and the two countries technically being at war. Entman (1991) detects two major frames—moral and technical frames—in the KAL and Iran Air incidents. For this study, using the deductive framing approach, I first counted repeated salient words and phrases. Categorizing those terms and the frequency with which they were used enabled me to identify dominant frames. As mentioned above, repeated words could be distinguished from day one.

As Table 5.2 shows, words about North Korea were highly prominent in international news. The same content in international news narratives was "Korea is in a state of war," "the disputed sea border, the NLL," "North Korea's nuclear ambition," "a tension between the two Koreas," "North Korea's threat," and "Three bloody skirmishes between the two Koreas." In other words, from day one, the international news used words related to conflict between South Korea and North Korea. Compared to the international news, the number of words related to North Korea or conflict was far lower in the Korean news media. North Korea was mentioned four times in *Yonhap*, but the content was that

**Table 5.2** Dominant words in the UK, the United States, and Korean Media

|  |  | "North Korea" (n) | "Neutral" (n) |
|---|---|---|---|
| US | AP | 95 | 5 |
|  | CNN | 44 | 3 |
|  | The New York Times | 43 | 3 |
| UK | BBC | 57 | 6 |
|  | The Guardian | 49 | 2 |
| South Korea | Yonhap | 6 | 2 |
|  | Dong-A Ilbo | 14 | 2 |
|  | Hankyoreh Shinmun | 7 | 3 |

there was no unusual sign from North Korea, suggesting a low probability that North Korea was involved (March 27, 2010); in addition, *Yonhap* reported only once that military officials said that they were investigating the North's involvement. In *Dong-A Ilbo*, terms related to North Korea appeared nine times on March 29, 2010 because it reported on the Korean Broadcasting System (KBS) broadcast on North Korea's reconnaissance aircraft, which claimed that the aircraft was seen flying toward the South about three hours after the incident, by reframing the KBS news as escalating the disastrous situation and placing the event in the context of a conflict with North Korea (March 20, 2010). *Hankyoreh Shinmun* used the term "NLL" in its first news story, but it said that the incident had happened far from the NLL, so it was unlikely that the North was involved; it quoted anonymous military officials. On the following day, *Hankyoreh* mentioned North Korea nine times because it reported on how the Korean mainstream media lead news stories toward North Korea's involvement. *Hankyoreh* also criticized South Korea's old military equipment and lack of military personnel by quoting the families of the victims. At the same time, it indirectly criticized the

**Table 5.3**  Dominant news frames in international news and national news media

| News sources | News frames |
|---|---|
| | **Conflict frame** |
| | The Cheonan happened near the disputed sea border, the NLL |
| AP | Korea is in a state of war |
| BBC | Conflict between the two Koreas |
| CNN | Three bloody skirmishes between the two Koreas on the same spot |
| The New York Times | North Korea's nuclear ambition |
| The Guardian | Tension between the two Koreas before the incident |
| | North Korea's threat |
| | North Korea's torpedo |
| | **Conflict frame and Human interest frame** |
| Yonhap News | Possibility of North Korea's attack |
| | Families and relatives of injured and missing sailors |
| | **Human interest frame** |
| Dong-A Ilbo | Amplifying theories and raising questions about the cause |
| Hankyoreh | **Responsibility frame** |
| | Criticism of the Korean mainstream media |
| | Criticism of the Korean mainstream media and the government by reframing Western media reports to support its own critical views |

government's approach to dealing with the incident. *Hankyoreh* referred to news articles written by Christian Oliver, who at that time was the Seoul foreign correspondent for *The Financial Times*. The articles criticized the Lee administration by citing Oliver's news report. He reported that the Lee government seemed to be returning to predemocratic conditions because the government provided official information only to the mainstream media and treated the families of the victims as troublesome (*The Hankyoreh Shinmun*, March 31, 2010).

From day one of the incident, as shown in Table 5.3, the *BBC*, *CNN*, *New York Times* and *Guardian* repeatedly reported that the Cheonan had sunk near the disputed sea border, the NLL, where three skirmishes had occurred in the past. Additionally, phrases such as "there is tension between the two Koreas" and "Korea is technically at war because the Korean War was not finished by a peace treaty but a truce" were used. The news included the remark that there was no sign that North Korea was involved in this incident. However, the international news made the conflict and tension between the two Koreas salient by repeatedly invoking the historical context of past North Korean attacks and skirmishes. Importantly, the dominant frame in the news coverage by the AP, *CNN*, *BBC*, *New York Times* and *Guardian* was the conflict frame. Some of the details are as follows:

The *BBC* reported that "The naval patrol vessel sank near the disputed maritime border with North Korea," (March 28, 2010, March 29, 2010, March 30, 2010), which situated the NLL in almost all of its news stories. Other international news outlets, such as the *AP*, *CNN*, *BBC*, *The New York Times* and *The Guardian*, also included this information in their news reports. Additionally, the news quoted Kim, Tae-Young, Defense Minister, who told the *Yonhap* agency that "The vessel appeared to have been split into half." Interestingly, the *BBC* cited an *AP* news agency report saying, "A group of 80 family members have sailed around the crash site and watched the rescue efforts." The *BBC* added, "However, some relatives are accusing the navy of a cover-up, saying the ship was in need of repair." A number of crew members had jumped into the water, *Yonhap* said. "Yells and screams filled the air," witness Kim, Jin-ho, a seaman who was on a local passenger ship bound for Bakryeong, told the cable news channel YTN. "Marines on deck were desperately shouting: 'Save me!'" The *BBC* mentioned that "North and South Korea are still in an official state of war because the 1950-53 Korean War ended only in a truce" almost every time it reported about the incident. The *BBC* finished its first story with "South Korea recognizes the Northern Limit Line, drawn unilaterally by the US-led United Nations Command to demarcate the sea border at the end of the Korean War. The line has never been accepted by North Korea" (*BBC*, March 28, 2010). The following day, nothing was found but theories and reports on the rescue operation.

Both the *BBC* and *CNN* emphasized the NLL as a controversial area. The *BBC* included this line more than three times in a row whenever it covered the Cheonan at the end of each article. This reporting stirred up the controversy related to the line. It also said, "South Korea recognizes the Northern Limit Line, drawn unilaterally by the US-led United Nations Command to demarcate the sea border at the end of the Korean War. But it has never been accepted by North Korea and the area has been the scene of deadly clashes between the navies of the two Koreas in the past (*CNN* also repeated this line), and fatal naval skirmishes in 1999 and 2002." *CNN* said that the two Koreas had exchanged gunfire in 2004 and 2009, framing the NLL as an area where the two Koreas had had clashes many times in the past. Notably, *The Guardian*, which is widely known as a liberal UK newspaper, used only the Korean conservative daily newspaper *Chosun Ilbo* as a news source, and its news about the Cheonan was very straightforward, unlike other news media, which tried to play it down. While the *BBC* tried to maintain a neutral tone, *The Guardian* news started with "The South Korean ship was apparently attacked near Baknyeong Island, near the North Korean demarcation line" under a graphic. It claimed that the damage may have resulted from an attack by South Korea's "neighbor," but Seoul sought to downplay such suggestions after claims that the ship may have been sunk by a North Korean torpedo (March 26, 2010, Tania Branigan in Beijing, Caroline Davies and Associated Press in Seoul).

In contrast, *Hankyoreh* reported the sinking location and noted that the Cheonan had sunk far from the NLL, indicating that North Korea was less likely to be involved in this incident (March 26, 2010). In this situation in which the actual cause was unknown, the international news was already suggesting (although reporting that Seoul downplayed suggestions that the North had attacked) that North Korea was involved. It is apparent that the international media viewed the incident as another naval skirmish between the two Koreas and that the two Koreas are technically at war because the Korean War was not ended by a peace treaty. Although there was no actual war to attract the audience's interest, terms related to war, such as attack, torpedo, warfare, and bloody skirmishes, were heavily and routinely used on almost a daily basis in news reports about the Cheonan.

## NEWS SOURCES

As Sigal (1986) states, examining the use of news sources in news stories is an effective tool to frame a new story. In addition, as discussed in the literature review, a news source is an important factor in framing a news topic and examining international news flow (Entman, 1991, 1993; Herman & Chomsky, 2002; Thussu, 1998). Entman says that the media tend to depend on official sources because they are comparatively easy to access, and journalists rely on information provided by officials because they are considered useful and legitimate sources (2004: 92). In addition, reporters can evade criticisms of bias and the threat of libel suits if they rely on officials rather than investigative reporting (Herman & Chomsky, 2002). For the categories of news sources, I referred to the third filter, sourcing mass media news, in the propaganda model (Herman & Chomsky, 2002) as well as Entman's (1991) comparative news narratives analysis. To identify news sources, I listed every source quoted or cited in each news story and classified them into groups. The officials were mainly Korean and United States, and these figures were classified and then calculated as percentages.

The results demonstrate how the news media depend heavily on government officials as news sources (see Moon, 2018). Of the sources cited, 88% in the *AP*, 92.9% in the *BBC*, 73.1 in *CNN*, 64.3 in *The New York Times*, 81.84% in *The Guardian*, 84% in *Dong-A Ilbo*, 84.2% in *Hankyoreh* and 55.6% in Yonhap were officials. Overall, Korean government officials were the most dominant news sources in the news coverage of the Cheonan incident. Notably, the news source distribution that the media do not use a variety of news sources. In addition, in terms of the percentage of U.S. officials, *CNN* in the United States and *Hankyoreh Shinmun* used more U.S. officials than other media outlets did (Moon, 2018). Based on news texts, the *AP* and *CNN* quoted U.S. officials directly in their reports, but *Hankyoreh* usually cited and reframed what the international news media had reported rather than interviewing U.S. officials independently. Additionally, in terms of the news narratives and the use of news sources, *The Guardian* was heavily dependent on the *AP*. As the dominant news frame in *Yonhap* was human interest, *Yonhap* gave more weight to families and relatives as news sources. There were citations such as "some analysts said" or "some experts" without specific names or institutions, so it was unclear exactly whom they were citing. In short, based on the results, both the national and international media were dependent on officials as news sources. Does this mean that the media support propaganda campaigns that have been established by the government? Next, I discuss propaganda campaigns using the propaganda model (Herman & Chomsky, 2002) in the case of the Cheonan.

The final conclusion concerning the cause of the Cheonan sinking was announced by the Korean government and the international-joint investigation team on May 20, 2010. The conclusion was that North Korea had torpedoed the Cheonan. However, news data for this framing analysis are reported from the first week after the incident occurred, when the real cause was unknown, but the international news repeatedly mentioned North Korea's threat and North Korea's nuclear ambition. The AP reported, "Friday's accident happened hours after North Korea's military threatened 'unpredictable strikes' against the United States and South Korea in anger over a report the two countries plan to prepare for possible instability in the totalitarian country" (March 27, 2010) and "On Friday morning, the military warned of 'unprecedented nuclear strikes' if the foes sought to destabilize the communist nation" (March 29, 2010). *The Guardian* said the same: "Earlier yesterday (Friday) Pyongyang had threatened 'unprecedented nuclear strikes' against the US and South Korea after reports that the two countries were to plan for potential instability in the North, but it often issues such threats when angered" (March 27, 2010).

Moreover, the same background information—"The Cheonan happened near the disputed sea border, the NLL," "Korea is in a state of war," "Conflict between the two Koreas," "Three bloody skirmishes between the two Koreas near Baknyeong," "North Korea's nuclear ambition," "There was tension between the two Koreas before the incident," "North Korea's threat," and "North Korea's torpedo"—was repeated in the international news media. This suggests that international media reporting is highly routinized. For instance, both the *BBC* and *The Guardian* noted, "Seoul sought to play down suggestions that the damage might have resulted from an attack by its neighbour, after reports of an explosion and claims that the ship may have been sunk by a torpedo" (March 29, 2010) and "Seoul sought to play down suggestions that the damage might have resulted from an attack by its neighbour, after reports of an explosion and claims that the ship may have been sunk by a torpedo," respectively (March 27, 2010).

As discussed in the literature review in earlier chapters, Herman and Chomsky argue that the force of anti-communist ideology faded with the fall of the Soviet Union and was offset by the market ideology (2002: xvii). However, the news text analysis presented in this chapter suggests that there is still a residual anti-communist ideology as well as market forces in the Korean Peninsula that act on news media. As Isabel Hilton said in a comment in *The Guardian*, London, "The Korean peninsula is the final holdout of the cold war" (April 1, 2010). From the very first report of the sinking of the Cheonan, international news media repeatedly made "anti-communist" ideology prominent by mentioning that North Korea's military had threatened the United States and that North Korea is a totalitarian country, a communist country, and South Korea's rival. They noted that "there is no indication that it was North Korea's attack but kept a vigilant watch" (March 27, 2010). The international news media consistently highlighted the North Korean engagement in past naval battles with South Korea and the tensions between the two Koreas by making the conflict frame salient in the news reports, while the national news used a human interest frame. In terms of news sources, Korean officials were dominant, and the second most dominant news source was U.S. officials. *The New York Times* and *Yonhap* used families or relatives as their news sources. This meant that the national and international news depended on incumbent government officials, who have better credibility. Additionally, based on the propaganda model by Herman and Chomsky (2002), dichotomized and established facts such as "threat," "totalitarian," "unpredictable nuclear strikes," and "torpedo" were salient. This incident should be differentiated from the KAL 007 disaster and the media's support for the Reagan administration's arms buildup. However, in particular, the international media seem to have played a role as a systemic partisan mechanism in identifying North Korea as a negative state by constructing the issue in ways favorable to the elites without any investigation of one of the most tragic incidents since the Korean War.

From the news data in this study, I was able to identify the frequency of news reporting and dominant news frames. Additionally, the use of news sources was examined by applying the filters in the propaganda model by Herman and Chomsky (2002). In the next section, to support a fuller discussion of the dynamic of international news flow addressed in Chapter 2, I conduct an additional news analysis, hoping to demonstrate the news flow within the news data.

## INTERNATIONAL NEWS FLOW

As discussed in the literature review and proposed in the research questions, the dominant Western international news agencies are likely to represent their views as a norm, and the domestic media have a tendency to indigenize international news texts by reframing global news content (Boyd-Barrett, 1998; Rantanen, 2004; Thussu, 2000). To test this theory, conducting only comparative news framing analysis and interviews was not enough to clearly demonstrate whether the news flow adheres to the traditional news flow from the North to the South. Hence, I further examine the international news flow in the case of the Cheonan. The traditional news flow structure is the flow from the dominant Western news media. Thus, one of the almost identically patterned and distinguishable issues in the news coverage of the Cheonan in the international news texts was the background information about the NLL. Thus, I searched news articles with the use of the keyword "NLL" in the national news outlets that were selected for this test during the same time period as the news framing analysis and followed the same steps for sampling the data. The outlets are *Yonhap, Dong-A Ilbo* and *Hankyoreh Shinmun*. The time period was the same as that used for the news narrative analysis, the first week after the incident, March 26, 2010 to May 31, 2010. To retrieve the news articles, I used the Naver news archives. NLL is an abbreviation for the Northern Limit Line, which is a sea border drawn by the United States; thus, the original phrase is English. In Korean, it is "Book Bahng Hahn Gye Suhn," but Korean news always includes "NLL" in English in a bracket following the loanword orthography.

The number of news articles that include the word "NLL" was as follows:

*Yonhap*, 41, *Dong-A Ilbo*, 7, and *Hankyoreh Shinmun*, 10. The significant fact is that *Hankyoreh Shinmun* first reported a news article that included "NLL"; next, *Yonhap* reported a news story with "NLL," and a *Dong-A Ilbo* report with "NLL" followed on the second day, March 27, 2010. Moreover, it was necessary to examine the ways in which the news represented the NLL. As shown above, the international news used the NLL to provide information that a few bloody skirmishes between South Korea and North Korea had occurred near the NLL in the past. To examine the news texts, I examined sentences that included the NLL. Due to the unequal number of news articles from each news outlet (e.g., *Yonhap* has a greater number of articles than the other two news outlets), I used a sampling procedure. I selected the first news article of each day for news narrative analysis. The important point is to compare and contrast news articles in the same time frame and how news framing about the NLL changed.

On the first day after the Cheonan incident occurred, only *Hankyoreh* included the NLL in the news story. At 11.13 p.m., the paper quoted a military-related official as saying, "The spot that the Cheonan sank was the southern sea, far from the NLL, so it is not clear whether North Korea attacked." The following day, all three media outlets included the NLL in their news stories. However, the *Hankyoreh* news website had the same news in an article uploaded at 11.13 p.m. on March 26, 2010. *Yonhap* also reported the same content at 12.28 a.m.: "the spot that the Cheonan sank is the southern sea between Bangnyeong Island and Daecheong Island far from the NLL." *Dong-A Ilbo* reported similar content by quoting another military-related source who said, "Given the plausible fact that the sinking spot is far from the NLL, it is clear that the possibility of North Korea's attack is small." Beginning on March 28, 2010, the Korean news media started to mention the same numbers for how far the Cheonan had been from the NLL—10~12 km—but still reported that the cause had been an internal explosion.

For instance, *Yonhap* reported, "Moreover, because the site of the incident is in the southern sea 10~12 km from the NLL, in the case of a North Korean vessel's infiltration, it is easily detectible, and based on the fact that the depth of water is approximately 20 m, a submarine's movement is also limited, the joint staff think that the cause is an internal explosion." *Hankyoreh* consistently said, "the site of the incident is far from the NLL" (March 28, 18: 44). *Dong-A* did not publish a news article that included the NLL on 28 March, but *Yonhap* reported, "It is the first time for a Dokdo corvette, which hit the water in July 2007, to implement its duty at sea near the NLL (a Dokdo corvette was placed for further investigation and rescue)" at 00.01. On the same day at 03.00, *Dong-A Ilbo* simply repeated the information that *Yonhap* had reported about a Dokdo corvette investigation and rescue near the NLL. *Dong-A Ilbo* published three news articles pertaining to the NLL at the same time, 03.00 on the 29th of March, reporting about the possible cause of the sinking. The paper said, "In preparation for contingencies against the ROK and US joint military drill, 'Key resolve,' a mine laid by the North Korean navy in their sea north of the NLL was swept away by the current and could have collided with the Cheonan warship." In addition, "Since the defeat in the DaeCheong naval battle on 10 November 2009, North Korea has raised tensions by announcing a peacetime zone of fire in the sea south of the NLL (21 December 2009) and firing shore bombardment (17 January 2010) near the NLL" and "For the nuclear issue resolution in the six-party talk ahead, it could be a provocation by North Korea that intends to remind the international community that the NLL is still a disputed area and press the US for a peace treaty." On 30 March, *Yonhap* quoted a policy maker as explaining, "it is unlikely to be a mine that has been swept to the downside of the NLL from the North due to hills under the sea near Bakryeongdo." *Dong-A Ilbo* reported an article with the subheadline "Was a North Korean observation aircraft flying near the NLL after the Cheonan sinking?" at 03.00 on 20 March. Again, *Hankyoreh* reported that the joint staff had said the incident spot was 12 km south of the NLL. On 1 April, *Dong-A Ilbo* mentioned the NLL in two articles (at 03.00): "the North laid mines north of the NLL" and mentioning the possibility that a North Korean semi-submarine that sometimes maneuvered near the NLL had torpedoed the Cheonan.

The data show that the NLL, which was reported to be "far from the spot of the incident" in the Korean media, had changed to the possibility of a North Korean mine being swept across the NLL, which is still a disputed area, as was repeatedly emphasized by the international news media. Additionally, by highlighting the line, North Korea's possible involvement in a disputed area was nuanced by all the Korean media, although the South Korean government was cautious about pointing at the North's involvement. This included *Hankyoreh* and *Dong-A Ilbo* reframed a *KBS* report as follows: "Right after the Cheonan sinking, a North Korean observation aircraft was flying near the NLL, but officials repeatedly denied it, saying, 'It's not true.'"

On 31 March at 02.00, *Yonhap* reported that Chinese fishing boats had illegally crossed the NLL between Bakryeongdo and Daecheongdo. In addition, like the other two media outlets, even *Hankyoreh* finally reported, "With regard to shooting, military officials said, 'there was no trace of a submarine near the incident spot, so if it was a North Korean submarine, we expected that it would run away toward the north, so the rescue ship – a Sokcho vessel – was driving toward the NLL and found an object that was moving quickly toward the north in the radar."

Above, I have specifically added the time when the news was uploaded to track which outlet reported first and which was therefore likely to set an agenda related to the NLL. In summary, the NLL was mentioned as "not related to the incident because the site where the incident happened was far from the NLL." However, the Korean media soon changed that assessment by providing the exact distance between the site and the line, and eventually, *Dong-A Ilbo* reported what the international media had repeated regarding the "disputed line" and the possibility that a North Korean semi-submarine had torpedoed the Cheonan. These results might not confirm that the international news media's consensus or dominant views directly influenced the domestic news's indigenized news framing because the data cannot show a visible path of the news flow as newly discovered facts and information were updated and reported. However, I attempted to test the news flow through what the international news highlighted consistently and aimed to examine whether the Cheonan case follows the traditional news flow structure in terms of the news content. Based on the findings of the news analysis pertaining to the Cheonan, including the NLL, the dynamics between the international news media and Korean media involved quoting and reframing each other's news reports and sources. Furthermore, the Korean media's change of view from "far from the NLL" to "near the NLL" implies that the international news media influence the domestic news media discourse.

As briefly mentioned earlier, there are limitations to conducting news analysis alone to examine what factors influence the ways in which news stories are framed. Hence, my aim is to explore the factors that influence how and why news reports appear as they do. To do so, I explore major factors that influence journalists' news frame in covering the Cheonan issue and investigate the nature of news production by placing these factors in a sociocultural context. In Chapter 6, I therefore turn to in-depth interviews with a range of journalists to discuss the processes of news production and the challenges faced by foreign correspondents and Korean journalists.

# REFERENCES

Boyd-Barrett, O. (1998). Media Imperialism Reformulated. In D. Thussu (Ed.), *Electronic Empires: Global Media and Local Resistance* (pp. 157–176). London: Arnold.

Entman, R. M. (1991). Framing U.S. Coverage of International News: Contrasts in Narratives of KAL and Iran Air Incidents. *Journal of Communication, 41,* 6–27.

Entman, R. M. (1993). Framing, Towards Clarification of a Fractured Paradigm. *Journal of Communication, 414*(4), 51–58.

Entman, R. M. (2004). *Projections of Power: Framing News, Public Opinion, and U.S. Foreign Policy.* Chicago: University of Chicago Press.

Herman, S. E., & Chomsky, N. (2002). *Manufacturing Consent: The Political Economy of the Mass Media.* New York: Pantheon Books.

Moon, M. (2018). Manufacturing Consent? The Role of the International News on the Korean Peninsula. *Global Media and Communication, 14*(3), 265–281.

Rantanen, T. (2004). European News Agencies and Their Sources in the Iraq War Coverage. In S. Allan & B. Zelizer (Eds.), *Reporting War: Journalism in Wartime.* London and New York: Routledge.

Semetko, H. A., & Valkenburg, M. (2000). Framing European Politics: A Content Analysis of Press and Television News. *Journal of Communicationn 50*(2), 93–109.

Sigal, V. L. (1986). Sources Make the News. In K. M. Robert & M. Schudson (Eds.), *Reading the News.* New York: Pantheon Books.

Thussu, D. K. (1998). *Electronc Empires: Global Media and Local Resistance.* London: Hodder Arnold.

Thussu, D. K. (2000). *International Communication: Continuity and Change.* London: Arnold.

# CHAPTER 6

# Reporting International Conflicts: Dynamics and Challenges

Drawing on the interview data, this chapter focuses on exploring the dynamics and challenges that international journalists face. Key themes were drawn from the interviews. First, this chapter will show the process of news construction in the news coverage of Korean conflicts to place the nature of journalism practices in the Korean Peninsula in a sociological perspective. Second, I aim to explore what kinds of news sources journalists use to construct a news story. Third, this chapter examines the primary factors that influence journalists' news frames in covering North Korea. Finally, in a global context, this chapter discusses the Korean conflicts, or "Korea," to reflect the current geopolitical power game in this region as well as foreign national interests through the eyes of international journalists.

## NORTH KOREA AS A NEWS VALUE

Former President of the Seoul Foreign Correspondent Club Yun-Suk Lim, noted that North Korean news topics are foreign correspondents' favorite news agenda in terms of their media audiences' interest and attention. In the same context, a former Seoul correspondent for the *Economist*, Daniel Tudor, said that he was resigning as a correspondent because Western news media disregard "real" Korean news; rather, they are obsessed with North Korean issues (Ohmynews, August 7, 2013).[1] North Korea is the primary news agenda for international news coverage of Korean issues.

© The Author(s) 2019
M. Moon, *International News Coverage and the Korean Conflict*,
https://doi.org/10.1007/978-981-13-6291-0_6

## CONTRA-FLOW?: THE CHEONAN EFFECT

Journalist 2, a writer and journalist who has lived in Korea for over 15 years, reports for UK mainstream media as well as U.S. mainstream TV and newspapers, described that night as follows:

> Was it Friday night? Actually, that night everybody, all the other foreign correspondents, had gone out drinking around here at Itaewon. I said, 'Tonight, I don't feel like coming out with you guys. I want to work on my book.' So I was sitting at home, doing some computer stuff, taking it easy, doing some work, but I got a call, it says from Atlanta, saying that they heard there's a ship sinking in the Yellow Sea. What kind of ship? We don't know; all we know is a ship sinking in the sea. Can you look into it and report it in fifteen minutes? There goes my evening. There was a one-line report by Yonhap or Reuters, South Korean ship sinking in the Yellow Sea. Report follows. (Journalist 2)

Another interviewee had similar recollections. Journalist 13, who has worked in Seoul for over four years, also recalled that night. He told me calmly how he found out about the incident for the first time:

> It was Friday night. I remember it really well. Having drinks with friends in Seoul. Around midnight or one A.M., I took a taxi going home. My boss from Paris called me and said there is a ship sinking and told me to cover it quickly. They have wires. I wrote a story within half an hour with very little information.

The ways in which correspondents found out about the incident were similar; either a phone call from their boss in their home-country head-quarters or the Korean news media. The responses above indicate two key points. One is that news agencies still play a role as news distributors to mainstream media outlets. Journalist 10 commented, "You certainly keep an eye on what *Yonhap* and Bloomberg and Reuters are reporting because if anything comes out from there, it's drawing attention to something new." Editors saw the news from news agencies and asked correspondents to report about the issue. Thus, the global news agencies still set the news agenda and play a role as the primary definers of international issues.

The other point is that very short time—fifteen minutes to half an hour—was given to correspondents for reporting. As Boyd-Barrett and Rantanen (1998) discuss, the consequences of decreased time for news gathering are a reliance on news agencies and increasingly homogeneous news texts. After they heard about the sinking, the first thing that correspondents did was to call the Blue House and the experts. Journalist 10 said that he called some professors, such as Lankov,[2] who know North Korea very well. Journalists 5 and 6 said that they returned to their offices along with the Korean staff to cover the story about the warship sinking. As the correspondents explained, little information was provided about the incident, but they had to prepare to report it as soon as possible. Journalist 9 described the situation as follows:

> Just all I can confirm is, yes, there is a ship sinking at the moment. We have no numbers of survivors. No, no, no further information. So s\*\*\*, I've got 10 minutes to report based on this one piece of information, so we knew where it was. I know about Bakryeongdo close to the NLL; there were firefights in 1999 and 2002, and it's a major flash point. I looked out the window, snowing that night. It was March but snowing. So my report was just, yeah, we confirmed from the presidential office that a South Korean warship is sinking.

Correspondents verified with the Korean government the fact that the Cheonan corvette had sunk, but there was a lack of further information because the cause was unknown. Nevertheless, they had to report on the incident as quickly as possible. All they knew about the cause was that, as Journalist 6 said, "Initially, the Seoul government did not suggest that North Koreans were to blame." Journalist 9 said, "The cause is unknown. But of course, we can't rule out North Korea, given where it happened."

> It's snowing, so anyone goes into the water tonight, it's gonna be a very narrow survival window. That was the report, and we just updated it every thirty minutes. I was 5 reports up that night with very limited information. What I could do is to give the content. What happened in Bakryeongdo; what happened in 1999? What happened in 2002? What's the weather like? All the stuff. You can actually give quite a bit of the picture 'cause you're here. If I was in Tokyo, Hong Kong or Singapore, I wouldn't have that information.

However, the skirmishes that he said he knew about in 1999 and 2002 occurred not in Bakryeong but near Yeonpyeong. In other words, in the first news coverage of the Cheonan, this journalist clearly confused

Bakryeong with Yeonpyeong. The AP included the information about the two earlier skirmishes in much of its news coverage of the Cheonan, and all of the other international mainstream news outlets also mentioned them.

## MEDIA INVESTIGATION AND MEDIA ROUTINES

Shoemaker and Reese (1991: 105–108) contend that journalists as gate-keepers who select news items from a large number of issues are often the greatest crusaders, but their standardized and patterned practices, especially those of television news production, are institutionalized as if in a news factory. They maintain that news producers have deadlines that preclude investigation, and journalists need to reach audiences with diverse backgrounds.

> When the incident happened, Bakryeongdo wasn't like somewhere you can go and actually see to report about it. It is different from those events like a building falling down in Seoul city or demonstrations. If it's at the demonstration site, you can be an eyewitness, reporting "who struck whom." However, even those soldiers [he meant those sailors] who survived the warship can't talk to us independently; you know, they are soldiers; those regulations always follow with them, right? And most of them died. I tried to meet and talk with the U.S. officials in Seoul, but it has its limitations. Basically, at that time, whatever journalist it might be, we all just wait for what the Korean government reports.

Journalist 11, who has been living in Korea since 1982, confirmed, "No reporter was on the Cheonan or exit or near the incident." However, he also said that no reporter received any report from the military or a reporting chain: "The captain of the Cheonan would report; they would radio a message to somewhere, I don't know who, and then those messages sort of go off up the radar eventually to the President. So he said that the reporters are only writing a story at the point when the Ministry of Defense or the Blue House issues a formal announcement."

Journalist 3 confirmed, "I never went to the scene, way out there in the Yellow Sea. Foreign journalists are allowed to go there in Pyeongtaek, where the rescued sailors were in Pyeongtaek, a big navy base." However, they did not go. Journalist 5 informed me that the

Ministry of Defense in South Korea sends video, audio materials and documentation to his office. The materials are in English, so the news outlets can use them immediately. As far as I know, Journalist 10 was the only one who went to the site near Bakryeongdo by boat: "I went to Bakryeongdo. Yeah, I went to the place where the Cheonan sank by boat. A week after the incident. It was arranged by the South Korean government. Nothing there, but how far from the coast...That's our job." This excursion indicates that, as other journalists said, the Korean government was open to journalists who wanted to investigate the cause of the incident.

Journalist 12 said, "After the Cheonan and also the Yeonpyeongdo incident, I was tick-tocked on Yeonpyeondo. It was a total mess, total chaos about the reporting, which about Cheonan, which happened before I got here, was totally erroneous." He talked about foreign journalists having to rely on fourth- or fifth-hand information, which often turns out to be wrong. "There is a chain of command for information reporting, and I think we've seen within the defense apparatus in South Korea that there is wrong information that gets fed up, misinformation, misinterpretation; when you have a crisis going on, there is a tremendous opportunity for things to be clouded, convoluted, misinterpreted, or sometimes deliberately misinforming, so you have to understand when these things happen, this is all possible. I mean, it's not just South Korea. It could happen anywhere."

As the interviewees said, it took approximately two months before the South Korean government released its final report. What did it uncover during this period? Where did it get its information? Journalist 8 said:

I'll be very frank with you. You've got to remember this. In a place like Korea, it is very difficult. Perhaps Seoul correspondents have already told you. It's whenever you... particularly anything to do with North Korean issues and a sensitive military issue, I wouldn't. I don't think the South Korean government is quite cooperative. They can make it very difficult for us. Governments all over the world, whenever it's a sensitive issue, dealing with rivals, the way they handle it is not cooperative, coordinal government. They are not. They only take those (correspondents) to or only show them relevant materials, which they think are conducive, or projecting an argument and their security interests. Any other country would be the same. This would happen in the U.S. or Australia. That's just the way it is.

He seemed to swallow, many times, what he wanted to say but further explained as follows:

> To be honest with you it's incredibly, incredibly, incredibly (he repeated the word three times for emphasis) difficult. It was in the middle of the Friday night. The first news we got was there was a meeting. The patrol was gone down. Obviously, there is a wave of suspicion. I think it was two months afterward. It took two months for the South Korean government to release their report to the public, the international report. To get information, what sort of information can you get in, you've got two months. Of course, the ruling government is spinning.

Journalist 8 stressed how hard it was to get any information from the government. He said absolutely, "you're not going to get any information out of the Defense Ministry." Basically, based on his experience, he said that "there are briefings with presidential advisors or other briefings with foreign ministries for journalists. But many of those briefings are just basic background information. They are not official briefings. Government will invariably give you what they perceive or 'say' may have occurred. A lot of it is sort of unofficial information which is being delivered." He covertly said again that

> In a place like Korea, you're not going to get it. You're just not going to get it. One is because they have closed up to the foreign media. Any military I'm talking about, even American military out there, really occasionally speak to the media. Any military, it's going to happen because they close it down. That's the military. That's the government. Obviously, Korea is open and a democratic country, but anything military they have to close it. (Journalist 8)

Journalist 9 commented, "You know it is important to be there to ask a question, the press conference, the international joint team reported the conclusion. It was televised live. Funnily enough, there were only two foreign reporters there: me for *CNN* and Ashley from *Stars and Stripes*." He said that he did not see his colleagues that morning except for the journalist *Stars and Stripes*, which is the American military newspaper. He said, "All ministries of defense are very bad with the media." However, he noted that *Stars and Stripes* was invited because it is American, and officials treat Americans well. He said that a *CNN* correspondent was invited because CNN is a big name. Journalist 10 simply said that the "Ministry of National Defense, it's also extremely protective about information, especially with foreign journalists." Journalist 11 agreed regarding the unfair treatment of foreign journalists. He provided the following criticism:

> Foreign correspondents don't have any, in fact, they have a disadvantage because they don't speak Korean. It is possible in the initial announcement there is some distortion because the military is notorious, I do not mean just Korean military, and any military is notorious to try to control information. For two reasons. One is for intelligence. They don't like to give their enemy information. The other is for their budget. They don't like to be criticized or have their budget reduced. They're very careful. Second thing is journalists who get their explanation from different sources by the foreign press here would contact the Americans. 'Cause the American military might talk to the press about it, or if they do, they talk in a very official way.

However, Journalist 2 spoke in contrast to other correspondents:

> Only our government has all the resources and data and sources. The government and civil joint investigation. Outside specialists had some partial information, and they did much speculation and guesses. I don't think that it's a good way. The important thing is what are scientific and reliable facts. The information that the government gives is the most important. There are many different sources for news related to North Korea. Most of what North Korean officials, representatives of civilian humanitarian aid, what the North announces (on North Korea Central News Agency (KCNA), which is heavily controlled by the regime) is propaganda. But some of them are right. We should catch some facts out of them. You know line by line. You should read them line by line. But the case of the Cheonan warship sinking is military conflict. Ordinary journalists couldn't get any information, I mean, for ourselves.

Journalist 2 thought that it was not unusual that the news story could rely only on government sources and information in the case of the Cheonan incident because it was a military conflict. Ironically, he believed that foreign correspondents did not trust Korean government sources or the final report about the Cheonan. The *AP* bureau in Pyongyang, the first Western news agency in North Korea, opened on January 16, 2012. Is the Associated Press in Pyongyang, North Korea, helpful? The *AP* bureau is located inside the KCNA building and heavily censored. The correspondents all said it was "no help" other than providing photographs of North Korea. What do journalists do other than quote what the Korean government reports? Journalist 11 said that American analysts or embassy diplomats and similar officials were in a much better position to explain to foreign correspondents what had happened. For example, "if you ring the French embassy, you're a French reporter, you're not going to get much in terms of the knowledge about it. Then, they ring analyst people who understand the context." Journalist 8 explained what he does to gather further information:

> What we can do, my colleagues might have told you the same too, I'm sure. You also have to rely on speaking to the diplomats. Diplomats live with various people, including South Korea. Many of us would be speaking to diplomats. Obviously, those diplomats are American. Off the record, they would tell you the information, but you can't use the source, so you should report disguising them.

Journalist 9 spoke about what he did the day after the Cheonan sank. He said that he met a senior naval officer, not from Korea but from another country. He asked the captain whom he met what could have caused the sinking of the Cheonan. The captain answered, "It's a torpedo."

As Journalist 12 said, the situation was chaotic. Foreign correspondents said that they believed the government's report, but they did not seem to trust the government and the Korean media in general. In addition, they routinely relied on diplomats, most of whom were U.S. officials.

## News Sources in Covering North Korea

The use of news sources is a significant part of framing a news topic. In addition, news sources are taken as the most important index, particularly in political news, to measure the balance of news coverage in terms of international news flow. Hence, the use of news sources can be a tool to assess whether the media play a role as a watchdog or a propaganda campaigner relying on officials, based on the propaganda model formulated by Herman and Chomsky (2002). I previously provided the percentage and categories of the use of news sources in news texts about the Cheonan incident in each form of media in the results section of the news framing analysis. This part offers a critical examination of the patterns of citing news sources on North Korean issues. News sources can be divided into two different types. One is the news source materials that a journalist uses to search for more information, such as other news organizations or internet sites, to make sense of an event. The other is the people whom a journalist cites or quotes in his or her news stories. Based on the interview data, the patterns of the use of news sources will be explored in this section.

Foreign correspondents reported that they use an array of people who can be quoted, but actually, the number of news sources was quite limited. As discussed above, the experts who understand North Korea are limited, and they cannot be more than analysts or observers because North Korea is so inaccessible. In addition, the biases and negative perceptions that journalists may have toward the Korean government or the military, assuming that they are not going to obtain any information, hindered further investigation. Moreover, the diplomats or other officials that journalists contacted asked to be interviewed "off the record," which meant the journalists could not officially use them as sources in the news. Rather, they had to refer to them as "analysts," even if they were diplomats, which meant there was no official way to cite or quote them as news sources. The source had to be disguised. Thus, the first type of news source involves obtaining further information on the internet. The other is to find someone who can be quoted for a news story. Since a very limited number of people could be found, the same news sources appeared repeatedly in many different news articles.

News sources have been addressed in two main ways in journalism studies. One is "What kind of news sources can correspondents contact for further information?" More specifically, in the new media era, there are many resources on the internet. The second approach considers that the internet and new media technologies have a significant impact on the profession of journalism (Bardoel & Deuze, 2001; Fenton, 2010). The correspondents interviewed for this study indicated that it was very rare for them to discover raw, original materials. They commented that obtaining information on the internet overlapped considerably with "media routine practices" and "routinized work," which is one of the factors that influence journalistic practices. Foreign correspondents all admitted that much of their work for news story creation is based on web information. The interviews as well as the news texts indicate that *Yonhap* news was predominantly used for their stories. Additionally, the interviewees all agreed that another internet news site was good. This site was Daily NK.

Daily NK is an online news site focusing on topics related to North Korea. It reported one of the most important stories out of North Korea in 2009, which was the report about the North Korean government devaluing its currency. It has North Korean refugee stringers in China and North Korea who are in contact with the Seoul office by cell phone. *The New York Times* reported that owing to Daily NK and underground stringers, important scoops about North Korea can be obtained. However, "many news proves wrong, although the mainstream Korean media regularly quote their stories. Daily NK and Open Radio each have 15 staff members, some of them defectors, and receive U.S. congressional funding through the National Endowment for Democracy, as well as support from other public and private sources" (*The New York Times*, January 24, 2010). Daily NK says[3] "the dynastic succession from Kim Il Sung to Kim Jong Il and Kim Jong Un is making a mockery of the democratic and historical progress we all support. Extreme human rights violations and the politics of fear continuously threaten the universal values that mankind has worked so hard to realize." Journalist 3 uses a few of his open contacts as well as Daily NK, run by Ha Tae Kyung and Howard Young,[4] members of the National Assembly in Pusan. Open Radio and missionaries,[5] "people know about North Korea. But I don't have any more contact than anybody else. Other people can talk to them too. All of those are important, but of course the Korean central news agency. It's been cut off. KCNA, you can't get it on the internet. Some people forward news about KCNA. *Yonhap* reports. Defectors. Daily NK, Open Radio for North Korea."

Journalist 10 said, "Very few people have direct information. Jeong Song Jeong at the Sejong Institute. It's one of the best. One of the rare guys. He has some contacts there (North Korea). He's good. Defectors. NGOs, I talk to Daily NK. They have some sources in the country. It's like a mix." In addition, Journalist 7 said, "Korean staff did most of the reporting. As I said, I have a lot of respect for *Yonhap* and also for the JoongAng Daily, which is an excellent paper. I couldn't read the Korean papers, but I watched their websites." Daily NK has a great impact on individual foreign correspondents in terms of providing information about North Korea. Journalist 1 said that he should look at the Korean media. "If you don't, you're going to be foolish because I'm here by myself, I should open my ears and eyes to see actually what's going on here. I should read the news as much as I can. I get some good ideas out of them. But the important thing is that you should do critical reading. In other words, you should read between the lines and compare to other news coverage to be able to do your own reporting." He is completely bilingual, so he can read Korean news, and when he wants to know or feels that he must know what is going on in the country, he tries to read the Korean news as much as possible, which most foreign correspondents cannot do.

First, the public obtains information from various media, and the media invest that information with their own framework and interpretation. If the sources from which each media producer obtains information and the ways in which those producers forge and encode the knowledge for dissemination are uncovered, this revelation will help the public understand the context and critically decode different messages. Journalist 11 said, "I get my information mostly from English Korean newspapers – Korea Times (Korean English newspaper), JoongAng Daily (Korean/English newspaper), Korea Herald (Korean English newspaper), International Herald Tribune, Wall Street Journal, Financial Times."

Journalist 7 said, "I used to watch the websites of Korean newspapers, also Daily NK, very good, and one or two others I can't recall. There's also a whole bunch of North Korea analysts, mostly U.S.-based, who have useful websites." He also said, "A news agency needs official sources, so we rely on the Defense Ministry, navy and Joint Chiefs of Staff for a story like this. *Yonhap* is also a good source, very professional and generally independent in its reporting. And we monitor the North Korean news agency."

Journalist 6 used body language to demonstrate typing on a keyboard. He said that "everything is from the web." He said, "I worked for the Washington bureau for more than five years before coming to Korea. We write a story about North Korea there in Washington. What do we do?" Again, he mimed typing as an answer. Likewise, Journalist 9 admitted, "Frankly speaking, that's true. I do frankly. A lot of news stories, you're right. In the days of the internet, everybody does it. Ways you're trying to add value. A lot of stories are from *Yonhap*. *Yonhap* has massive resources. Their reporters are everywhere. Very, very fast. They are a wire service, so they tend to be very, very fast with Korean news, so often I would write saying Kim Jung Un was caught in bed with a very young, beautiful Korean starlet, according to *Yonhap*. Then, I'll continue."

We generally expect correspondents to obtain "original" and "offline" news, but as they said, much work is based on the internet. This means that the site they use can be a significant factor that influences journalists who investigate events, although it has been argued that in lieu of providing a variety of information and opinions, the internet reinforces what readers already believe by polarizing attitudes (Sunstein, 2002). However, correspondents for the international mainstream media found *Yonhap* useful and responded that they rely on this convenient and resourceful news source.

Journalist 8 commented, "I know Daily NK. But do I believe everything in the library? Absolutely not. Do I believe reading, some, in the South Korean newspapers or their website? Not necessarily. Absolutely the same applies to anything to do with North Korea. When it comes to any news reporting on North Korea, anyone who says 'they know what's happening in North Korea' doesn't know what they're saying. If someone wants to tell, 'I know what's happening in North Korea,' I would say, absolutely, rubbish. No one knows what's happening in North Korea."

The interviewees said that there is an array of people whom they can cite. However, in reality, the sources cited in the news were extremely limited because there was very little variety. Additionally, there are not, and perhaps cannot be, various people to act as official sources from South Korea, and much information from officials can be restricted or secretive in terms of permission to cite or quote it. Most international journalists mentioned Daily NK, meaning that they knew this website as a dominant news source. Andrei Lankov published an article about the book "Cryptography from the Third-Floor Secretariat" written by Thae Yong-ho, a former North Korean deputy ambassador to the UK who defected to South Korea in 2016. This book is written in Korean, and the correspondents said that they were waiting for it to be translated into English on Twitter—mainly former and current international journalists and news sources were cited in mainstream newspapers, but Andrei Lankov shared a memoir published on NKnews.org, formerly called Daily NK. NKnews plays a key role in providing and sharing information about North Korea, as did Robert Koehler's Marmot's Hole blog, which started in 2003 and closed in 2015. Even if international journalists neither cited NKnews in their news stories nor believed everything it published, they found the all-English internet news that concentrates on North Korean issues useful in making sense of the North. It has become a type of online community for international journalists and native-speaking analysts. For instance, Oliver Hotham has been the managing editor since 2016. He works for Muck Rack, a PR company based in New York, U.S., which helps journalists create spheres for the stories that they cover using the networking power of social media.[6]

Journalist 9 explained that American newspapers are more professional than British newspapers in terms of news source citations because American newspapers have specific rules for such citations. For example, every news story has more than three news sources. He mentions that British newspapers tend not to cite news sources, making them appear as if they are the original news source—their "exclusive news story," which is not always true. Additionally, he said, "There is that element, but it's okay to do that if you cite a source, so as a journalist, where you add the value, what you need to do is you call sources, experts, sources who can comment on that, and that's the way you differentiate your stories from other stories." Journalist 8 said, "Diplomats" because it was easy to contact diplomats, whether academics or analysts who work in government-related think tanks, for quotations. I asked whom he meant by the "analysts" to whom he often refers in his news stories about North Korea. He said, "It could be diplomats and a lot of information."

> People that don't want to be named. People we would use, many of them are actually directly related to Victor Cha. It (news source) would be various. (You could) tap it for information. They can steer you in the right direction. These people are consulted by the government. U.S. government. You take, for instance, what's my Russian friend's name, the Russian academic, Andrei Lankov? Classic case. One of the U.S. governments used him as an adviser; Lankov tries to help them. Of course he does. Victor Cha. They were opinionated. Do I just want them to tell me, to parrot what the government tells me or the U.S. government? To use, like our brain, trying to understand whether or not I agree with their opinion; Lankov is left. Victor is right. I know that. These are the opinions, we think. Unless I have evidence, sometimes information coming from a very high authority, you can use it, but "you can't identify me." Often that's the case. Some might call it leaks – information which people are fully aware is going out to you.

Journalist 1 answered "U.S. officials," and he added, "university professors like John Delury? He's good." Delury is a professor of international relations at Yonsei University in Seoul, South Korea. I asked, "Why is he good?" He said, "He's quick." Journalist 1 remarked, "For me, looking at the conflicting news, based on what they reported, I wrote news, confirming what's evident. For the Cheonan news, news sources were from two major sources. One was the announcement from the official channel of the government. The other was from vast speculative information." Based on his remarks, he has been writing stories by checking what the Korean media say together with what government officials say. Similar to other interviewees, Journalist 10 named Andrei Lankov. He said that Lankov makes a good quote. He has a good grasp of the North Korean political system.

> No one has the truth. The Defense Ministry is overprotective. Every country. Ministry of National Security Defense, obviously, it's quite closed up. They want to protect the information. They always say it's national security. We can't say. Basically, they can't say anything. It's a disaster. I'll use AFP, Reuters. The main story. They launch a rocket. KCNA. Go to experts. Yonhap is the basic for us. We add what they say with some more analysis. (Journalist 10)

Journalist 9 listed names that he used as news sources. He said that he had a source, an "off the record" major in the Defense Ministry. John is staff, so he quotes him. "The Blue House guy (he meant Cho, the PR person)," he said. "All my other military sources are off the record. The guy who's the most quoted, Andrei Lankov, he's now well known as a North Korea specialist, but he's more politics. He was at Kim Il Sung University. So he really knows Pyongyang well. So Andrei is a good source, and the guy who's called Ki Tae (Kim Tae-Woo) is a good source. The guy in the Korea Institute for Defense Analyses[7] is a good source. I've got guys from Korea University and Yonsei University I can talk to. The guy in Daily NK who was a North Korea defector. Those are the main ones."

As shown above, as in the news articles, there were a few experts or specialists who could be quoted. The news sources to whom journalists could turn were mainly U.S. officials, but they referred to them as "analysts" because their comments had to be "off the record." In addition, other main news sources were academics, but again mainly two professors—Andrei Lankov and John Delury—or analysts—mainly U.S. officials and people in institutes on a level with observers. The news media focusing on North Korea are also limited. That area is not filled with resources that a journalist can use because it is difficult to obtain information from North Korea. Importantly, *Yonhap* citations in international news media seem to be a "basic" or convenient device to create a story with the journalists' own analysis. From its responses and interviews, it is difficult to perceive that *Yonhap* plays a contra-news flow role despite frequent citation of it in international news. The citation of *Yonhap* seems to be a conjuncture of media routine practice with online English news services, such as *Yonhap* in English online and Daily NK online news in English, which provide information and resources that correspondents can use and highlight the lack of available news sources. Journalist 10 talked about his frustration with the news sources when he covers news about North Korea. Because he cannot do any fact-checking, which is a basic practice for a journalist before writing, he often cannot write a story about North Korea. There are always rumors or noise, but there are seldom any facts.

> The North Korea issue is a dream or a nightmare for a journalist. It's a dream because it's a secret country. We don't know anything, so many crazy things are happening. It's exciting for a journalist. People want to read about North Korea. They get excited about North Korea. But it's a nightmare because you can't do fact checking. Very difficult to go there. I've been there, but on the day of, like, a rocket launch, you only rely on information coming from the North. What they say, you can't check and there's, you know, a lot of propaganda. But on the other hand there are a lot of rumors spreading out over North Korea, sometimes crazy and impressive rumors, but the problem is often you can't check them. I have this problem, and all the journalists who are covering North Korea, we hear a lot of noise. Some people say there was a coup d'état against Kim Jung Un. Someone says that. How can I check? (Journalist 10)

Consequently, why were the news stories about the Cheonan in the international news media almost the same? How does a journalist use the news sources? We discussed the reasons for these factors. Journalist 16 frankly concluded, "If you look at most stories, our stories, Times stories, Reuters stories, most of the North Korean stories have a few paragraphs of the news and then lots of background to explain what's going on, and the facts aren't changing much. So in a way, writing about

North Korea is one of the easiest things to do because there is such limited information." In terms of the use of news sources, he said, "If you pick John Delury to speak to, you would get a different story to if you pick Brian Myer to speak to because they have different viewpoints, so when journalists write that analysts say North Korea wants to come to the negotiation table, it's prepared to sit down in good faith, you know that you've spoken to the left-wing analysts. If you see a paragraph that says that analysis showed that North Korea has no interest in dialogue and just want to be treated as a nuclear power on a par with us, you know that's probably been spoken by the right-wing analysts. Both of the stories are valid. Which one is correct? I don't know. I have my opinion, and that's what becomes a story." Journalist 16's comments transparently describe foreign correspondents' news-making practices and how they use news sources with limited information as well as the difficulties of fact-checking North Korean news.

### UK Media vs. U.S. Media

There were surprises, thoughts, and debates among the journalists when comparing U.S. and UK media regarding how and why the *BBC*'s reports on the Cheonan issue used "alleged." The interview about this focused on why the *BBC* might have reported this incident as "alleged" even after the final conclusion by the Korean government together with the joint international investigation team. Some journalists said, "maybe for a couple of months" or "they just say it because of their policy." In short, they did not know that the *BBC* still used "alleged" and "allegedly" in its news about the Cheonan, and they were surprised to learn that this was the case. They looked as if they were trying to think of a reason when answering the question of why that term was used.

Journalist 1 said he was quite surprised that the *BBC* used "allegedly" in news reports about the Cheonan because he usually perceived the British media as rather more "careless" than the U.S. media except for the *BBC* and the *Economist*. For him, most of the British media have a tabloid tendency, even those that are broadsheet newspapers. If he compares the equivalent U.S. newspaper, the case is the same even for *The Financial Times*. He said that sometimes when he reads British news, he thinks, "I can never write like that for the American news because the editors would never let it be." He emphasized how much stricter the American news is than the British news. He added that British ways of writing a news story can be offensive or somehow condescending. However, he was also careful to add, "I don't mean what's good and what's bad." In his opinion, the British news media, including broadsheet newspapers, have a strong tabloid character.

> The British media is freewheeling. Their use of words and expressions. I can never write like that. I'm not talking editorials but a reporting piece. The British media don't know about North Korea. For instance, it was the Telegraph. Probably. They had quite a big photo of Kim Jong Un in the news, explaining the photo, which was Kim Jung Un with a Mickey Mouse hat. But it was not Kim Jong Un. It was Kim Jung Nam (his brother). Moreover, the original photo didn't have a Mickey Mouse hat. It was made with Photoshop by someone. The reporter who covered the story didn't check it. They don't know anything, to a surprising degree. I don't doubt that BBC reported the incident with speculation as well because they are aware of the cultural and historical background.

Journalist 1 said, "I always say South Korea says that North Korea attacked...or Seoul says...I never write North Korea attacked the Cheonan." Journalist 3 said, "We used to, for a long time, but we don't say that anymore. But we used to have to say that."

> That's BBC policy, I guess. I mean that's what they do; they still do that? I didn't know they still do that. American media and most other media have stopped saying "allegedly." I don't know when BBC said that. Maybe for a while they didn't, I mean, of course, the first couple of months. (Journalist 3)

In fact, the *BBC* consistently used "alleged" in almost all of its articles about the Cheonan, even after the final report that North Korea had torpedoed it. Journalist 10 supported the *BBC* choice:

> BBC is right to say "allegedly." Me, too. Because I saw the torpedo, in my opinion, I tend to believe that this is a torpedo from North Korea. But I'm not 100 percent sure. It's so controversial. North Korea says that; South Korea says that. We say allegedly South Korea says that.

Journalist 8 also said, "I never say that North Korea attacked the Cheonan either. I always say that the Seoul government, South Korea says." Journalist 5 commented that the news using "alleged" is from the news in the UK, not from Seoul. He was surprised as well, saying, "It can't be..." Journalist 9 admitted, "I'm probably slack on it. I mean, to me, it seems fairly clear that by process of elimination, all it could have been was North Korea's torpedo, but given that North Korea still vehemently refused to admit it, we have to say, 'it's alleged' 'cause it's not proven. Or you should say in an article, 'North Korea continues to deny the attack.' *BBC* might have an internal rule that if it's not proven, they have to say, 'alleged.' So in this case, as a journalist, you can't say, 'There is no doubt.' That's true with pretty much every North Korean story."

Journalist 11 thought that the reason the *BBC* uses "alleged" is that there has been much criticism of the government report, with experts pointing out contradictions; thus, the *BBC* itself is not a 100% sure. Therefore, the *BBC* uses "alleged," whereas the American media are much more confident.

Journalist 2 said, "I guess the UK doesn't like the United States. At that time, Korean journalists were very competitive. Over 100 media companies. We were struggling to get scoops, very competitively. All the journalists were covering the issue so closely, observing government research. Perhaps *BBC* journalists have never actually seen anything, and they only get restricted information. I mean, rather, they can't see closely the processes of the government investigation, like us. We talk to each other, and we ask every day. It was like the investigation, the Korean press and the government were implementing the investigation together." Anonymous Journalist 5 said, "We're not much different from U.S. news. The reason that the news journalists write 'alleged' in the UK is to be safe because there are a lot of criticisms around the incident." Although the government announced the final report, the BBC and Reuters reported it in the third person, writing, "the Korean government said this" or "Seoul says that" rather than presenting a conclusion as their own opinion. As my interviewees said, "it was controversial," and there were criticisms.

## FACTORS THAT INFLUENCE NEWS FRAMES

Among the factors that influence the news frames shaped by journalists, as discussed in the literature review, the external factors were individual, media routines, news institutions, extramedia, and ideologies. A major internal factor was the news organization that a journalist belonged to, which was related to the journalist's autonomy and independence of media institutions. Except in media routines, which were discussed above in the interview data, a journalist's autonomy and ideology were very important. Hence, in the following section, I address to what extent journalists are independent of their media institutions and the ways in which a journalist's ideology affects news frames.

At a national level, Journalist 4 emphasized an individual journalist's independence of a media institution. He said that *Hankyoreh* did not have a hierarchy system but rather had an equitable, horizontal system, unlike Korea's three top conservative dailies, "ChoJoongDong," which had "higher-ups" and bosses. He added, "The ownership is important. *Hankyoreh* doesn't have a President. We are run by shareholders. So no need to be aware of what higher-ups want. Of course, journalists work for a certain company that shares their ideology. Thus, the company and the journalists who work for them are ideologically the same; ideologically similar companies and journalists work together so news organizations don't need to pressure journalists." He continued, "There are what is called 'Choolip,' journalists from 'ChoJoongDong' – mainstream right-wing newspapers at the Defense Ministry. They are like spokesmen for the Defense Ministry. What do you think the relationship between the Defense Ministry and those 'Choolip' reporters would be? They're like spokesmen or representatives of the Defense Ministry." Further discussion of the Choolip Kija system will follow in the Korean journalist section.

At the international level, most foreign correspondents stressed that they are independent of their news institutes and governments compared to Korean media. This means that different correspondents in the same news institution can have different frames for their news stories. Most correspondents said that there is no pressure or force. However, the U.S. correspondents added that in when a journalist works for the White House or the State Department, he or she might be influenced by the institution. In this regard, Journalist 6 said, "I've worked for more than five years for Washington *AP*. You know, you can't write something different from what U.S. officials say." He said only that. Journalist 1, who had worked at the *AP* for more than 10 years as a correspondent, said, "When I write about the Cheonan, do I get any influence from the government or my company? Absolutely, no. They (*The New York Times*) have not that much interest in North Korea." However, Journalist 10 commented that generally, editors trust correspondents who are in the field, but if a news topic such as "Dokdo"[8] is controversial, then an editor in Paris would change an article.

The American news is not so careful about North Korea. They never sue you over anything when it comes to North Korea. You can write whatever you want. North Korea wouldn't do anything. No one would sue you over whatever you say about North Korea. No one has any evidence. Usually, the American news is very cautious. Americans love lawsuits. I'm very careful with liability. But you don't have to worry about anything about North Korea. In the United States, North Korea is a rogue state. News about North Korea is a source of fun, a source of entertainment. It's a weird country. They have this cultural prejudice. As for the Cheonan, they just easily say, of course they (North Korea) did it. I don't know; I'm not sitting in their mind or head. But due to that prejudice, I think they just write whatever they think is right. (Journalist 1)

Journalist 15 had a similar opinion of foreign, especially Western, journalists, saying that it is no surprise that they (Western journalists) do not even know that there is a hotline (telephone line) between South Korea and North Korea. This comment shows that in general, Korean journalists believe that foreign journalists have little interest in North and South Korean issues. In particular, from the Asian journalists' perspective, both Korean and Japanese journalists thought that North Korean issues are not "their" (from Western journalists' perspective) issues but "our" issues.

Bourdieu stresses that a writer's background is important in constructing news. Thus, at the individual level, Shoemaker and Reese (1991, 1996) note that a journalist's ideology influences news construction. In the same vein, Journalist 10 explained the differences between journalists; usually, for him, "what one's originally from, more ethnic background, was the key factor." He said, "Journalist 1 and Martin Fackler write differently, don't they? Even if they work for *The New York Times*. I and Journalist 1 would probably say, 'South Korea accused...' in a story about the Cheonan because we tend to believe probably North Korea, but we're not 100% sure. I wrote, 'South Korea accuses North Korea for allegedly attacking.' That's what I try to do. But I'm sure Martin, a bureau chief in Tokyo, is far away. Maybe he has more, a bigger picture. He doesn't go into it. Maybe a guy in New York City would be even worse. He's gonna exaggerate. You know, in newspapers, in journalism, I noticed the closer you are to the field, the more nuanced you are because life is complex, you know, with complexity, nothing is black and white. It's very rare."

Journalist 10 talked extensively about a journalist's background as well as ethnic background. His comments imply hegemonic power between countries in that where a journalist is from plays into journalistic practices. That is why, depending on a journalist's background, news stories about the same topic can differ from each other even in the same media institution. In fact, Journalist 10 was the only one who also mentioned the audience interest.

> When the U.S. went to Iraq, all the U.S. media were extremely kind of supporting the Bush administration, even The New York Times, completely supporting a lot of bullshit from the government; you know, if you look at reports in France, it was all the opposite. All the newspapers were against the war, writing a lot of articles against the U.S. So it's depending on the opinions of your readership. It does influence. You know objectivity doesn't exist. You have to write something you think is accurate. You don't know all the things, but at least what you write should be what you think is accurate; it's close to the truth.

Journalist 10 emphasized that a journalist's ideology and his/her individual background are key factors that influence news making. In addition, he explained that journalists' perceptions of audience preferences, external pressure, play a key role in news making. Journalist 1 commented,

> Usually, American journalists don't work by political ideology; they simply don't know much about it, so they don't care, so they just write it at face value, being careless. You know America didn't have that much interest in the Cheonan. It's not like the Iraq War. So national interests are not influenced in any way by the Cheonan issue. Well, they might have some kind of prejudices, though, as I might have. They think North Korea is bad, but they can trust South Korea, like that. It happens to South Koreans as well. Some people think that way.

As Thussu (1997) argues, there was a distinction in the presentation of friends—South Korea—and foes—North Korea already exists, as in Israel "good guy" and Iran "bad guy."

Based on the interviews, in covering sensitive issues such as territorial conflicts as in the case of Dokdo (island), it seems that a journalist cannot be free from the editorial board. This does not mean that editors force journalists to write in the way that they want them to.

However, negotiations seem to occur with correspondents in the case of a controversial issue. As Journalist 6 said, correspondents are on the spot, but it seems that they cannot be completely independent of news organizational views and directions as well as government foreign policies (e.g., Washington). In addition, a journalist's ideology and news framing (how they view the issue and make a judgment) are important factors. As journalists said in the interviews, even if journalists are from the same news institution, depending on who wrote a story, the news frame can be different. Therefore, the correspondents said that a journalist's background, which influences a journalist's ideology, is an influential factor in news framing.

## The Disputed Area, NLL

The most cited and reported words in the international news about the Cheonan corvette were related to the NLL. Journalist 11 addressed the actual problem of the NLL. He thought that both the Cheonan and the Yeonpyeong Island incident happened due to the problematic demarcation of the sea borderline. "Those happened because of the NLL issue. The way to resolve or to prevent those happening again with North Korea is to try to solve it, the NLL issue." In news that showed the NLL as a serious problem in the area, knowledge about the NLL was no different from what the news stories reported—that the line had been drawn unilaterally by the United States and had been the site of skirmishes in 1999 and 2002. Journalist 11 said, "Dealing with North Korea is a waste of time and it's counterproductive. North Korean people and the country are part of the broad Korea, the future and unified Korea. The government ruling the country right now is the enemy. It's the enemy. They would kill everybody in South Korea if they had to."

> Actually, I think some of the best things that Roh (Roh Moo Hyun, former president) did in Korea, I think it was North Korean policy. I think he started that policy. I think it's a big mistake for Lee Myung Bak not to follow up on the agreement he (Roh) had on that summit at the end of his term. There were a lot of promising things in there which the incoming government, they just nixed. (Journalist 9)

Journalist 1 also mentioned Roh's attempt to create a peace zone. "He did persistent engagement, step by step, trying to make an incremental peace zone. That's the only way. That's what diplomacy is all about, right?" He explained that the North Korean regime is based on creating external tension. That way, North Korea grasps power. The core ideology, "JooChe self-reliance ideology," is built on extreme national pride and a sense of crisis. There should always be an external enemy. He said, "If there is no external enemy, you have to create one." Therefore, he thought that the Northern Limit Line is the best place to create conflict because it is a disputed border line. "It's like a hot spot for them. That's the basic nature of the North Korean regime," he said.

From a Korean perspective, Journalist 2 was not happy about the NLL disputes. He was opposed to foreign journalists, and he thought that "foreign journalists create some disputes around the NLL." Journalist 17 said that the NLL issue is similar to the Dokdo issue with Japan. "If you were asked about the issue, even if you don't have any great knowledge about the island, you have no question. You would answer 'of course, it's our island. The Japanese talk nonsense.' 'I think the NLL issue is like the Dokdo issue. Korean people would say, They say the NLL is not territory on land. But the NLL is a South Korean area, even if the concept is slightly different between water and land.' There is no clear logic about the line, but we live in South Korea, and South Koreans are guarding the area, so it's our land. Foreign correspondents can bring all sorts of materials to argue the area. Japanese people would know possible failures or some problems in 'Abenomics' (a portmanteau of Abe and economics, the economic policies advocated by Shinzō Abe, the current prime minister of Japan); they have it for economics, they have it for survival (boosting economy). Foreign journalists can bring all the economic logic to criticize 'Abenomics' as well."

However, Journalist 12 said emphatically, "Daniel Pinkston is American, He is U.S. Air Force, and he was a Korean language intelligence officer. He's definitely a U.S. patriot, and he's very knowledgeable about North Korea, and he's definitely anti-North Korean, but he'll tell you the NLL, the North Koreans have a point. It was drawn unilaterally by an American military official; North Koreans for many decades de facto agreed to it and then decided one day they weren't going to agree to it anymore, but there's never been any treaty signed about the NLL. It's just an arbitrary point in the water that has been respected for many decades, and so, obviously, North Korea saw this as a vulnerability from the point of view of the United States and South Korea. So they now tend to use that. I think North Korea desperately wants to be taken seriously, wants to be seen on an equal footing with the United States, the most powerful country in the world."

Domestically, the NLL issue is enormously important and has continued to be a hot topic between the Democratic Party and the Saenury Party to the present day. It is one of the most serious political issues currently being debated. The debate is about whether the Democratic Party, when Roh was in office, was going to give up the area, yielding it to the North. In Korea, the line was not the issue that was discussed after the Cheonan sinking. However, international journalists have perceived the NLL as problematic because the controversial line partly caused the sinking. Both nationally and internationally, the line is a problem, but it has become as important a political issue as the Dokdo Island conflict between South Korea and Japan.

## North Korean Issues in the South Korean Public and Media

By the time I interviewed journalists, the conclusion that the Cheonan had been sunk by a North Korean torpedo had been officially announced by the Korean government based on the report by the international joint investigation team, and the Yeonpyeong artillery attack by North Korea had already happened. However, among journalists, personal opinions about "who had done it—what caused the sinking of the Cheonan" differed. They told me, as a journalist, why they had framed the news as they did. Most of them were very cautious about telling me their opinion about the Cheonan incident because it could also mean that they were suspicious about the Korean government's conclusion. Indeed, it is telling that the journalists who still had some questions about the veracity of the final report lowered their voices slightly when they talked about the Korean government and their personal opinion on this topic. Journalist 2 said, "I know a journalist at *Hankyoreh Shinmun*, the most progressive, radical newspaper, who covered the Cheonan. He told me that after the final conclusion was announced, he said, 'I believe now.'" He explained that the *Hankyoreh* reporter had not believed that the North was responsible at first, but after the final report, he said that he believed the results of the government investigation because he had observed the process very closely. For two months, the journalist raised all the questions for the government. However, after the official report was issued on May 20, 2010, he reported that the government's reports were correct. He had tried hard to find an alternative to the conclusion that the government reported, but he accepted the official report after observing the two-month government investigation. He compared foreign journalists to progressive young Korean people who oppose government reports. He said that they are the same. Korean elites who are over 40 years old, power elites, and conservatives believe the government conclusion. Journalist 1 simply answered, "Actually, I don't know the truth. What's the truth? I still don't know what happened. I can't make a conclusion about the incident but can only try to report truly as much as possible as a journalist."

Journalist 1 pointed out the lack of information in the official conclusion of the probe by the international joint investigation team. He said that he found an aspect of the conclusion interesting. First, the report was signed by a U.S. general, although it was a joint statement. In addition, the joint investigation group had two investigating committees. One committee said that it had found a torpedo that was labeled "No. 1" in Korean and was North Korean-made. It did not report any further. However, the other committee reported that a North Korean submarine had fired the torpedo, saying, "according to our intelligence..." Journalist 1 also believed that a neutral country that had participated in the first committee was not represented on the second committee.

> They're not close to North Korea. You know it's not like a China or Russia joint team. The second committee said that according to intelligence... How can you convict with this evidence in a lawful court? (Journalist 1)

*Hankyoreh Shinmun* emphasized, and the general public probably agrees, that Sweden is a neutral country, considering that Sweden has an embassy in North Korea. However, the country that was missing from the second investigation was Canada. The international investigation team consisted of the United States, Australia, Sweden, and the UK. Originally, Canada joined the first committee. However, as Journalist 1 said, for the second committee, Canada was not on the list. Journalist 10 also said that he was not sure about the committee reports. He said, "South Korea says that it was an international investigation. But the countries they picked are Australia, Sweden and Canada. So they're all like friends, U.S. allies."

> I can tell you one more item of information. It's not released anywhere, but it can tell you the mind-set of the South Korean government. For example, France proposed to help the investigation, and South Korea rejected it. Sounds like they don't trust France. France is officially like an ally of South Korea and the U.S. You know, France is not exactly the line on the U.S. South Korea politely and secretly refused, so that's interesting, you know. *AFP* is French. But Simon Martin (who covered the Cheonan as a correspondent for *AFP*) is British and writes in English for Seoul. (Journalist 10)

He explained that the *AFP* bureaus work with different languages and different people. "French, English, sometimes Spanish, sometimes German also, depending on the country. In Asia, it's very British. It's very English speaking. So basically in Seoul. Even there, there is no French speaking in Seoul. The head of the office in Seoul is British. But the head office in Beijing is French with French flags. Some are French, and others are English. So an original news story written in English goes to Hong Kong, and there is the regional office there. Then, French colleagues will pick a story and translate it into French. That's how *AFP* news production works in Asia. Then, the copy that goes to *AFP* from Korea is all originally in English."

> It doesn't mean that what South Korea says is not true. I'm just saying that the investigation, so-called international investigation, is not that international. I mean, that doesn't mean that it's a bad job. I'm saying that it shows that South Korea picked the one they want. South Korea always goes to the international states and says, look, we have an international investigation. So it's true. The fact is that yeah, it's international, but they are all your friends. That's why. If it was, for example, the UN, it would be more credible because the UN is more credible, more balanced. Russian did their own investigation, not part of the team. I'm not an expert, but I saw the propeller. When I see this, it's impressive, but for me, it was too good to be true. (Journalist 10)

Journalist 10 said that since then, he had had some doubts. Therefore, he had talked to French military naval experts who were not in Korea but in Norway and asked what they thought. They told him that it was a torpedo "because they said if you looked at the shape, the way the boat cracked, there was for them no question. It's a torpedo. It cannot be something else. Maybe it's a mistake torpedo from...ha ha...I tell you, I don't have the truth about the Cheonan. I don't know someone who has the truth. Maybe North Korea has the truth. No one knows the truth. But from everyone I talked to, I end up with the conclusion, I tend to believe that 80% or 90%, this is a North Korean torpedo. But you know..."

Journalist 9 said that because running aground was highly unlikely, he believed that the North was responsible because after the government statement, he asked the British, American, Canadian, and Swedish journalists sitting with him in the first row, "'Do you gentlemen fully endorse everything that has just been said?' And they said, 'Yes.' That's credible," he said. "I don't disbelieve the South Korean government, but on these kinds of issues, generally Western governments are quite credible. But the most critical thing was there was Swedish participation. On that, there were two points. Sweden has a lot of experience in anti-submarine warfare. They've taken the Russians and NATO. Sweden was in there. Yes. They were part of the report." He pointed out again that Sweden seems to be known as a "neutral" nation. However, he said, "I mean Cheonan even to this day is still a mystery. No one's 100% sure what happened, Yeonpyeong was obvious, I mean a terrorist strike. The North Koreans are not denying that. But they're still denying Cheonan, which is a bit odd, a bit of a mystery."

In the interview, Journalist 9 was usually very sure about the matters that he was talking about, and he had many years' experience as a journalist in South Korea. Additionally, he had been a columnist for *Chosun Ilbo*, one of the top-selling Korean newspapers. However, he explained that North Korea's attack on the Cheonan was very confusing. He said that the probability of "running aground" was very low, and Sweden, the most independent and neutral country in international affairs, signed on to the conclusion of the joint international investigation team. However, in contrast to Yeonpyeong, North Korea vehemently denies responsibility even to the present day; thus, the Cheonan sinking is a mystery.

To me, it's obvious that it was North Korea. I mean, I was a little bit suspicious, but they found the actual missile, all of that, OK. They're trying
so hard. Very obvious from an analyst's point of view. It's obvious. I mean,
it's not gonna be Taiwan that is gonna torpedo them or the Americans –
who is gonna torpedo them? If it was a mistake that the Americans torpedoed a Korean ship, that'll come out. They can't keep that a secret. To me,
it's obviously North Korea. Running aground? I don't know, but people
are trying hard to find another explanation because there is a certain thing,
what's the saying: "Occam's razor – also written as Ockham's razor." Let
me just check with Wikipedia here. It's basically a principle that there is,
it's about different theories about something, you choose the most logical.
Obvious. You know, for all the other theories, running aground or hitting
a mine, it's people who don't trust government. (Journalist 11)

He said that in a free environment, journalists are controlled to some
extent by the rules of credibility. "The source is always important. When
the military announces something, you usually believe them unless you
have a good reason not to believe them. The military, a company, and a
government, they may twist the truth or exaggerate a lot, but they are
kind of an authority. If the government announces about the Cheonan,
and the investigation shows it was North Korea, if your Korean government supports that investigation conclusion, you usually, as a journalist, you would accept that unless there is a very, very good reason not
to. For 9/11, no one says 'alleged.' You are also examining the rules of
the game." These comments were slightly confusing and contradictory
because earlier, he had said that "you should trust foreign correspondents and the government, especially military officials who do not give any
information to foreign correspondents." Journalist 3 said that there was
no question. "Who else?"

Many of us, including journalists as well as a lay public, are concerned
about the Iraq War. And the evidence also shows that the Americans
should stop the Iraq War. Now, you are probably getting the point that
I'm trying to make here. Because they found a propeller in the ocean
with number one on it. Does that mean that North Korea attacked the
Cheonan? I don't know. I would say, certainly, pretty good evidence.
But is it 100 percent evidence? No. Absolutely not. How can it be unless
someone actually witnessed it and had proof of its attack? Let's say that
you could prove it, between you and me. But who said it was fired in
error? Who said a rogue general ordered the torpedo to be fired? There are
so many questions. (Journalist 8)

Journalist 10 said "South Korea doesn't seem to question the Cheonan incident, although it still matters to know what happened. We'll know, maybe we will never know, I don't know, or we'll know much later. We're still looking for answers. It would be amazing if there is some evidence from the North side, some sources or some evidence to show that the North indeed orchestrated it and how they did that. Maybe one day, we'll find that we know. Maybe when North Korea collapses, we'll find that we know. We still don't know how they do it. Even the story is fascinating. I talked to sailors and so on. They told me that if a North Korean submarine went there, they took amazing risks because the Yellow Sea is extremely shallow. It's a very dangerous place to navigate, especially for a submarine, so basically submarines normally just don't go there, and I can tell you that if they did it."

Journalist 13 criticized how "global media embarrasses it up during the last two months[9] on North Korea because without naming news sources, I think a lot of international TV and the media and network made clear that they didn't understand the dynamics here. They didn't understand when North Korea says there is going to be a war tomorrow, that's not actually what it means." He continued,

> The news media, they left all the conditions they would say North Korea says it will start a war. They ignore the fact that there was a conditional statement. I think that's very irresponsible journalism. So many journalists came. more than 40? It was a waste of money. It made me angry. It's misinformation and misleading. North Korea began to use the international media as a tool, so, for example, North Korea wanted to damage South Korea's reputation as a place to live and invest. North Korea potentially starts the announcement by saying we recommend all the foreign residents in Seoul to leave. All the international media say, oh, great story; they just report it. What shall I report today? Say, let's report this, that's great. So that becomes a tool in their hands of the North Korean government, which I think is ridiculous. So I hope people learn lessons from that.

These comments show the nature of covering North Korea, how important it is to ensure that the context and nuance are correct. That is why some Korean journalists think that international journalists do not understand Korean society and, therefore, North Korean issues. On the other hand, international journalists think that Koreans do not have much interest in North Korea and that they do not commit to critically questioning officials, in contrast to most Western journalists.

While conducting interviews, I noticed that the relationship between international journalists and Korean journalists is not particularly collegial. Rather, there seemed to be a clear division between foreign journalists and Korean journalists, with the boundary indicated by "we" and "they" as they criticized and were frustrated with each other. Thus, in the next section, I show the main views of international journalists of Korean society and Korean journalists' practices in a sociocultural context.

## INTERNATIONAL JOURNALISTS VS. KOREAN JOURNALISTS

As defined in Chapter 2, news is not a mirror of a reality but a social construction (Allan, 2004; Tuchman, 1997). Hence, exploring how journalists shape an issue and what aspects journalists make salient is important. In particular, the ways in which foreign correspondents frame South Korea are important because they work for the primary definers, which are global news agencies, and news framing influences public attitudes (Entman, 1993). Thus, it is helpful to identify the ways in which correspondents view Korean society and Korean journalists' practices in sociocultural and political contexts. Correspondents explained what they have observed by describing the differences between Western journalists and Korean journalists.

Correspondents found that there are sociocultural differences between Western journalists and Korean journalists. Journalist 9 said, "particularly, guys (journalists) from ChoJoongDong – *Chosun Ilbo*, *Joongang Ilbo* and *Dong-A Ilbo* (conservative daily newspapers) – they see themselves as members of the establishment, whereas Western reporters see themselves as critics of the establishment. There are some reporters, Boris Johnson being a good example, who go into politics. Winston Churchill is a good example."

> If you go to a press conference, it is very interesting. Western reporters would stand up and say, "Mr. Minister, what do you think about A, B, or C?" That's it.... Korean reporters would get up, and they give 2 or 3 or 4 speeches, saying, "You know, minister, I think this, and I think that, da da da da da, I think this," and then finally, they would ask a question at the end.

Considering the Korean culture regarding asking a question of one's senior or boss or higher-ups, I suggested that this approach could be a way of politely asking a question. Journalist 9 answered, "It might be true. It could be a very indirect way of asking tricky questions. They just received materials from the Defense Ministry. They web search." Journalist 8 agreed that "it's a very cultural thing that I mentioned earlier. They don't question authority, they respect authority, and you can see that in the structure of government authority; it is highly respected in Korea. You don't question government, you don't question the security apparatus. Domestic politics. I saw that when we had news conferences. Koreans wouldn't ask tough questions. Foreign media would ask all those tough questions." Journalist 10 also explained that Korean journalists do not confront but ask general questions. Furthermore, Journalist 1 concluded that although Korean journalists have more staff and better access to news sources than correspondents, "their weak point is they are very much confined within their news organization. Compared to the press in the U.S., the news organization has quite a lot of influence on journalists' practice."

Journalist 11 also indicated that Korean reporters are more embedded in their nationalism. He stressed that

> One thing to bear in mind, I think, is the Korean press and also the Japanese press, in my experience, they care about their national interests. American and British journalists don't care much about their national interests. Korean reporters are far more likely to be influenced by the government. Even their own ideas are in their national interests more than Western reporters. In the Cheonan case, to me, the root of this problem is the level of trust in Korean society. That's what it comes from, I think.

Journalist 11 noted that Korean journalists play a certain role that the government should be playing, and the relationship between the Blue House and journalists is interdependent. Journalist 15 said he feels that "sometimes, *Yonhap* reports in the administration's favor. I can't believe sometimes how this sort of news about the Korea conflicts can be reported by *Yonhap*, compared to the Kyodo news agency that sometimes criticizes the government. But in Korea, if you're a reporter for the news agency, that's a basic." Foreign correspondents were also very antagonistic toward the Korean journalists for some reason. The Ki Ja Dahn system is a very sensitive issue in the Korean media. The system was mentioned by several Seoul foreign correspondents who have worked in Korea for many years. For instance, Journalist 12, who had many years of journalist experience in Japan, said,

> In Japan, there is also a Kija Club system; here, it is Kijadan. So it's sort of similar to pack journalism with all the reporters for major publications. They report the same thing; they keep out from the Kijadan if the news organization is not part of the media oligarchy. They tend not to be investigative in nature; the reporting very much relies on quoting reports of officials with numbers, and they are very focused on the numbers rather than contexts. Their reporting is very one-sided. Another saying when something involves Japan and South Korea, they are very much reflecting what their own government is reporting inasmuch as it is an objective story. (Journalist 12)

Comparing South Korea to Japan, Journalist 12 pointed out that there are differences in the structure of the media. He noted that most Korean media were under government control for many decades; thus, Korean reporting that is independent of the government had started much later than in Japan. Journalist 16 had journalism experience in Japan as a copy editor. He pointed out that the Kija system creates unhealthy tension because with both the Kija Dahn (Korea) and Kija Club (Japan), there is a very close relationship between journalists and news sources, and in some sense, it is too close.

He observed, "Journalists are spending most of their time with the news sources, and they develop good relations. When they have tough questions and tough stories to write, that can be a problem."

> The problem is, they are too close to the...In this case – the *Yonhap* reporters in the foreign ministry are too close to the foreign ministry, and the foreign ministry may have pressured them. *Yonhap* is the largest news organization in Korea, so they have resources, they have good contacts, and they do write a good story. I don't want to say they don't; I'm just saying that in some situations, their independence is an issue. It's also an issue because they're partially government funded. That creates some unhealthy tensions. (Journalist 16)

Steve Herman at VOA, who had worked in Japan, said, "The Kija Dahn System I saw in Japan. If you're part of the Kija club, there is self-censorship that's imposed. If you violate the rules, the group journalism rules, then you potentially could be excommunicated. To me, South Korea is more slightly leaky than it is in Japan. Japanese reporters almost agree what to report together. There is much more sense that it is a little bit more independent and competitive here because of ideological division, and there is more willingness of Korean reporters to criticize people inside the system, where in Japan, criticism usually comes from outside first. Oshukahn, weekly magazine will be the first to break some scandals even if the information might have been fed by the people in the Kijadahn or people in Kijadahn writing under a pen name..."

Additionally, Journalist 16 pointed out the ownership of the media and its influence on journalists' practices. The close relationship between journalists and news sources can be problematic because it may make reporters challenge the views of news sources. Hence, he added that reporters in a media organization such as Hankyoreh can ask tough questions because they are independent of outside funding.

In contrast, from a Korean perspective, based on his experience, Journalist 17 said, "The Ki-Ja Dahn system is like a double-edged sword. For journalists, it's necessary to be part of the system because we can get a rich stock of information and have 'deep-background' briefings under an embargo. There are limitations, such as reporters have to follow the time and date when we can or cannot report due to the embargo. In a way, for reporters, having good and close relationships with news sources seems to be our right for more information even if we don't write a report about it right away. For foreign correspondents, because they can't be part of the system, it would look like a very closed system." Journalist 18 commented on the system by saying that "having a good relationship with news sources is helpful because you can ask questions in private, for example, while having a meal together."

Correspondents noted the Ki-Ja Dahn system and the close relationship between Korean journalists and news sources. In addition, some correspondents pointed out that Korean journalists tend not to challenge the government and news organizations. They concluded that the Ki-Ja Dahn system hindered Korean journalists' independence of the government and news organizations and that the ownership of a news institution affects journalists' practices. If reporters are too close to news sources, correspondents believed that it is very difficult to report negative news about those sources, especially if a news organization is funded by them. As a result, they concluded that Korean journalists do not question the government, although a journalist's main role is to act as a watchdog. In addition, the correspondents said that Korean journalists' national interest is very strong. In the correspondents' views, Korean journalists care deeply about their country compared to Western journalists. Hence, they are likely to be influenced by the government. Regarding the Ki-Ja Dahn system, as Korean journalists responded, on one hand, the system looks as if reporters defend the government and their news organizations from the viewpoint of correspondents who cannot be part of it. On the other hand, it is a privilege for selected reporters to be able to obtain information from close news sources because the purpose of the close relationship with news sources is not necessarily to criticize them but to receive important information or updates on a particular issue from them.

## North Korea: Geopolitics, National Interests, and Foreign Policy

Rhee (2010) argues that the Korean mainstream media routinely take sides with political parties and that the incumbent political party influences public service broadcasters. Consequently, he concludes that the Korean media's ideological cleavage has caused a decline in public trust of the mainstream media. In the same vein, Journalist 1 said that Korean people tend not to trust government official reports because of South Korea's experience with military regimes. This section shows correspondents' views on the Korean conflict in Korean society. Another key theme drawn from correspondents was the ideological division of Korean society.

> Whether you believe the final result (of the Cheonan probe) or not is a political issue in South Korea. Some people say, "I can't believe it or it's a fabrication or distorted," and others question why you don't believe it. In this sense, South Korea has failed for integration. (Journalist 15)

Correspondents explained that the society is extremely ideologically divided into a left wing and a right wing, as two opposite ideological news sources tend to be consulted for every news story, so they thought that the speculation that circulates is also divided by the opposing ideologies. Hence, according to Journalist 1, the Cheonan incident was the worst case because when it happened, rather than investigating "who's done it," a left-wing newspaper would criticize the ruling party and the government, and the right-wing newspaper would act in counterpoint. They used the incident as a political weapon by attacking their counterpart rather than searching for facts. "It's like an election," said Journalist 3. He contended that Korean politics are about regional conflicts, where people are from; for example, someone from Jeolla Province will criticize a current government official who is from Kyungsang Province. He said, "It's unfortunate that regional prejudices dominate scientific findings." Journalist 1 also explained,

> You've probably seen the recent news about the leaflets that the South sends, and North Korea said that they would be shelling. If it happens, the conservatives would say that it's time to get tough. Look at what the North does. We should vote for a conservative. Also, the left wing would argue that the Lee administration is damaging peace, making the North reckless and creating tension with North Korea.

Most correspondents mentioned that in the Korean media, conservative and progressive newspapers are very polarized ideologically. In addition, they said that North Korean issues have become political agendas. The political aspect of a North Korean issue seems to demonstrate a regional as well as an ideological division in Korean society. Moreover, the ideological division seems to be deeply rooted not only in the Korean media and Korean politics but also in the Korean public. Journalist 11 commented,

> It's unfortunate. People will assume, "Do you agree with the government's report about the Cheonan? You therefore agree with everything else to do with the government." The reason you agree with the government's report is not because you thought about it but because you're pro-government. And the same for the opposite. If you disagree with it, the reason is you disagree because you're antigovernment. That can be very true in a lot of cases, but it also can be unfair to people who are trying to look objectively. It's childish.

Therefore, according to the interviewees, the North Korean issue is viewed in South Korea as a political agenda that brings political division and ideological contestation to Korean society. Moreover, reactions to the Cheonan implied the Korean public's trust in or mistrust of the government, as Journalist 1 explained, probably due to Korea's historical political background. In addition, in terms of politics, both oppositional political parties use North Korea as a political tool for their political purposes. Furthermore, Korea's never-ending and deeply embedded regional division, which is similar to the relationship between Lancashire and Yorkshire, has been a political issue for a long time. Journalist 8 said that in the new era, social media are transforming the political media role, as shown in recent mayoral and presidential elections. He perceived that the alternative media in South Korea play a role in changing Korean society from a political perspective.

It was noticeable that news texts mentioned how China reacted to the result of the international joint investigation. There were some criticisms of China's lack of response to North Korea in national and international news. In particular, the U.S. media included the Obama administration's condemnation of China's inactivity. In response to my questions, Journalist 18 clearly explained the current situation in the Korean Peninsula with the new great power, China. She said that China is using North Korea as a buffer because if North Korea is under U.S. control, China will find the U.S. influence as a neighbor at its border. In short, because China has expanded its influence in East Asia, the United States will attempt to restrain the increasing Chinese expansion in the region. That is why the United States has attempted to solidify the alliance between Japan and South Korea, which is closely bonded to China. Thus, the Korean Peninsula can be a buffer between the G2 nations. She said, "North Korea knows that North Korean issues are to deal with the U.S., and North Korean brinkmanship means negotiations with the U.S."

> In the Obama administration's first term, North Korea was not part of the U.S. interest because the U.S. was involved in the Iraq War and many other conflicts in the Middle East, and they outsourced, hoping that China or South Korea would take care of the North and that the situation would stay as it is. North Korea needed aid. For their economy, they had to negotiate with the U.S., but the U.S. didn't try to listen. So North Korea raised the tension. (Journalist 18)

In addition to the United States, which was considered to have influential power in the region, most journalists emphasized the important role that China could play in the region's stability in relation to North

Korean issues. Journalist 3 said that the relationship was "wrapped up in a whole thing. China repeatedly said about Cheonan that they want stability. It is hard for China to be harsh to North Korea. It's a great deal of aid, fertilizer oil. China is still a big ally of the North. Of course. China is their only ally. Source of arms, oil, food; some people think so. Russia getting increasingly close to North Korea. Russian big interest in North Korea. Russia had a dream about a railroad from Busan to North Korea to Europe."

However, Journalist 1 considered that China would not play the role in the Korean conflict that the United States and South Korea want it to play:

> The Cheonan motivated a turning point. Considerably many people also thought that we should be closer to the U.S. to hold China in check. In other words, the incident gave Korean people a better understanding of the importance of military alliance with the United States. As China becomes a regional power, they'd like to host a six-party talk and make their image or identity. (Journalist 1)

Even in the post-Cold War era and after the fall of the Soviet Union, it looks as if a second or new Cold War lies in the Korean Peninsula. The relationship between China, North Korea and South Korea and its ally the United States is an important element in maintaining, technically, a state of war but, practically, peace.

> South Korea and Japan, I don't want to say pawns of the U.S. But they are, you know, regional actors for the U.S. North Korea could be used in some ways by China against the U.S. as well. (Journalist 14)

In response to Chinese ambition, the U.S. President Barack Obama announced that the United States was "rebalancing" power in the Asia Pacific region, which is called the pivot to Asia. Journalist 12 explained, "Because of Korean history, Korean people feel very vulnerable and very defensive and react very strongly emotionally to things, worried about the survival of Korean culture. Look at Korea's position geographically. It's always been vulnerable to China. It's been caught in between." He said that Korea's geographical location and weak economy enabled South Korea's overthrow by Japan, which might have been worse if it had been China.

Korea is like the Balkans in Europe before the First World War, in other
words, an area wherein the interests of various great powers meet. It's
always been that way in the last hundred years because China and Japan
at the end of the 19th century were fighting for control of Korea, then
you had Japan and Russia fighting for the control of Korea and then the
Japanese war in 1894, the Russian and Japanese war in 1905, then obviously the Korean War, which was a war between America and China, so
you know, this is a historical pattern that is happening and continues to
happen. What now is happening (increased tension between the two
Koreas in March 2013) is that you know China is expanding regional
power just the same way imperial Germany was for the First World War,
and obviously, Korea is a sphere of influence for China. (Journalist 14)

As Journalist 12 said, "The Korean War was the start of the Cold War.
Definitely, the Cold War is over; that was a Soviet Union versus U.S. ideological conflict. That's over. It's a geographical conflict for the future
between two powers or two power bases. Obviously, the power base in
the East will be led by Beijing. The power in the West will be led by
Washington, but Washington, it can project power, but it must have a
number of strong allies around the world who share common values and
in a military conflict, all our NATO are willing to fight alongside."

These remarks by journalists indicate that North Korean issues such as
the Cheonan sinking reflect issues of national interest, national security,
foreign policy, and geopolitical power. Moreover, the Cold War seems to
still be alive in the Korean Peninsula. In their view, South Korea is quite
vulnerable, and China is a rising power; thus, depending on the powers,
South Korean stability could change.

Journalist 13 explicated, "It's hard to know exactly what the interests
(of the U.S. and China) are. But it was interesting, North Korea said
recently that they think the U.S. is using North Korea as an excuse to
move military assets to the region as part of its pivot to Asia. I think it's
important to know, if you actually look beneath all the talk about the
U.S. pivot to Asia, because of all the budget cuts, there is hardly any
military assets being moved, but nonetheless, clearly, the U.S. and China
both want to build strategic influence in the region, and the Korean
Peninsula is the point where the influence meets."

The Korean Peninsula is divided into two stands between the great
superpowers. As shown earlier, Korea historically has been under the rule
of powerful countries. As the journalists repeatedly said, the Cold War

has ended, and the world is now in the post-Cold War era. However, China's economic power is on the rise, and Beijing is emerging as a superpower. It is not certain yet that China will eventually supplant the world's dominant superpower. However, the United States keeps China in check, and China is balancing its power by promoting cooperation and building trust with the international community. As shown in the international news reports analysis, the media blamed China for not reacting to North Korea regarding the Cheonan sinking. In other words, China did not blame North Korea for torpedoing the Cheonan warship and rather blamed the United States for escalating tension. The situation was similar to the situation of 60 years ago, as it seemed that China and the United States were confronting each other along their ideological lines—democratic and communist. Hence, the Korean Peninsula is still caught between the superpowers in their power struggle. In summary, domestically, a North Korean issue has been used for political purposes, and internationally, the Korean conflict shows the geopolitical dynamics between the great powers in the region. The appearance of the divided Korean Peninsula seems to show the unfinished Cold War in the post-Cold War era in the Korean Peninsula.

## SUMMARY

It has been shown how news gathering, investigating and news sourcing by foreign journalists are performed and what limitations journalists experience in covering Korean conflicts. International journalists said that they are independent of their organizations, and the Korean government does not pressure them. However, their responses showed that the journalists tended to trust U.S. officials and third-party officials. In addition, to a great extent, the news sources that they can use in news stories are somewhat limited in relation to North Korea, which is highly inaccessible. Therefore, foreign correspondents said that they turn mostly to U.S. officials or the English versions of internet news sites because they believe there is no other way to obtain materials for news stories. For more information, they used websites that were not substantiated, mainly Daily NK, because no one had original information about North Korea. Thus, these practices show that the new media, particularly English versions, have affected correspondents' media practices. Moreover, most of the foreign journalists said that they knew that they could not obtain any information from government officials or military officials, while Journalist 2 said that these sources are the best sources for North Korean news. Additionally, there is some degree of antagonism between Western journalists and Korean journalists, who do not view each other as fair competitors or colleagues. Importantly, depending on a journalist's ideology—what they believe, their social universe—and background, the news frame for the cause of the Cheonan sinking was different based on their beliefs and whom they talked to. Accordingly, the news frames were shaped differently.

Moreover, some interviewees were unsure of what had caused the incident. They said that was why they did not say that "North Korea attacked the Cheonan" in their news stories. Rather, they emphasized when they wrote that "the Seoul government blamed the North" or "the South Korean government accused North Korea." Journalists somehow must make a decision or choose a direction regarding how they will frame a news topic. Moreover, some international journalists, in particular, said that they were not sure who was responsible even after the conclusion of the joint investigation was reported. Most international journalists perceived that they would not obtain any more information even if they investigated further. Consequently, it yielded media routines. A great volume of research on news analysis adopts a framing theory by providing a rationale that news frames shape the public mind (Scheufele, 1999), but studies about news framing effects are scarce. The Cheonan as a case study shows that journalists' routinized media practices and indecision regarding the cause of the incident affected the framing of the news agenda, as reiterated disputable elements were repeatedly reported without further investigation; thus, the news frame of uncertainty about the cause shaped the public perception. Therefore, it is possible that the public who were exposed to the news could also be suspicious and question the cause of the sinking of the Cheonan warship due to journalists' indecision regarding who is responsible.

As Hamilton and Jenner (2004) found in the foreign correspondence landscape, by hiring local foreign correspondents who are able to communicate in Korean and read local news, international news media seem to incorporate local views and local sources into their news stories. However, within the same environment, with a lack of available news sources about North Korea and only limited news, North Korean issues in South Korea seem to accelerate media routine practices. In this research, the direct effects, the news effects on the audience, are not shown. However, based on the theories that we have discussed—news framing, the role of the news media and the impact of such frames on society—it can be argued that journalists' questions might be a reason that the public—national and international—questioned the final report by the government. Consequently, it is possible that the news reports that emphasized the unanswered questions amplified suspicion of the investigation's conclusion because the news media shape public opinion and public perceptions, as discussed in the literature review. Correspondents commented on the ideological division in the Korean media as well as society, while in many other countries, such divisions are meaningless. As interview data show, the historical background of the current situation in the divided Korean Peninsula and political development toward a democratic country has influenced the unfortunate ideological division in Korea. In this chapter, based on interviews with international journalists and Korean journalists, I have described the complexity of current journalism practices, North Korean issues, and the geopolitical power game in the Korean Peninsula. In the next chapter, I will discuss the critical analysis of the data and the implications of the study.

## Notes

1. http://www.ohmynews.com/nws_web/view/at_pg.aspx?CNTN_CD=A0001893524.
2. Andrei Nikolaevich Lankov is a Russian scholar of Asia who attended Kim Il-sung University in Pyongyang, North Korea. He has taught at Kookmin University in Seoul since 2004. He is a regular columnist for the oldest English-language daily, *The Korea Times*, in South Korea. He is one of the most quoted news sources in international news coverage about North Korea (www.koreatimes.co.kr, www.wikipedia.org, and www.kookmin.ac.kr).
3. http://www.nytimes.com/2010/01/25/world/asia/25north.html?pagewanted=all&_r=0.
4. Howard Young is a South Korean radio station founder. He said, "It is clearly terrorism and suggests that the attacks were part of an escalation in aggression toward South Korea." He cited a torpedo attack on a South Korean naval ship and the shelling of a South Korean island near disputed waters in 2010 (September 26, 2011, October 10, 2011, Barbara Demick, *Los Angeles Times*).
5. Open Radio reports from Seoul, aiming to be a voice of change by airing information to counter Pyongyang's propaganda and passing messages from friends and relatives to North Koreans (April 12, 2009, John M. Glionna, *Los Angeles Times*).

6. https://muckrack.com/.
7. The Korea Institute for Defense Analyses (KIDA) is an independent civil-ian research institution funded by the government under a special law to support the policymakers of the Ministry of National Defense (MND) and the Joint Chiefs of Staff (JCS) (www.kida.re.kr).
8. It is an island in Korean territory, but Japan named the Korean islands "Takeshima" and has claimed that it has ownership. Thus, this territory has been disputed for decades. Japan suggested to South Korea in 2012 that a case be filed with the International Court of Justice (August 11, 2012, *Yonhap*), http://news.naver.com/main/read.nhn?mode=LSD&mid=sec&sid1=100&oid=001&aid=0005752353.
9. North Korea announced that it would invalidate the Armistice on March 11, 2013, when South Korea and the United States conducted joint annual military drills called "Key Resolve." The North threatened the South and criticized the drills (March 11, 2013, *Yonhap*).

# REFERENCES

Allan, S. (2004). *News Culture*. Maidenhead and New York: Open University Press.
Bardoel, J., & Deuze, M. (2001). Network Journalism: Converging Competences of Old and New Media Professional. *Australian Journalism Review, 23*(2), 91–103.
Boyd-Barrett, O., & Rantanen, T. (Eds.). (1998). *The Globalization of News*. London, Thousand Oaks, and New Delhi: Sage.
Entman, R. M. (1993). Framing, Towards Clarification of a Fractured Paradigm. *Journal of Communication, 414*(4), 51–58.
Fenton, N. (2010). *New Media, Old News: Journalism & Democracy in the Digital Age*. London: Sage.
Hamilton, M. J., & Jenner, E. (2004). Redefining Foreign Correspondence. *Journalism, 5*(3), 301–321.
Herman, S. E., & Chomsky, N. (2002). *Manufacturing Consent: The Political Economy of the Mass Media*. New York: Pantheon Books.
Rhee, J.-W. (2010). The Rise of Internet News Media and the Emergence of Discursive Publics in South Korea. In J. Curran (Ed.), *Media and Society* (5th ed.). (pp. 348–364). London and New York: Bloomsbury Academic.
Scheufele, A. D. (1999). Framing as a Theory of Media Effects. *Journal of Communication, 49*(1), 103–122.
Shoemaker, J., & Reese, S. D. (1991). *Mediating the Message: Theories of Influence on Mass Media Content*. New York: Longman.
Shoemaker, J., & Reese, S. D. (1996). *Mediating the Message: Theories of Influence on Mass Media Content* (2nd ed.). White Plains, NY: Longman.

Sunstein, R. C. (2002). The Law of Group Polarization. *The Journal of Political Philosophy, 10*(2), 175–195.

Thussu, D. K. (1997). How Media Manipulates Truth About Terrorism. *Economic and Political Weekly, 32*(6), 264–267.

Tuchman, G. (1997). Making News by Doing Work. In D. Berkowitz (Ed.), *Social Meanings of News: A Text-Reader* (pp. 173–192). Thousand Oaks, CA: Sage.

CHAPTER 7

# Discussion and Conclusion

This chapter discusses the major findings in the news analysis results and contemplates the implications of the data collected in the interviews with journalists. Applying the hierarchy of influences model by Shoemaker and Reese (1996), this part aims to draw a conclusion about the news production processes and, based on the results of the news framing analysis and the interpretation of the interviews conducted in this study to discuss in depth the core factors that influenced journalists' news production practices and news frames in covering the Korean conflict in a sociocultural and political context in light of theoretical debates. Additionally, the Korean media and society through the eyes of foreign correspondents will be addressed in this conclusion.

## NEWS FRAMES IN THE U.S. AND UK NEWS REPORTS

The images and themes that the media create construct associations in the public mind (Castells, 2009). In particular, considering the significance of the role of the international news media and their impact on both public perceptions and foreign policies (Livingston, 1997), it is imperative to examine the ways in which news is constructed and shaped by journalists in the international news media. Furthermore, the public dependence on international media for news about North Korea is even greater because North Korea is the most reclusive society in the world. This study examined news content related to the Korean conflict and explored the key factors that influenced the news frames. For

© The Author(s) 2019                                                        173
M. Moon, *International News Coverage and the Korean Conflict*,
https://doi.org/10.1007/978-981-13-6291-0_7

the empirical research, I selected news institutions in South Korea, the United States and the UK because traditionally, the United States and the UK are the two prime leading players in global news communication. Specifically, this study focuses on the international news media because they are major news distributors, particularly in relation to international conflict, and agenda setters.

In the results of the news framing analysis, as the frequency of news articles demonstrated, the number of news stories about the Cheonan in news media outlets in the United States, UK and South Korea indicate to what degree each nation's news media configured the North Korean issue as prominent. This study also examined the dominant news frames embedded in the sampled news data. The words used in each news article were examined thoroughly. The common frames detected in the media by Semetko and Valkenburg (2000) were employed to identify the primary news frames. They were the conflict, economic consequences, human interest, and morality frames. The results showed the differences between national and international news texts. The dominant news frame in the international news media was the conflict frame, while the human interest frame was more prominent in national news texts. From day one, the international news mentioned "North Korea" more than five times in each article and included similar background information, which could increase tensions in the Korean Peninsula because of the repetition of sensitive issues such as "the disputed area, NLL," "three bloody skirmishes" that happened in the past between South Korea and North Korea, Korea has been "in a state of a war since the Korean War," and "the day before the incident, Pyongyang had threatened unprecedented nuclear strikes against the U.S."

According to Semetko and Valkenburg (2000), the conflict frame emphasizes conflict between two opponents in an effort to capture the audience's attention. Thus, the findings show that there is a possibility that international news treated the incident as a media agenda to draw the global audience's attention by highlighting the tension between the two Koreas and the previous conflicts between South Korea and North Korea even when the actual cause, the North Korean attack, was unknown. National newspapers did not mention any possibility of North Korea's engagement in the incident. For instance, *Yonhap* did not completely exclude the possibility that the North had attacked. As the data show, there was only one line on the first day of the incident mentioning that the defense minister did not exclude the possibility that North

Korea was involved. However, on the second day of the incident, *Yonhap* quoted an anonymous military source as saying, "there is a possibility of a North Korean torpedo ship because there was a hole penetrated at the rear of the ship" (March 27, 2010). However, the national news media did not repeat background information about the conflict between the two Koreas, as the international news did. Instead, the dominant news frame in national newspapers was the human interest frame. They prominently framed the emotional state of the devastated families who had lost their sons and relatives. However, *Yonhap* had a combined conflict and human interest frame that aroused emotional attributes because both the conflict frame and human interest frame are intended to attract audience attention (Semetko & Valkenburg, 2000).

What I learned from identifying the prominent news frames in news texts was that it is essential to address how the news frames changed as the investigation developed and the cause of the incident was revealed. The news content for those three designated days—the first day after the incident happened, the day of the interim report and the day that the final conclusion was announced—was updated in terms of attributing responsibility for the cause of the tragic incident. Accordingly, the news frames were changed. In particular, as the Korean government officially reported the conclusion of the joint international investigation team that North Korea had torpedoed the Cheonan warship, the ramifications aroused global concern. The UN reported the conclusion of a Security Council meeting with the title "Security Council condemns attack on Republic of Korea naval ship 'Cheonan,' stresses need to prevent further attacks, other hostilities in Region" (July 9, 2010).

The *BBC* news, especially as reported in London, had been trying to maintain a "neutral" or "safe" stance, as Journalist 5 said, by writing "alleged" every time it released a news story about the Cheonan. *The Guardian* also wrote about the Cheonan using the term "allegedly," even after the final conclusion, although it had news content very similar to that of the *AP* prior to the final report. As Journalist 1 said, the reason is probably not that the UK news media have much knowledge about the conflicts between the two Koreas but that they have no national interest there compared to the United States. However, the U.S. news media seemed to link the Cheonan and denuclearization, calling for North Korea's denuclearization and six-party talks following an announcement of economic sanctions against the North. Later, the news media in the United States, as well as South Korea, condemned China by mentioning that China was not reacting against the North's "provocation" and thus creating increasing tension in the relationship between the United States and China.

For example, Andrew Jacobs and David E. Sanger wrote in an article in *The New York Times*, June 29, 2010, that President Obama had accused Beijing of "willful blindness" toward North Korea's military provocation, "the sinking of a South Korean naval ship." Regarding Obama's remarks, a Chinese spokesman, Qin Gang, contended, "China is a neighbor of the Korean Peninsula, and on this issue, the Cheonan sinking, our feeling differs from that of a country that lies 8,000 km distant. We feel even more direct and serious concerns." After President Obama's remark, the condemnation of China's failure to control the North with regard to the incident and North Korea's provocation was primarily framed in news. In June 2010, it was noticeable that the news media reported as if the two superpowers, China and the United States, were confronting each other over this issue. The atmosphere was similar to a return of the Cold War, not between Russia and the United States but between China and the United States On Saturday, during the G20 summit meeting in Toronto, "Mr. Obama announced that the United States would extend by three years, until 2015, an agreement under which American commanders would take control of South Korean forces in the event of a military clash with the North." It was confirmed that the United States had agreed to return wartime operational control to South Korea in 2012. However, due to the Cheonan, it was necessary to consider postponing that return (*Dong-A Ilbo*, April 17, 2010). Regarding the transfer of operational control of South Korean forces, there had been a debate in 2006 over whether it should happen in 2009 or 2012. However, in 2006, North Korea conducted a second nuclear test, and it was agreed to extend U.S. control for three more years, which would make the return date 2012 (*Yonhap*, October 19, 2006). Then, due to the Cheonan incident, South Korea and the United States reviewed the postponement of the transition of operational control authority (OPCON), and President Obama agreed to postpone the transfer of wartime operational control from April 17, 2012 to December 1, 2015 (*Yonhap*, October 24, 2014). Since then, the South Korean government has seemed to prepare for the transition of OPCON to the Republic of Korea (*Newsis*, July 26, 2018). In the process of the news framing analysis, I learned that the dominant news frames change depending on the period and the presence of other mediating factors. It would be useful to consider the factor of changing frames depending on the time period in conducting future news framing analyses.

## INVESTIGATIVE JOURNALISM

The correspondents' journalistic practices were highly routinized. A nearly identical paragraph about the NLL and "technically at war" was repeated in many news stories and by many different news outlets. The results partly imply that investigative journalistic practices were deemed to be inapplicable. It is not the case that the news reports lacked facts and that the journalists' routine work caused public disbelief and suspicious attitudes toward the government's final report based on the international investigative group's conclusion because this thesis presents no strong evidence of how the news reports affected public beliefs and attitudes.

However, through news analysis and in-depth interviews conducted with journalists, the findings suggest that the news reports on the Korean conflict were not constructed in an investigative way but rather were constructed with the same background information simply repeated and a couple of controversial issues highlighted frequently. As Shoemaker and Reese (1991) state, some news texts are almost identical, which means that journalists' practices were routinized (Shoemaker & Reese, 1991). Moreover, Bennett says, "Despite some obvious differences involving the nature of assignments and personal writing styles, American reporters tend to cover news events in remarkably similar ways" (2012: 166). In this regard, Bennett (2012) states that a journalist's routinized work contributes to the standardization of reporting formats and cooperation with news sources and daily information. Thus, based on the findings, in line with journalists' routinized work practices, officials, as the most frequently used news source for newsgathering, can be an important indicator of routine work in the discussion that follows.

## NEWS SOURCE MECHANISMS

As emphasized in journalism theories, news sources are a significant index of the investigative news frames employed in news texts and of the international news flow. However, finding new news sources is not an easy task in terms of accessibility, as this study discussed, due to the limited news sources about the North. Thus, the findings regarding the use of news sources indicate that the news stories were heavily dependent on government officials, mainly from the Defense Ministry. This issue was the same in both national and international news. If there was any difference, the national news tried to hear more of what family members and relatives had to say. Regarding news sources for quotations, Korean and U.S. officials were frequently cited because the journalists said it was difficult to obtain information from North Korea. Schudson (2011: 128) states, "Government sources are not alone in seeking to satisfy the media's hunger." Journalists need official sources to write a story. Furthermore, Schudson says, "Among government sources, 'routine government sources' matter the most—press releases, public speeches, press conferences, and background briefings for the press" (2011: 128).

In the divided Korean Peninsula, given a situation in which there is no communication between the South and the North, I raise the question of what valid news sources other than officials would be in constructing a news story. With the sole results of the dominant official news sources used, can we conclude that the news delivers only the views of the powerful and that media routine is the usual practice. Moreover, based on the news sourcing filter, experts are in the same category as government officials if they are associated with government-funded institutions. Hence, quotations from academics as news sources were very limited. Thus, only a few, such as Professor Andrei Lankov and John Delury, were frequently quoted in North Korean news by the international news media for a long period. Since 2017, Robert Kelly has become well known as a news source. He became a humorous video star after his analysis from his home office was interrupted by his child on air during a *BBC* news live segment. He was a main news discussant for the Singapore Summit as well. I enjoyed the video, but I believe that the incident showed the nature of news construction in detail—a professor wearing a suit to report the news from his own room with a world map hung on the wall as a background, sitting in front of a computer with a camera. Correspondents also revealed that even if more professors were available, verifying the facts is another issue. This problem similarly applies to citations of other news outlets as news sources. *Yonhap* was heavily cited in the international news. Does that mean that the frames of *Yonhap* were dominant in the international news? As discussed in earlier sections, I concluded that correspondents cited *Yonhap* because the English version of *Yonhap* was conveniently updated frequently, and it is the largest news agency, with many staff all over the country; in addition, unlike *NKnews*, which journalists commonly refer to, *Yonhap* is an official news source. Correspondents replied that *Yonhap* is very good because it has many resources. However, *Yonhap* does not upload all news reports in English, and only selected news topics are translated into English online.

As the *Wall Street Journal* uploads news online, *Korea Real Time*, Korean news media post free readable news in Korean on their websites and reframe the international news to report it. The major international news media set an agenda that can become the Korean media agenda; consequently, it could affect the public agenda. As Journalists 12 and 16 said, Koreans are sensitive to how the outside world perceives them; hence, how the international news reports about Korea is important to them. Thus, government officials sometimes promptly respond to critical comments on their policies international news media, although criticizing government policies is a basic role of journalists as watchdogs. In a globalized world, coupled with new media technologies, the world appears to be under constant surveillance as people watch each other sitting in the Panopticon architecture, if I may adopt Foucault's (1979) insightful observation. Alternatively, this may mean that officials and elites view other parts of the world through the media. Consequently, they are likely to depend on the reality that the media construct. Therefore, news framing can affect foreign policy making. However, the superpowers are equipped with satellites and have major international news agencies, which are agenda setters (Thussu, 2000). Hence, a country such as South Korea should rely on reports of North Korea's military movements or its preparations for a nuclear test, as Journalist 12 explained. Therefore, military information and communication from the most powerful country in the world, the United States, can be very important to other nations such as Korea. Even if we observe a contraflow in international communication, for example, Al Jazeera, Telenovela, or K-pop such as Psy's Gangnam Style and BTS, an information flow from the North to the South is seen.

## THE IMPACT OF THE NEW MEDIA

The nature of news production, especially regarding North Korean issues, seems to have adapted to the technical use of the new media in accordance with the journalists' needs. To collect information, foreign correspondents referred to *NKnews*, a South Korean online news site. Almost all journalists mentioned that they used it, and many of them instantly said, "They're good." However, as *The New York Times* reported, "many of their reports are wrong while some news is very original and noble information"; therefore, *NKnews* does not necessarily provide good-quality news. My point is that most foreign journalists, in particular, who cannot comprehend Korean tend to understand "reality" through what *NKnews* reports. Additionally, most correspondents did not know the Korean language, even if they had lived in Korea for many years. That is why most news articles written by foreign correspondents credit contributors at the end of the article. Usually, two or three Korean names appear. They are stringers who help foreign correspondents find further information, especially Korean materials, by calling officials or contacting other Korean sources. It was rare for the correspondents whom I interviewed to speak basic Korean even after more than five years of living in Korea. Sawada at the Mainichi Shimbun spoke perfect Korean. Many signs and social systems are translated into English, and many social and cultural systems even give priority to English speakers. Thus, the correspondents might not need to learn Korean. One of the major difficulties that interviewees said they faced was the Korean language. Even if they have Korean staff reporters, it is different from writing a story in South Africa or Singapore. Hence, for news gathering, they are likely to visit English-language websites. The language was still a major challenge for international journalists.

The English version of *Yonhap* has been quickly updated in real time over the last few years, while mainstream newspaper companies have English-version news, although only some of their daily news is uploaded. *Yonhap* translations are now at the native English level, while other newspapers have a literally translated English version, which is not as fluent. The use of English on the *DailyNK* website also gives it more value than other sites. As discussed above, foreign journalists were highly dependent on materials in English on the internet. Moreover, an anonymous interviewee said that he gets almost all of his information from the web to write a story about any country in the world; significantly, he said that "you can't write in a different mind-set from U.S. officials in Washington." When he was in Washington, he wrote a story about the Cheonan based on information from the internet. This implies that on the one hand, locally based correspondents might possess more credibility because they are "in the region" of the conflict even if they rely on the internet, and journalists in their home countries can write about international conflicts by using stable official news sources from the internet with. As the journalists indicated, news gathering and reporting were dependent upon the internet.

As the journalists also mentioned, apart from its ownership, the state-owned *Yonhap* has the most extensive news resources, which cannot be compared to those of any other media within South Korea, making it somewhat equivalent to *Al Jazeera*. Additionally, it is noticeable that the international news media adopt news agencies' news almost unchanged; thus, for example, *The Guardian*'s upload of a news article looks almost the same whether it prints "AP news" under the title or incorporates it into its own article. However, *Yonhap* citations in international news stories are used to add factual information that *Yonhap* discovered and quotations from officials or to make an argument. The findings do not demonstrate the contra-news flow discussed in this study or whether the view of *Yonhap* can compete with the dominant Western views. However, in the aspect of being a news source for international news, it is clear that the *Yonhap* agency plays a leading role. The new media have had an impact on the changes of news production processes and facilitating interactions between national and international media to a great extent. Furthermore, they seem to play a significant role in blurring the lines between news agencies and the news media from the perspective of competitive news distribution because there is seemingly not much difference between journalists in news agencies and in the mainstream media in news gathering and access to news sources at the national and international levels.

## THE HIERARCHICAL INFLUENCES MODEL REVISITED

The internal factors of journalism determine how journalists and their news institutions frame issues. National journalists seem to be independent, even if the editor at *Hankyoreh* said they might not be due to a hierarchy system. The journalist at *Dong-A Ilbo* said that he informs the Blue House of secretive movements in North Korea based on his sources, and he seemed to be independent in covering North Korea. A journalist may have more information and be able to alert officials to matters related to national security. As Journalist 4 said, there is no need to apply pressure because journalists' and their companies' ideologies will be the same. In addition, a *KBS* journalist answered in reference to journalist autonomy, "That question should go to the Chinese journalists," meaning that the

*KBS* journalists are not under pressure by media institutions. However, journalists at *KBS* were very cautious about commenting and expressing their personal opinions because they work for a public broadcasting company.

For foreign correspondents, there seems to be no pressure from their companies. Rather, they feel distant from their home bases after living in South Korea for many years. Editors in their home countries trust what they do because they are the closest to the field, as Journalist 10 said. Correspondents observed that Korean journalists do not criticize the government or ask tough questions. I do not wish to conclude that Korean news media place constraints on journalists based on four interviews with Korean reporters. My work experience in the media industry in Seoul indicates that journalists as well as the public are very careful about expressing their opinions, in particular on North Korean issues because they are sensitive issues related to national security that could remind the Korean public of North Korea's invasion on June 25, 1950, and they do not want to be stigmatized as left wing and pro-North or right wing. As discussed in this study, ideological division is severe in Korean society. Thus, members of the public benefit from appearing neutral in their social life. Hence, correspondents said that it is unfortunate that regional prejudices and the dichotomy of being pro- or antigovernment, whether or not you agree with the government, dominate the country.

Boyd-Barrett (1998) acknowledges that globalization and modernization imply that a country has adopted a Western hierarchy. In a global era, a country such as South Korea must adapt to developed countries' modernized and globalized systems as well as its own culture. Korean culture is not so much about debate; rather, Koreans respect their seniors whether they make perfect sense or not. In Korean culture, a person's age is important. That is why Korean people often ask a person's age when they are introduced. It is not because they are rude but because they have to change the language terms in Korean depending on the individual's age—whether they are older than you or not. Not asking a woman's age is, in fact, a Westernized cultural practice. Korean people do not want to argue with each other. This avoidance might be owing to Confucianism. In fact, it was extremely difficult for me to talk with Korean journalists about this issue in depth due to its sensitivity. However, I should mention that North Korean issues are too sensitive to be criticized or for people to express their opinions in Korean society. It is very different for Korean journalists, or the Korean public, to express their opinions other conflicts, such as the Israeli–Palestinian conflict, in terms of "proximity" and "news value" because the North's issues are closely related to Korea's tragic history, the Korean War, which has led to the division of the Korean Peninsula.

Through this investigation of newsgathering, news sourcing, and interviews, foreign journalists said that they were independent of their news organizations to a great extent, while a reporter in a home country can be influenced by official reports. Correspondents heavily cited the Korean news agency *Yonhap* and conveniently used U.S. officials,' military officials,' and government officials' reports. Moreover, because of a lack of Korean language skills, English-speaking journalists were dependent on web-based English-language sites to gather further information for their news stories. Additionally, it seemed that correspondents had focused on drawing global audiences' attention by highlighting the tensions between the two Koreas and setting a media agenda because in the past, except for North Korean news, there was not much interest worldwide in South Korea, although there has been growing interest in the country since the Korean Wave globalized Korean popular culture such as K-pop and Korean television dramas. There are physical limitations and restrictions on accessing news sources in covering North Korean issues. Frequently, those news sources cannot be quoted, and while they are "technically" experts and analysts, in reality, they do not know what is happening in North Korea because it is one of the most inaccessible countries in the world. Hence, there are always limitations on journalists' investigations of what has actually happened. Influential factors that restrict journalists' investigative work are not only journalists' lack of access to news materials about North Korea but also correspondents' reliance on U.S. officials in terms of credibility rather than Korean news sources. Correspondents showed that there was no external pressure, such as pressure from the Korean government, that affected journalists' news framing, but all journalists addressed one significant factor as hindering their professional work. There was a "cultural difference"—a "Korean culture" that does not confront and is not open with the knowledge and information that individuals have as well as Korean journalists' nationalism.

Overall, foreign correspondents and Korean journalists are not influenced by their news organizations. The journalists' autonomy is preserved, and they are independent of editors' restraints. However, my interviews with journalists indicate that individual ideology is still an influential factor in determining the news frame in covering the Korean conflict. The comments about and resentment toward North Korea and China in conversation, mocking them, indicated a certain ideological division in journalists' minds. They tended to believe what they wished to believe and trust rather than basing their conclusions on factual materials and findings, paradoxically, because it is difficult to fact check. Consequently, they cited limited news sources in their stories based on unchecked materials. Hence, the most influential factor that determined a journalist's news framing of the Korean conflict was the journalist's ideology. That is why, in the same news institutions, depending on who wrote the story, there was an ideological divide in the news. As all the interviewees pointed out, Korean journalism has a political divide. Correspondents said that Korean people are divided left or right, black or white, politically and ideologically. Hence, the news sources they use and those they cite as the most important sources show that there are ideological differences and patterns between individual journalists. However, from the responses of journalists in the interviews, I very often noticed that there was hostility between Korean journalists and foreign correspondents. I interviewed only four Korean journalists, but Korean journalists perceive foreign journalists as "exaggerating news with limited information" and "not knowing much about their subject." Foreign journalists regard Korean journalists as "not doing what a journalist should be doing," "not asking tough questions" or "wanting to promote themselves." Even more, correspondents were divided into two distinct groups.

As part of this study, I adopted sociocultural approaches to examine the news about the vessel and the factors that influenced the news framing, that is, why the incident was reported in a certain way. Correspondents, except for two interviewees, questioned the final conclusion of the investigation. They said that they trusted the South Korean government, but they could not just say that the North had attacked the Cheonan. However, they had no strong evidence to counter this finding and could not provide reasons regarding why they did not believe it. They simply said that they had not witnessed the incident. There was the spent torpedo found by South Korea. They did not try to investigate it, but they said they did not believe the conclusion. Correspondents said that they wanted the Korean government to open up slightly more and communicate better with them in terms of providing information; nonetheless, they relied heavily on official news sources.

The news about the incident was a stalemate, similar to the situation in Korea. How the incident was treated by the media seemed to contribute to the growing public questions as a framing effect. Additionally, the issue became a political news agenda for the national and international media. Moreover, the Cheonan issue reflected Chinese foreign policy, showing China's continuing "neutral" position as an ally of the North and a close trading partner with South Korea. As we observed in the interviews, journalists find the incident mysterious even to the present day. In lieu of more information and investigation, international news reports contained repetitive text about the NLL and mere descriptions of what officials said, and the UK as a third party kept reporting the incident as "alleged." "The Cheonan effects" with the "alleged" cause reflect a lack of investigative journalism practices and the exploitation of politics by the media to attract an international audience. The news media should not exploit Korean conflicts because the news media influence governmental institutions and foreign policy (Baum, 2003; Bennett, 1994; Graber, 1997; McCombs & Shaw, 1972), nor should they set an agenda to draw audience attention and interest because they should be a watchdog.

## A NEW COLD WAR

The rising superpower, China, stands on North Korea's side, and the Russian investigation team blamed the South Korean government for the early final report announcement of the probe by the international joint investigation team. North Korea vehemently denies its involvement. The United States is strengthening its military alliance with South Korea, and Japan is ready for any nuclear weapons test by the North. The North Korean issue seems to be re-establishing a new Cold War order in the post-Cold War era. The news reflects the society. Through journalists' eyes, especially from foreign correspondents' perspective, the current Korean society and Korean media were explored in a sociocultural and political context. This study also examined what other factors influenced journalists' news framing and why those factors had an impact on the news. The research findings show that despite much speculation, most of the news that foreign correspondents covered or reported was not based on investigative work but was dependent on information from government officials.

In summary, this is an investigative study on the international news coverage of the sinking of the Cheonan. Through news article analysis and in-depth interviews with foreign correspondents as well as Korean journalists, the news production about the incident from news gathering to reporting was examined in detail. The overall goal of this research was to explore the nature of news production in relation to the conflict between the two Koreas—South Korea and North Korea—in particular, studying the case of the sinking of the Cheonan, which created ceaseless speculation and questions in Korean society and on a global scale. The journalism literature has been developing as global society undergoes historical, economic, and cultural changes. It has adapted its theories through a post-Cold War era, a neoliberal era, hegemonic power, and a new imperialism, along with new technologies, in order to generalize or rather to produce a universally applicable theory that encompasses the recent news phenomena in journalism. However, in the case of the Cheonan in the divided peninsula, the situation has not changed according to the different "world eras" (i.e., the post-Cold War era and the neoliberal era), and a paradigm shift does not seem to have occurred. Additionally, the findings show that the propaganda model by Herman and Chomsky (2002) was applicable to the news coverage of the Cheonan issue.

At a national level, factors that influence journalistic practice have been extensively discussed. At an international level, the political economy of international communication has developed, arguing for the dominance of Western media over developing countries and their shaping of how peripheral nations are perceived. However, news about the conflicts in the Korean Peninsula, which has been divided into South and North since the Korean War that followed the Second World War, cannot be examined solely by analyzing news texts or by interviews with journalists who cover news stories about the South and the North and the adoption of those theories. The conflicts in the Korean Peninsula involve the United States, Japan, China, and Russia, in particular the power struggle between China and the United States. There have been not two-party talks but six-party talks whenever there are clashes or skirmishes in the Korean Peninsula. Whenever issues related to North Korea arise, for global security, the outcome is that the UN, the United States, and Japan blame the North, imposing sanctions and stopping food aid, while China tries to defuse the situation. The impact of the news on making social policies and on public beliefs and attitudes has been discussed. Thus, it was crucial to explore the ways in which journalists reported the Cheonan incident.

As an anonymous journalist told me, news content about the same topic at the *BBC* can be different between TV news and radio news. He informed me that a news producer can provide differently framed news content for a different medium. Therefore, a comparative study of news reporting in different media, such as TV, newspaper, or radio could be crucial to understanding different news frames, depending on the medium. In other words, news can be framed differently depending on the media channel—the type of media. The type of media can be a crucial factor that influences the audience. Finally, it is imperative to consider the impact of the new media not only on audiences but also on journalists in news production. This study clearly shows the ways in which the new media currently affect journalists' news production practices.

The internet has two faces. In terms of infrastructure requirements, it costs much less, so it is easier to access fairly equal resources for knowledge and to produce original materials online. However, once the infrastructure of internet penetration is established, it will become easier to share international news at the same time on mobile phones as well as on the internet. According to Newzoo, there are 3 billion smartphone users across the globe in 2018. The population of South Korea is 5.180 million, and nearly all South Koreans have smartphones. As 96.2% of Koreans in their twenties have smartphones (94.2% in their thirties, 81.3% in their forties, 51.3% in their fifties and 85.5% in their teens) (*Yonhap*, July 3, 2014), it has become much easier to read reports from the major news agencies and international mainstream news on smartphone applications in bed, on the subway or anywhere outdoors immediately and for free.

News provided through apps is short and condensed, with video and pictures. By using stylish modernized applications and reading the news on the application itself, an individual is exposed to, and in the end becomes used to, highly developed and fine technology. People are becoming accustomed to such high-technology and modernized Western cultural practices from a young age. The internet seems to function as an equal distributor, but at a macro level, the current political economy is likely to continue or might be expanded in the new media era. Thus, it is currently essential to examine the representation of international conflicts by the international news media, including the global news agencies as agenda setters and primary definers and their investigative journalism as news distributers in utilizing their resources to cover, particularly, international conflicts. In addition, it is noticeable that there were no citations of Kyodo, the Japanese news agency, or Xinhua, the Chinese news agency, in either national or international news. It would be helpful to be able to share information across those media channels because the two countries are close neighbors to Korea and would likely be affected by any Korean conflict.

## CONCLUSION

Traditionally and historically, international news agencies have played a crucial role in investigative journalism, in particular in international conflicts worldwide, although there has been criticism that the global news agencies' wholesale news distribution constructs a homogeneous "Western" view and functions as a propaganda campaign. Nevertheless, many international journalists sometimes risk their lives to report international conflicts and make events known to global audiences under various situations so that we can gain knowledge and information about these conflicts wherever we are. Thus, a "Journalistic Field" can be a significant element (Benson, 2006).

The Singapore Summit with Trump and Kim Jung Un in June 2018 was an unprecedented and historic moment, although there has been no sign of active dismantlement of North Korea's nuclear weapons and no concrete timeline to investigate it from the United States. However, the man who a year ago was called "rocket man" is now called "Chairman Kim" and treated as a leader of a normal state by President Donald Trump, abandoning their hopeless provocations and brinkmanship. No one is sure yet whether Kim Jung Un's current gestures toward South Korea, the United States and China through meetings and summits mean that he will seriously dismantle nuclear weapons or bargain with the United States. However, the prospect model shows that the United States treating North Korea as a normal state brought the two countries to the table. Alternatively, this means that if the United States treats Kim as a rocket man, then he must behave in an uncivilized manner (He & Feng, 2013).

Bandow (2010) argues that the U.S.-South Korean military alliance has no purpose in the present day. For over sixty years, South Korea has been dependent on the military alliance with the United States, but there is a growing opinion that the United States should not intervene in the Korean conflict. He maintains that in the end, it seems that the North Korean issue as a threat is ultimately an issue for Korea and its peripheral countries. Therefore, he argues that it is pivotal for South Korea to prepare its own defense and equip itself with strategies for an independent vision for the sake of its people. Throughout global history, Korea has learned that strengthening its military forces will encourage North Korea to further develop nuclear weapons. While the ultimate goal would be to bring peace to the Korean Peninsula, a fundamental change in North Korea's regime might have to come first. A survey conducted by *The Financial Times* shows that the younger generation has much less interest in reunification than older generations. What they are interested in is finding better jobs in the current period of economic downturn. However, no one wants their nation to become a battlefield.

After the joint international investigation concluded that North Korea had attacked the Cheonan warship, the South Korean government imposed economic sanctions called the "5.24 measures" on North Korea in retaliation for the sinking. Moreover, in preparation for further retaliation, the South Korean government and the United States jointly deployed heavy weapons and built up arms across the border. Reactions such as economic sanctions and arms buildup have been South Korea's best options, and small and large clashes between the South and the North have continued. When the President of the United States, the most powerful country in the world, officially announced and condemned North Korea as part of the "axis of evil" and a "belligerent country," tensions in the Korean Peninsula increased because of North Korea's unpredictable provocations that might follow abruptly. Likewise, South Korea's "war control" has been in the hands of the United States The Cheonan incident occurred when the ROK-U.S. annual military drills were ongoing, which was reported in June 2010. The superpower United States and South Korea's military drills must have threatened the North, but they are necessary for South Korea's defense and the region's security. We have seen these chronic routines, such as naval battles, military exercises, arms buildups, and economic sanctions, for nearly 70 years since the Korean War. Would South Korea see its own people victimized for another 70 years without any peaceful negotiation other than strengthening its military defense? *The Economist* boldly suggests that there is hope for "the world's most oppressed people." It says that since Kim Jung Un, a "modernizer," has taken over the country, capitalism should be an answer. He might not go as far as Deng Xiaoping in China, yet the article says that as the West did in Eastern Europe during the Cold War, outsiders, including China, should help expose North Koreans to the "prosperity and freedoms of the world around them" (February 9, 2013). As seen in the Singapore Summit, what North Korea wants is to secure its regime and economic prosperity (Wee, 2018).[1]

## DIGITAL MEDIA AND SOCIETY

Correspondents, especially those who have been in Seoul for over a decade, seem almost tired by North Korean issues in terms of the ongoing conflicts that never seem to be resolved and that have become a cycle—North Korean brinkmanship, tensions, six-party talks and no resolution, a return to North Korean brinkmanship after a few months, and then tensions. At the time of writing, North Korean issues were in stalemate, and North Korean brinkmanship was no longer creating tensions in this region, but the international news still reported it as a new and breaking issue. Journalists report on "growing tensions" and "unprecedented tensions and crisis in the Korean Peninsula," but they have never believed that there would be a war of any kind, which is contradictory. Among the factors that influence journalists' framing is an individual journalist's ideology. Ideology is an attribute of a living organism—a human being as a whole. It cannot be explained by the several parts that comprise an ideology. An individual journalist's ideology can be affected by his or her social background, education or race or experiences. Therefore, a journalist's "field," a Bourdieu term, can be different even within the same media institution. The greater the discrepancies in frames are between journalists in various media channels, the more the division in society is exacerbated. Thus, ideology is individualistic.

Many previous studies are concerned with political and ideological divisions in South Korea. Likewise, correspondents themselves had ideological divisions, especially on North Korean issues. What must be focused upon is not the fact that there are ideological divisions but the fact that one side does not respect the other's dissenting views (Moon, 2018). Dissenting views should coexist, and the struggle between different opinions in a public forum as a process of deliberation is an essential element of a functioning democracy. One should not have to make the other completely agree with them and become one.

Considering Korean history, culture, and security, ideological polarization cannot be regarded as the sole element hampering Korean democracy. However, the current state of Korea being a country that is divided in two and at war could preclude it from becoming a fully democratic country. Regarding the Korean conflict, it would be extremely difficult to conclude or suggest what policies should be made to prevent any more losses in the Korean Peninsula and the Yellow Sea. Nevertheless, given the impact of the news media in the conflict between the two Koreas in this study, the role of the international news media cannot be overemphasized because the global public is tremendously attentive to their reports, and international media agendas could shape government policies and public perception, as when we witnessed thousands of rallies and violent protests on the day after it was reported that U.S. President Donald Trump had recognized Jerusalem as Israel's capital on December 7, 2017. Western correspondents criticized Korean journalists for their lack of critical views, and Korean journalists mentioned that correspondents have no knowledge of or interest in Korean news. In terms of the role of national and international journalism in South Korea, instead of ignorance, it is desirable for national and international journalists to share resources and respect each other's roles.

Although there are criticisms of inequalities and imbalance in electronic communication, the common feature of the media that the public recognizes as credible is not to rearticulate what has already appeared on the internet but to uncover a news topic with investigative journalistic practices regardless of media ownership. The public seems to be aware that media institutions construct ideologies differently, and it seems to recognize the attributes of credible and trustworthy news media in a digital media environment influenced by big data and flourishing fake news. The public perceives media institutions as credible and trustworthy if they construct a news report with balance and investigation. Therefore, I hope that mechanisms to detect news based on facts and investigative journalism can be formulated soon so that people can read not 'fake' news but 'real' news critically. I emphasize what will need to be revisited in journalism practices in the globalized and the new media era. The internet opened a democratic arena where people can interact and communicate online easily and quickly. However, as in the case of Babel (Lule, 2015), the globalized world with multiple channels and multiple modalities has become even more highly competitive, and concentrated media ownership and core nations' advanced communication technologies in global communication have made 'globalization' critical from the political economy perspective.

Video-art pioneer Nam June Paik, who fled to Hong Kong and eventually Japan when the Korean War started, has foreseen the electronic highway and the importance of interaction with an audience through his art since his first solo show with electronic piano and thirteen televisions at Galerie Parnass in Wuppertal, West Germany, in 1963. Hence, his artwork has been appreciated in various prestigious galleries worldwide even to the present day. He coined the term "electronic superhighway" and designed a fifty-one-channel video installation with one closed-circuit television feed called "Electronic Superhighway"[2]; "Continental U.S., Alaska, Hawaii" (1995) showed a concrete map of the future networked world. Nam June Paek's "TV Buddha (1974)," with a bronze Buddha sculpture facing a closed-circuit video, also provides us with "a live and immediate experience" (Walsh, 2018).[3] We are experiencing a live and immediate reality with augmented reality (AR) and virtual reality (VR), as shown in the film "Ready Player One" (2018) by Steven Spielberg. What type of new media will come next? Our imagination of the future new media modality and content should be limitless. I cannot wait to see. There might not be a form to make everyone equal, but in pursuit of the humanity, dignity, and respect of each individual, the media and journalism will play pivotal roles for the public interest and will eventually make the world more transparent and bring it closer to the ultimate core value, democracy.

## NOTES

1. https://www.cnbc.com/2018/06/11/how-kim-jong-un-wants-to-develop-his-economy-and-secure-his-regime.html. Accessed on September 2, 2018. How Kim Jong Un wants to develop his economy and secure his regime, CNBC.
2. https://americanart.si.edu/artwork/electronic-superhighway-continental-us-alaska-hawaii-71478.
3. https://news.harvard.edu/gazette/story/2018/07/harvard-showcase-for-korean-artist-nam-june-paik/.

# REFERENCES

Bandow, D. (2010, July 14). *The U.S.-South Korea Alliance: Outdated, Unnecessary, and Dangerous* (Foreign Policy Briefing No. 90), pp. 1–12. CATO Institute.

Baum, M. (2003). *Soft News Goes to War: Public Opinion and American Foreign Policy in the New Media Age*. Princeton: Princeton University Press.

Bennett, W. L. (1994). The Media and the Foreign Policy Process. In D. Reese (Ed.), *The New Politics of American Foreign Policy* (pp. 168–188). New York: St. Martins Press.

Bennett, W. L. (2012). *News: The Politics of Illusion* (9th ed.). New York: Pearson Education.

Benson. (2006). News Media as a "Journalistic Field": What Bourdieu Adds to New Institutionalism, and Vice Versa. *Political Communication, 23*, 187–202.

Boyd-Barrett, O. (1998). Media Imperialism Reformulated. In D. Thussu (Ed.), *Electronic Empires, Global Media and Local Resistance* (pp. 157–176). London: Arnold.

Castells, M. (2009). *Communication Power*. Oxford and New York: Oxford University Press.

Foucault, M. (1979). *Discipline and Punish: The Birth of the Prison*. New York: Vintage Books.

Graber, D. A. (1997). *Mass Media and American Politics* (5th ed.). Washington, DC: CQ Press.

He, K., & Feng, H. (2013). Xi Jinping's Operational Code Beliefs and China's Foreign Policy. *The Chinese Journal of International Politics, 6*(3), 209–231.

Herman, S. E., & Chomsky, N. (2002). *Manufacturing Consent: The Political Economy of the Mass Media*. New York: Pantheon Books.

Livingston, S. (1997, June). *Clarifying the CNN Effect: An Examination of Media Effects According to Type of Military Intervention* (Research Paper R-18). Cambridge, MA: The Joan Shorenstein Barone Center on the Press, Politics and Public Policy at Harvard University. Retrieved from http://genocidewatch.info/images/1997ClarifyingtheCNNEffect-Livingston.pdf.

Lule, J. (2015). *Globalization and Media: Global Village of Babel* (2nd ed.). Lanham, MD: Rowman & Littlefield.

McCombs, M., & Shaw, D. L. (1972). The Agenda-Setting Function of Mass Media. *Public Opinion Quarterly, 36*(2), 176–185.

Moon, M. (2018). Manufacturing Consent?: The Role of the International News on the Korean Peninsula. *Global Media and Communication, 14*(3), 265–281.

Schudson, M. (2011). *The Sociology of News* (2nd ed.). New York: W. W. Norton.

Semetko, H. A., & Valkenburg, M. (2000). Framing European Politics: A Content Analysis of Press and Television News. *Journal of Communication, 50*(2), 93–109.

Shoemaker, J., & Reese, S. D. (1991). *Mediating the Message: Theories of Influence on Mass Media Content*. New York: Longman.

Shoemaker, J., & Reese, S. D. (1996). *Mediating the Message: Theories of Influence on Mass Media Content* (2nd ed.). White Plains, NY: Longman.

Thussu, D. K. (2000). *International Communication: Continuity and Change*. London: Arnold.

Walsh, C. (2018, July 13). Exhibit Foregrounds Video-art Pioneer Nam June Paik. *The Harvard Gazette*. Retrieved from https://news.harvard.edu/gazette/story/2018/07/harvard-showcase-for-korean-artist-nam-june-paik/.

Wee, H. (2018, June 11). How Kim Jong Un Want to Develop His Economy and Secure His Regime, CNBC. Retrieved from https://www.cnbc.com/2018/06/11/how-kim-jong-un-wants-to-develop-his-economy-and-secure-his-regime.html.

# INDEX

**T**
Territorial dispute, 9
Terrorism, 64, 102
Trump, Donald, 13, 188, 191
Tuchman, Gaye, 23, 39, 45, 158
Twitter, 88, 89, 140

**U**
U.S. media, 144
UK media, 144

**V**
Voice of America, 106

**X**
Xi, Jinping, 10, 14
Xiaoping, Deng, 5, 190

**Y**
Yeonpyeong, xix, xxi, 131, 150, 152,
    155
Youtube, 86, 88, 89

Printed by Printforce, the Netherlands